Mainstream Education for Hearing Impaired Children and Youth

Mainstream Education for Hearing Impaired Children and Youth

EDITED BY
GARY W. NIX, PH.D.
Associate Professor and Director,
Education of the Hearing Impaired,
Texas Tech University,
Lubbock, Texas

GRUNE & STRATTON
A Subsidiary of Harcourt Brace Jovanovich, Publishers
New York   San Francisco   London

Library of Congress Cataloging in Publication Data
Main entry under title:

Mainstream education for hearing impaired children and youth.

Includes bibliographies and index.
1. Deaf—Education.   I. Nix, Gary W.
[DNLM: 1. Education, Special—Congresses.
2. Hearing disorders—In infancy and childhood—
Congresses. 3. Hearing disorders—In adolescence—
Congresses.   HV2437 M225]
HV2430.M28   371.9'12   75-40319
ISBN 0-8089-0925-8

©*1976 by Grune & Stratton, Inc.* All rights reserved. No part of this publication may be reproduced or transmitted in any form or by any means, electronic or mechanical, including photocopy, recording, or any information storage and retrieval system, without permission in writing from the publisher.

Grune & Stratton, Inc.
111 Fifth Avenue
New York, New York 10003

Library of Congress Catalog Card Number 75-40319
International Standard Book Number 0-8089-0925-8

Printed in the United States of America

Contents

Contributors vii
Preface viii
Introduction 1

Section I Auditory-Perceptual and Psycho-Social Aspects of Mainstreaming Hearing Impaired Students

1. Whose Schools: Educational Expediency/Educational Integrity? 11
   Grant B. Bitter

2. A Rationale for a Mainstream Education for the Hearing Impaired 23
   Perry T. Leslie

3. Residual Hearing—The Yeast of Communication 39
   Derek A. Sanders

4. The Audiologist As Educator: The Ultimate Hearing Aide 53
   Barbara A. Hanners

5. Psycho-Social Aspects of Mainstreaming for the Child and Family 75
   Ruth R. Green

6. Maximum Cultural Involvement for the Hearing Impaired: Environmental Impact 87
   Grant B. Bitter

7. Assessment of the Hearing Impaired Prior to Mainstreaming 101
   Mark Ross

Section II Mainstream Problems and Practices

8. Mainstreaming the Preprimary Hearing Impaired Child, 0-6: Practices . . . Progress . . . Problems 111
   Winifred H. Northcott

9. Mainstreaming Problems and Procedures: Ages 6-12 135
   Donald I. McGee
10. The Mainstreaming of the Junior High and Senior High Student .. 147
    Charles H. Cosper
11. In the Current—With Only One Oar 157
    Gloria M. Matter
12. What Do You Do If The Mainstreamed Hearing Impaired Child Fails? or Mainstreaming: Sink or Swim........................ 169
    Helen R. Golf

Section III Administrative Aspects of Mainstreaming

13. Administrative Concerns For Mainstreaming 181
    Leo E. Connor
14. Mainstreaming in Southwestern Michigan...................... 191
    Lee F. Auble
15. Components for Normalization of Hearing Impaired Children in a Public School Setting 197
    Andrew R. Gantenbein

Section IV Exemplary Programs and Materials

16. Deaf and Hearing Children at the Lexington School for the Deaf or—Mainstreaming the Special School 209
    Leo E. Connor
17. The Central Institute for the Deaf Demonstration Home Program . 217
    Audrey Simmons-Martin
18. Model Educational Cascade for Hearing Impaired Children 227
    Mark Ross
19. Deaf Children Can Learn to Hear 239
    Helen Hulick Beebe
20. Mainstream Education for the Hearing Impaired—Promises to Keep 247
    Grant B. Bitter

Summary 255

Index 271

Contributors

Lee F. Auble: Former Superintendent, Berrien County Public Schools, Berrien Springs, Michigan

Helen Hulick Beebe: Director, Helen Beebe Clinic, Easton, Pennsylvania

Grant B. Bitter, Ed.D.: Coordinator, Teacher Education, Area of the Deaf, Department of Special Education, University of Utah, Salt Lake City, Utah

Leo E. Connor, Ed.D.: Executive Director, Lexington School for the Deaf, Jackson Heights, New York

Charles H. Cosper, Jr.: Berrien County Day Program for Hearing Impaired Children, Sylvester School, Berrien Springs, Michigan

Andrew R. Gantenbein: Head Teacher, Berrien County Day Program for Hearing Impaired Children, Sylvester School, Berrien Springs, Michigan

Helen R. Golf: Program Consultant-Coordinator, Bill Wilkerson Hearing and Speech Center, Nashville, Tennessee

Ruth R. Green: Director, Counseling and Social Services Center, New York League for the Hard of Hearing, New York, New York

Barbara A. Hanners: Bill Wilkerson Hearing and Speech Center, Nashville, Tennessee

Perry T. Leslie, Ed.D.: Assistant Professor, Department of Special Education, The University of British Columbia, Vancouver, B.C., Canada

Gloria M. Matter: Resource Teacher, Shorewood High School, Shorewood, Wisconsin

Donald I. McGee, Ph.D.: Program Specialist, Programs for Hearing Impaired Children, Fairfax County Public Schools, Fairfax, Virginia

Winifred H. Northcott, Ph.D.: Consultant, Early Education for the Handicapped, 0-4/5 Years, Minnesota Department of Education, St. Paul, Minnesota

Mark Ross, Ph.D.: Professor of Audiology, Department of Speech, University of Connecticut, Storrs, Connecticut

Derek A. Sanders, Ph.D.: Professor of Audiology, State University of New York at Buffalo, Buffalo, New York

Audrey Simmons-Martin, Ed.D.: Professor of Education of the Deaf, Washington University and Director of Parent-Infant Program, Central Institute for the Deaf, St. Louis, Missouri

Preface

As legislative mandates, an accumulation of case law, and a general special education trend toward mainstreaming developed momentum, administrators, teachers, and other professionals engaged in the education of the hearing impaired have found the need for more information on the problems and practices of mainstreaming. In order to collect and disseminate current information on the mainstreaming of hearing impaired children and youth, a national symposium was held at the Peabody Hotel in Memphis, Tennessee.

This book is partially based upon the information presented at the four-day symposium and a one-day pre-symposium workshop held for administrators of regular education programs. The volume disseminates current information on both the practice and technology of mainstreaming hearing impaired children. The contributors include outstanding professionals from the fields of psychology, audiology, language pathology, regular education, and the education of the hearing impaired. Auditory-oral, total communication, public, private, day, and residential programming are all reflected in the contributors' present professional involvements. While all of the contributors are professionals, one is also the parent of a hearing impaired daughter and two of the contributors are themselves hearing impaired.

Diverse viewpoints on mainstreaming are offered for examination. It is possible that more than one approach to normalization may be effective. In addition to the variety to be found in this volume, some commonalities of approach and effect are seen to emerge.

Although the book is divided into four sections, it will be readily seen that several of the chapters could be cross-referenced to more than one section.

Gary W. Nix

Gary W. Nix

Introduction

During the decade of the 1970s, considerable momentum in the direction of placing hearing impaired children in classrooms with hearing children has occurred. Legislation in over one-half of the states has been changed to reflect the movement to educate exceptional children "as a part of rather than apart from" their nondisabled peers whenever possible.

The terminology, which includes "mainstreaming," "normalization," and "integration," is used to specify the regular class placement of exceptional children. Mainstreaming in the current context will be used to designate the *assimilation* of a hearing impaired child into a hearing peer group. The assimilation of a hearing impaired child into a group denotes more than the term "integration." The integration of a hearing impaired student into a regular class situation has frequently meant a concurrent education with a class of hearing children. The integrated hearing impaired child may not perceive himself nor be perceived by the teacher and hearing pupils as belonging to the class.

The usual temporal lag between educational technology and educational practice has been dramatically reversed. The educational practice of mainstreaming has outpaced the diagnostic and educational technology of mainstreaming. A rapidly developing body of case law, new educational legislation, and an increasing trend toward administrative legal accountability have placed many professionals in a very difficult position. Connor discusses some of the administrative concerns in Chap. 14.

The mainstreaming of hearing impaired students is not a new phenomenon. A number of programs have used a mainstream placement alternative for some time with varying degrees of success. However, just a decade ago, the Babbidge report (1965) noted that over one-half of the deaf school age population was receiving instruction in residential institutions (p. 9). Day schools and classes accounted for the enrollment of 40 percent of the population (p. 13). The statistics on fully mainstreamed hearing impaired children were not reported by the Babbidge committee. The population of mainstreamed hearing impaired students who have been assimilated into regular classrooms have generally not been reported in statistics on the education of the hearing impaired. As a case in point, the 1973 Annual Report of the National Advisory Committee on Education of the Deaf stated: "Slightly less than 50 percent of the deaf children within the United States are enrolled in residential schools for the deaf. The rest are enrolled in day schools and classes for the deaf (p. 3)."

In many respects, the academically and socially assimilated hearing impaired learner is the most successful "deaf" student. He has minimized the constellation of handicapping conditions surrounding his hearing disability.

Assimilated hearing impaired students are frequently transferred from programs for the hearing impaired and assigned to a regular school in their attendance district. They are no longer carried on the rolls of the special program. This sorting process is apparent in the chapters by Ross, Northcott, McGee, Cosper, Matter, Golf, Bitter, Connor, Gantenbein, Simmons-Martin, and Beebe.

A reading of the research literature indicates that, almost universally, the assimilated hearing impaired student is excluded from the population samples of studies on "the deaf." The data is, therefore, truncated and does not reflect the capabilities of the entire spectrum of hearing impaired students.

The current thrust for mainstreaming hearing impaired children is discussed in detail in the chapter by Leslie. It is partially a result of the general trend in special education. In 1971, two model state laws were drafted and published in *State Law & Education of Handicapped Children: Issues and Recommendations* by the Council for Exceptional Children. The model laws have provided the framework for the enactment of legislation affecting all exceptional children at the state level.

Concurrently, a body of case law has accumulated which directly affects educational practices and has added impetus to the increased movement to mainstream hearing impaired children and youth. A landmark case entitled *Pennsylvania Association for Retarded Children vs State Board of Education* resulted in a decision which stated that placement should be in a regular classroom, if possible, and that the second choice was in a special classroom in a regular school (334 F Supp 1257, 1971 and 343 F Supp 279, 1972).

A case in the Federal Court in Alabama titled *Ricky Wyatt vs Stonewall Stickney* yielded a decision which has importance for all exceptional children. The Federal Court held the primary function of special education was integration into the community as a whole and that the schools must implement the principal of normalization (334 F Supp 1341, 1971 and 325 F Supp 781, 1971).

Attorney Herbert P. Feibelman (1974) in a paper presented at the Alexander Graham Bell Association national convention in Atlanta, Georgia stated: "The principle has been clearly established that public education must be provided in the least restrictive environment, designed to maximize the abilities of the child, and with a view toward normalization (p. 11)."

While the landmark legislation has been primarily concerned with retarded citizens, the legal principles established apply to hearing impaired citizens as well. The National Center for the Law and the Handicapped through their publication *Newsline* issued the following statement:

"The right to treatment and community service cases in which the Center has been involved signify the right to treatment and the right to services in the setting least restrictive to the individual's personal freedom and liberty. These principles apply to all handicapped persons—blind, deaf, epileptic, mentally ill, and mentally retarded among others (p. 6-7)."

The legal mandate for providing an education in the least restrictive environment possible immediately poses several questions and problems for everyone involved with the hearing impaired student. This volume is organized around the questions and problems which have been raised.

Section 1 focuses upon the developmental aspects of mainstreaming a hearing impaired child or youth. It also examines the crucial problem of assessment of a hearing impaired child or youth in order to achieve an educational placement which is the least restrictive and most appropriate for the particular individual involved.

Bitter reviews the literature on mainstreaming from the nursery level through the college level. Three mainstreaming patterns appeared most frequently in the literature and are discussed in the chapter. The service components necessary for a successful resource program are delineated. An increased emphasis on preschool mainstreaming is noted with particular emphasis given to the development of auditory function. The work of several pioneers of the auditory approach is discussed.

Leslie examines a developmental rationale for mainstreaming hearing impaired children and youth. As a part of the rationale, he presents the adjustment patterns to a disability which an individual may adopt. Alternative educational placements are discussed along with the current ground swell of support for mainstreaming.

Sanders considers the effect of early auditory intervention and its implications for cognitive development and later communicative functioning. The early development and maximal use of residual hearing is viewed as one of the important parameters for successful mainstreaming. He presents the need for determining a child's auditory functioning and the subsequent selection of communication modalities best suited to the individual.

Amplifying points raised by Sanders, Hanners presents the need for audiologic management in early intervention with hearing impaired children. She illustrates some of the inadequacies of current management programs. The role of the audiologist in an educational setting serves as a major focus of the chapter.

Mainstreaming a hearing impaired student establishes for him a psycho-social and educational climate which is different from a self-contained or residential environment. The development of a positive self-image through early mainstreaming into a nursery group of hearing children is viewed as more easily accomplished than delaying mainstreaming to a later age. Green discusses the effect of early mainstreaming on the social maturation of profoundly hearing impaired students. Higher expectancy levels and hearing peer personality models are two of the important parameters which can effect the psycho-social functioning of the mainstreamed child. Green examines the role of the family and its impact on mainstreaming the hearing impaired child. She has included the transcripts of interviews conducted at the New York League for the Hard of Hearing which discuss some of the benefits and problems.

The effective use of environmental parameters is also viewed as important by Bitter. In his chapter on environmental impact, he describes a cultural model which enhances the development of a positive self-concept, social adequacy, and competent educational skills. He makes several recommendations for effectively using the environment for normalizing the development of hearing impaired learners.

The determination of the setting which provides the least restrictive alternative for a particular individual yet provides fully all of the services needed is a difficult one at best. The greatest void in the available information on mainstreaming is in the area of instrumentation for the selection of students to be mainstreamed. Rudy and Nace (1973) have developed a Transitional Instrument which yields a transitional quotient as one predictor of success in a mainstream placement. The Transitional Instrument was published in *The Hearing Impaired Child in a Regular Classroom* which was edited by Northcott.

In the current chapter on student selection, Ross considers the assessment which should precede any educational placement and the alternative placements which must be available to children who are not candidates for full assimilation into a regular class. He discusses the criteria for determining a successful mainstream placement.

Section 2 attends to the problems and current practices of mainstreaming for the individual birth to age 21. Suggestions are presented for minimizing the problems involved in implementing a mainstream placement.

Northcott in the chapter on mainstreaming the preprimary child advances a "Bill of Rights" for every parent of a hearing impaired child. One of the important items is the right to an intact family. The idea of regional public school programming which permits home care and an active parent-school interaction is viewed as a preferred alternative to an institutional placement.

The author considers the effect of communicative modalities and the selection of a method of instruction for the preprimary child on the later assimilation of the child into a regular class setting. The data presented by Northcott on the importance of the degree of hearing impairment to mainstream success stand in disagreement with the Ross observations and data.

The delineation of the common characteristics of successfully mainstreamed children is presented along with the implications for programming which stem from them. Attention is also given to those preprimary children who should not be considered as candidates for a mainstream placement.

McGee tackles the problem of monitoring the mainstreamed student at the elementary level. The difficulties involved in establishing a feedback system and preparing the regular class teacher for the management of a hearing impaired child present challenges for the mainstream specialist. A program which provides alternative placements is used to illustrate various levels of mainstream placement.

In his chapter on the mainstreaming of junior and senior high students, Cosper outlines three characteristic types of student functioning. Educational tracking is viewed in relation to the three characteristic types. Cosper reviews the advantages of early mainstreaming for later success in junior and senior high school. Age is not seen as a critical factor in the placement of hearing impaired youth. Academic or vocational placement at a level which will permit success is seen as the primary placement determiner.

He discusses the normalization of communication skills and their importance for regular class enrollment. The difficult task of monitoring junior and senior high hearing impaired students in a departmentalized setting is covered in the chapter. A number of the problems involved in mainstreaming hearing impaired youth are enumerated along with suggestions for their solution.

The Shorewood (Wisconsin) Public School program serves hearing impaired children on a regional basis. Students are returned to their own school districts and full-time regular class placements as soon as possible. The students who are incapable of being fully mainstreamed are retained in the program for the hearing impaired. Matter details the high school resource room program at Shorewood and the types of assistance given to the hearing impaired students. Suggestions are given for a feedback system between the regular and resource classrooms. Possible adaptations in assignments to be made in the regular classroom (involving reading and language levels which are too difficult for a hearing impaired youth) are illustrated.

Participation in co-curricular activities provides the student with the opportunity to be a part of the athletic and club life of the school. A follow-up study of the students leaving the Shorewood program over a fourteen year period demonstrates the success possible through partial mainstreaming and resource support.

Golf focuses her attention on the use of an age/level service continuum which extends from birth to 21 years of age. In her chapter, she discusses inappropriate mainstream placement and the conditions which can lead to the hearing impaired student's "failure." The author presents and disputes some of the major "myths of mainstreaming."

In the third section of the book, the administrative aspects of mainstreaming serves as the topic. Organizational patterns, administrative procedures, and concerns are included in the section.

Connor discusses the concerns which general and special education administrators have regarding the initiation of a mainstream program. After legislation, litigation, and leverage, the administrator is faced with the implementation of a mainstream program and a new set of complex problems.

In his chapter on administrative concerns, Connor gives a set of administrative guidelines to provide direction on the complexities involved in the implementation of a mainstream program. Connor presents his own observations on the parameters which contribute to the successful mainstream placement of a hearing impaired child.

Auble, as the superintendent of a county school system, shares his experiences in the development of a regional program for hearing impaired children which emphasizes mainstreaming. He discusses the establishment of administrative policies which foster program growth. The author also presents the expectancies his administrative staff has for regular classroom teachers regarding their acceptance of mainstreamed hearing impaired students. The perennial problems of pupil transportation and financial matters are discussed.

Gantenbein addresses his comments on components for the normalization of hearing impaired children to administrators faced with responsibilities for mainstream programming. The Berrien County Day Program for Hearing Impaired Children offers educational alternatives which provide for varying degrees of mainstreaming. A diagram of the program appears as figure 1 in the chapter. Five plans for mainstreaming, cross-mainstreaming, and reverse mainstreaming are included in the chapter.

Section Four of the book covers three exemplary early intervention programs, the results of Project NEED, and a final summary chapter. Each of the early intervention programs approaches early mainstreaming in a different way.

The Lexington School for the Deaf in Jackson Heights, New York has, for over 100 years, served as a leader in the education of hearing impaired children. Connor in his chapter on "Mainstreaming the Special School" presents an innovative model for changing a school for "the deaf" into a school for children and youth some of whom are hearing impaired. Segregated, day/residential schools for the hearing impaired can be altered to provide a mainstream education for hearing impaired children in a facility which was designed as a segregated institution. The chapter by Connor demonstrates the change possible in a long established educational institution.

A "mainstreamed special school" can, in a sense, offer the best of both the segregated and mainstreamed settings. The hearing impaired children and youth are truly mainstreamed yet have all of the audiological, etc. support services readily available to them. The close monitoring of the mainstream placement is possible on a daily basis without the necessity of a traveling resource teacher.

The Lexington program seeks to return pupils to their own neighborhood school setting as rapidly as possible. Connor outlines the several levels of the program from the parent-infant program through the adult level.

The chapter by Simmons-Martin describes the demonstration home program which is operated by the Central Institute for the Deaf in St. Louis. Simmons-Martin presents a number of case histories of hearing impaired children. The effects of premature mainstreaming of hearing impaired children who do not possess functional communication skills or the linguistic competence necessary for success in a regular class placement are illustrated with case histories.

The author presents the criteria used by the Central Institute for the Deaf in deciding upon the appropriateness of a mainstream placement. The structure and contributions of the parent-infant program to the successful educational placement of a hearing impaired student is discussed in some detail.

Beebe presents the approach which is used in her private clinical program. The stimulation of the auditory sensory apparatus of hearing impaired infants serves as the basis for the Beebe program. A number of specific teaching suggestions for the development of auditory-oral and linguistic competance are given.

The chapter includes suggestions for the role to be filled by private practioners in the support of mainstreamed hearing impaired children. The reciprocity between the development of good communicative functioning and a mainstream placement is noted throughout the chapter.

In "Promises to Keep . . .", Bitter traces the advancement of human rights for the handicapped and presents the training dimensions necessary to meet the needs of the professionals and parents involved in mainstreaming hearing impaired children and youth. The Systems O.N.E. multimedia training package and its effective use to facilitate a successful mainstream placement serve as the primary focus of the chapter.

The editor has synthesized the information presented in the book and reported the current state-of-the-art in the summary chapter. It is intended that the book will provide an information base to be built upon as advancements are made in this important area.

BIBLIOGRAPHY

Babbidge H: Education of the Deaf, A Report to the Secretary of Health, Education, and Welfare by his Advisory Committee on the Education of the Deaf, Washington, D.C., 1965

Council for Exceptional Children: State Law & Education of Handicapped Children: Issues and Recommendations, Reston, Va., 1971

Feibelman HP: You, The Law, and Your Child. Paper presented at the Alexander Graham Bell Association National Convention in Atlanta, Georgia on June 21, 1974

National Advisory Committee on Handicapped Children: Basic Education Rights for the Handicapped. The 1973 Annual Report to the Secretary of Health, Education, and Welfare, U.S. Govt. Printing Office, Washington, D.C., 1973

National Center for Law and the Handicapped: Newsline. Vol. 3, No. 1, South Bend, Indiana, January, 1975

Northcott WH (ed): The Hearing Impaired Child in a Regular Classroom: Preschool, Elementary, and Secondary Years. The Alexander Graham Bell Association for the Deaf, Inc., Washington, D.C., 1973

Pennsylvania Association for Retarded Children vs State Board of Education: 334 F Supp 1257 (1971) and 343 F Supp 279 (1972)

Wyatt vs Stickney: 334 F Supp 1341 (1971), 325 F Supp 781 (1971); 344 F Supp 387 (1972)

SECTION I

Auditory-Perceptual And Psycho-Social Aspects Of Mainstreaming Hearing Impaired Students

Grant B. Bitter

1
Whose Schools: Educational Expediency/Educational Integrity?

"It is in fact nothing short of a miracle that the modern methods of instruction have not yet entirely strangled the holy curiosity of inquiry; for this delicate little plant, aside from stimulation, stands mainly in need of freedom; without this it goes to wrack and ruin without fail."
Albert Einstein.

Whom do our schools serve—the elite, the intelligent, the slower learner, the fast learner, the nonlearner, the parents, the children?

Does unnecessary labeling have an adverse effect on the children in our schools? Does segregation hurt children, or does it enhance learning?

How are educational programs and systems organized to meet the needs of children? What determines political and/or educational expediency? What is required for educational integrity?

Evidently, there are great numbers of our youth who find the educational environment unrewarding and somewhat "strangled."

According to James A. Harris (1974), President of the National Education Association,

- Nearly 2 million school-age children are not in school. Most of them are in large cities.
- Of the students attending classes, more of them will spend some portion of their lives in correctional institutions than those who will attend all the higher institutions of learning.
- On any school day of the year, one will find 13,000 school-age children in correctional institutions, and another 100,000 in jail or police lock-up.

- Of every 100 students attending schools across the nation, 23 drop out, 77 graduate from high school, 43 enter college, 21 receive a B.A., 6 earn an M.A., and 1 earns a Ph.D.
- Many states spend more money to incarcerate a child than to provide him with an education: Iowa pays $9,000 a year to maintain a student in the juvenile home at Eldora—and $1,050 for a student in the regular classroom. Maryland spends $18,000; Michigan $10,000 per year to maintain a child in correctional institutions, yet far less on children in regular classes.

Although the U.S. system of education is considered to be outstanding and unique, there are obviously some grave areas of concern as pointed out by Harris.

Furthermore, vast numbers of exceptional children remain segregated who might find regular school placement far more enriching and meaningful. For example, figures from the Bureau of Education for the Handicapped (Northcott, 1973) revealed that of 41,109 children studied in regard to educational placement, only 10.6 percent of them were involved in any kind of integrated placement which permits functional involvement in the normal environment.

It is my contention, therefore, that unnecessary segregation and labeling violate the rights of exceptional children to equal educational and social opportunities. Fortunately, many systems of education in the United States are now initiating program modifications which will offer more effective delivery of services to children.

Obviously, the *mere* placement of an exceptional child in a public school classroom is not the answer. However, appropriate remedial steps are necessary when prevention is neglected which can remove both inefficiency and expediency in the administration of mainstreaming programs. Indeed, the incredible complexity of our bureaucratic process is frequently so confusing and unwieldy that appropriate services to children are frequently curtailed or simply not provided. Lack of funds, staff, time, tools, space and/or the absence of *administrative readiness* are generally causal factors of an unpleasant, static educational and social environment.

In my opinion, one of the first prerequisites for successful mainstreaming must be "administrative readiness." This is considered to be critical to the successful implementation of effective mainstreaming programs. Readiness minimizes expediency and enhances educational integrity.

It implies a state of preparedness, an attitude of acceptance and respect, and a personal commitment to the modification of any given educational system to meet emerging needs in accommodating exceptional children.

Many contemporary administrators of educational programs are vitally concerned with appropriate deliveries of services to their consumers. In view of the issues of the times (legislative mandates and court decisions) regarding mainstreaming, these responsibilities are becoming more complex and challenging. Had the exceptional child never been segregated, desegregation would not now be an issue. Nonetheless, "what might have been" is not the concern. How best to implement meaningful service "now" is the issue.

The following review of literature describes how some educational systems are implementing services. This information can be of value in enhancing both educational integrity and administrative readiness.

A review of the literature (Bitter et al, 1973) disclosed the use of many approaches to the mainstreaming of the hearing impaired. Among those most frequently mentioned were standard mainstreaming, cross-mainstreaming, and reverse mainstreaming. These approaches are identified by the degree of interaction between hearing impaired students and their hearing peers as follows:

Standard mainstreaming is the approach whereby hearing impaired children are instructed for all or part of the school day in the regular classroom with hearing peers under the direction of a regular classroom teacher.

Cross-mainstreaming is a teaching arrangement similar to a team-teaching concept which involves the regular classroom teacher and the teacher of the hearing impaired, or resource room teacher. However, in cross-mainstreaming, the teachers do not occupy the same room. The regular classroom teacher may take one or more of the members of the special class into her own room for a period or periods of instruction. As a reciprocal measure, the teacher of the hearing impaired includes one or more children from the regular class in one or more periods of instruction in his/her classroom with hearing impaired children.

Reverse mainstreaming refers to the strategy of bringing one or more hearing children into the classroom with the hearing impaired for one or more periods of instruction each day.

In any of the above-mentioned approaches to mainstreaming, the resource room may also be utilized. The resource room concept for hearing impaired children works precisely in the same way as it does in similar programs for other exceptional children. Indeed, the hearing impaired child spends the major portion of his time receiving instruction in the regular classroom, but goes to the resource room teacher for specialized instruction in those areas which require more individual attention (Bitter et al, 1973).

According to Jenkins and Mayhall (1973), the delivery of services through emerging resource teacher programs, if they are indicative of quality educational programming and practices, must possess the following components: "(a) identified criterion performance, (b) daily instruction and assessment, (c) individual instruction, (d) management of tutors." All of these may enhance the opportunities for the adequate educational achievement of children.

Furthermore, approaches to mainstreaming should involve the services of support personnel, i.e., the itinerant teacher and/or the academic tutor. The itinerant teacher concept permits the hearing impaired student to remain in the regular classroom while receiving periodic visits from an itinerant teacher who may serve several different schools. The responsibilities of this specialist are definitely oriented to meeting the child's individual needs, but in addition this person must serve in a liaison and public relations capacity as well.

The term "academic tutor" is used in a number of ways in the literature pertaining to mainstreaming. Generally, it refers to individualized support in those skill areas wherein the child needs special assistance. Although the role is generally occupied by specialists in the field, the review of literature indicates that this function is sometimes accomplished by classroom instructional aides, regular classroom teachers and/or parents. It must be remembered that none of the above-mentioned titles denote mutually exclusive job descriptions.

Although the approaches previously discussed generally refer to the elementary and secondary levels of instruction, a notable thrust toward mainstreaming is also evident at the college level. Several articles reviewed describe approaches to the academic and occupational mainstreaming of students in universities or technical colleges. For example, Berg (1972) described the facilitative program for mainstreaming hearing impaired students at Utah State University. He summarized four requirements that students must satisfy upon entering the program. These include

1. Consistent academic motivation
2. Competent reading skills
3. Competent lipreading skills and intelligible speech
4. Commitment to communicate and socialize with hearing as well as hearing impaired individuals

Many educators favor gradual involvement of the child into the whole mainstream process. For example, as soon as the child gains usable vocabulary and language skills, he is placed in the regular classroom for some part of the school day. As skills develop, the degree and extent of involvement into regular classes increase (Bowling, 1967).

Bowling (1967) stated that when mainstreaming is widely practiced in the schools, fewer handicapped children are clustered together in the same classes; thus, regular classroom teachers are able to provide more individual attention to each child.

The importance of the use of hearing aids and auditory equipment by hearing impaired students in the regular schools was reviewed by Warnke (1972). It was concluded that the use of a binaural auditory trainer used during class and individual aids worn on the playground and at home assists in the mainstreaming process. Warnke (1972) supported the contention that success in mainstreaming is enhanced through the consistent use of appropriate auditory training equipment.

There is increased emphasis in the literature on preschool training which tends to increase the child's ability to cope with a regular school environment (Pollack and Ernst, 1973).

Acoupedic programs described by Pollack (1964, 1973) and Stewart et al (1964) include

1. Early detection of hearing impairment
2. Early fitting of aids
3. A unisensory approach
4. A normal learning environment
5. Development and use of an auditory feedback mechanism
6. Individualized teaching
7. The development of language through exposure to normal auditory language patterns
8. Parental acceptance of the child and his hearing loss
9. The involvement of parents as his primary models of communication

Whorton (1966) emphasized that extreme educational deficiencies or educational problems need not occur if hearing loss is discovered early and appropriate compensatory measures are provided immediately.

Additionally, Johnson (1967) concluded that educators should see the child as a person rather than a specimen who characterizes a particular clinical type of deafness with a defined degree of hearing loss. Rather, emphasis should focus on how the hearing impaired child functions which should, in turn, determine the type of educational placement.

Jones and Byers (1971) used a theoretical model of classifying hearing impaired children enrolled in the classroom. They concluded that the hearing deficit does not appear to be the central factor for predicting the child's success. The most striking factor appears to be the ability of the individual child to function in his total academic environment.

A significant focus on the utilization of listening and hearing skills through appropriate amplification is offered through the use of the auditory approach. Professionals using this approach stress the functional potential of hearing impaired children through the use of a variety of auditory techniques (Regional Conference on The Auditory Approach, 1973; interviews with Griffiths, Horton, Stewart, Gantenbein, Ling, and Northcott).

Effective educational systems utilizing the mainstreaming concept continue to provide support services in the areas of speech, speechreading, and language as well as in other academic areas after mainstreaming has been initiated. According to the literature, prescriptive educational placement should be based on academic skill and social stability.

Whorton (1968) recommended that sensory deficits be classified in terms of psychological and educational handicaps inasmuch as the regular teacher may not recognize the educational implications of various degrees of hearing loss.

According to Bowling (1967) orientation of regular classroom teachers and hearing peers must be arranged so that they will be prepared to accept the hearing impaired child into the classroom.

Weinstein (1968) reported that years of experience with the deaf caused teachers to be aware that, in teaching deaf youngsters to speak, it is essential to have them intermingle with hearing children—the earlier the better. Therefore, the primary goal of the specific school mentioned in this report was to help the hearing impaired child find his place in the normal everyday world.

According to a declaration made by the A. G. Bell Association (1968), the educational and social benefits are reciprocal between hearing and hearing impaired children. Hearing children have much to contribute in understanding and accepting someone who is different. The mainstreamed hearing impaired child comes to a basic and vital understanding that his needs and feelings are very similar to those of hearing children.

Weiss (1968) concluded that the effects of mainstreaming are twofold in that hearing children become sensitized to hearing impaired children and learn to accept them; while at the same time, hearing impaired children acquire basic language experiences and socialization skills. Hearing children also learn skills for facilitating interaction, i.e., facing the hearing impaired child while speaking.

Weinstein (1968) observed that a benefit derived from mainstreaming is that deaf children become increasingly self-sufficient as they experience exposure to hearing classmates, and hearing children learn to accept the fact that some people are handicapped and a person's disability is not the most important concern, but that human beings learn to live comfortably with individual differences.

In referring to the general social adjustment of all children within the peer group, Spidal and Sheridan (1972) concluded that children have the opportunity to test their strengths and weaknesses. They compare their values and attitudes with those of their friends, and ultimately structure a value system of their own. Therefore, the school can and must play a crucial role in providing the opportunity for this kind of interactive, interpersonal experience.

There are many teaching aids available to the regular teacher who has a hearing impaired child in her classroom; these include visuals such as films, books, transparencies, and charts. Support personnel also should be available such as the resource teacher or the special teacher who provides assistance in language and speech development. Teacher aides are sometimes employed to help with group activities thus permitting the regular teacher to devote more time to individualized instruction (Bowling, 1967; Weiss, 1968).

In identifying hearing loss, environmental clues are very important indicators as to whether the hearing impaired child is comprehending what is happening in the environment. Many mildly hearing impaired children remain undetected and undiagnosed until an alert teacher identifies their problems. For example, Whorton (1966) emphasized that inattention and indifference are not common traits of a correctly diagnosed and well-taught hearing impaired child. If the child appears to be inattentive, indifferent, or "lazy," the teacher should contact the special personnel on the staff to arrange for hearing tests and an evaluation of both the child and the learning situation.

Weinstein (1968) reported that in a school in New York City that provides services for the deaf, hearing children assist hearing impaired children by signaling the beginning and ending of activities. These "buddies" relay directions given by the teacher when necessary. Teachers in that program report that hearing impaired children appeared to follow directions effectively and seemed relaxed in the regular school.

Weinstein noted further that some deaf children relate to other children of their own age more readily than to adults. Therefore, there is a very natural flow of language among children. Some teachers report that hearing impaired children were less dependent upon authority figures for guidance, and that the children's adjustment to social situations was better than was the adjustment among those children whose classmates were all deaf.

Reports of early infant education programs that focus attention on the child and his parents are found in the literature. Niemann (1972) described the Acoupedic program where parents are taught to assume the role of the child's primary model of communication. However, she indicated they may need help from the specialists in effectively fulfilling their responsibilities.

Garrett and Stovell (1972) voiced the belief that the hearing impaired child's future education is the combined responsibility of both the parents and the educators; they must work together as a team. Many parents strive for the mainstreaming of their children into regular classrooms because it helps the children socially and educationally. The aspirations for their children are just as high as those held by a parent of a hearing child. Therefore, in order to cope with their concerns, parents should seek counseling as soon as they become aware of hearing impairments in their children.

Bowling (1968) and Weiss (1968) stated that involvement of the parents is a primary goal. They suggested that parents attend monthly "adult only" meetings, as well as come into the classroom to observe or to help with school activities. Later when children are in the primary grades, parents may be asked to attend conferences with the regular teacher to discuss progress and concerns.

Rosenthal (1966) emphasized that the parent plays a very important role in the early life of the child, and since the social adjustment is more difficult for a hearing impaired child, the parents must give special attention to this aspect of growth to help them overcome their frustrations. The child not only must cope with his own frustration but the occasional frustrations of those with whom he interacts. Rosenthal's recommendations to parents of adolescent hearing impaired children are

1. Do not assume that your child is always, or never at fault.
2. Acquaint others with the challenges of communication yet emphasize he is a child and a person like anyone else.
3. Whenever possible, prepare him for social situations so he will be more at ease.
4. Do not shield the child from new experiences. Teach him to be aware of his capabilities, and let him try.
5. Be as consistent and patient as possible in fulfilling the parental role.

It is well recognized that there are many factors which determine the success of mainstream programs. Many of them, as viewed by those who have served in various roles of mainstreaming, are termed successful because students flourish academically and socially to one degree or another. Truly, the final determiner of whether mainstreaming is successful or not is dependent upon what happens socially, academically, emotionally, and vocationally to the individual. Indeed, the hearing impaired students and their parents in any given educational program are the ones who, along with the educators and other appropriate specialists, should be able to evaluate strengths and weaknesses and determine the degree of success achieved.

Mrs. Constance Garrett (1972), the mother of a hearing impaired child who attends a private hearing school, suggested that the key to successful mainstreaming is that of early identification, early amplification, early education, and early parent counseling. The ultimate goal for her daughter, Linda, is to have the broadest possible options available as an adult—academically, vocationally, and socially. Mrs. Garrett maintains that the best way for Linda to achieve this goal is for her to grow up with her hearing peers and to stay in the hearing world from the beginning (Garrett and Stovell, 1972).

Mrs. Nell Cole (1971), declared that the problem she and her husband had was in finding adequate services for their son Paul. She said, "Some teachers wanted to work him and others didn't. One teacher treated him as any other child in her class and he thrived." In retrospect, the Coles concluded that it becomes a delicate function of tolerance to help a child experience the satisfaction and security that all children need, yet at the same time, face squarely the reality of the handicap.

According to Mrs. Leah Stambler (1973), mother of two hearing impaired children, the use of the auditory approach is proving to be of inestimable value in the successful involvement of her children in mainstream education.

Successful cultural involvement is recounted by numerous hearing impaired individuals who participated in various programs of mainstreaming in the public schools. For example, Linda McArthur (1967), expressed the strong desire to be like others and to be able to compete. She found that the process of growing in social experience involves participating in a variety of groups within society, each adding a new experience and each building more self-sufficiency. Miss McArthur gives credit for her successful involvement to her skill of lipreading, her use of her residual hearing through her hearing aid, and her use of speech along with the help of her parents in learning self-sufficiency.

Charles Sullivan (1967), who was deafened at age 12, indicated that attendance in a regular public school was critical in his achievement of success. At first, he was sent to a state school for the deaf; however, he ultimately withdrew from the institution and returned home where he attended public school with no special program or teacher. He stated that he lives and works completely in a hearing environment. He said, "If you can make yourself understood, if you can understand others, you need not limit the horizons of your life to a closed little world. No one achieves happiness or success without effort."

The survey of the literature indicated that many students who participated in regular schools are now in college or are successfully employed in the world of work. Some of these young people are broadening their educational, vocational, and professional horizons in such areas as psychology, science, dentistry, accounting, business, etc. through further education in universities and junior colleges across the country (*The Volta Review,* "Report of Graduates," 1973).

Numerous approaches to the mainstreaming of the hearing impaired into public schools are reported in the literature. Although descriptive terminology and the degree and time of mainstreaming differ from program to program, the rationale supporting the mainstream concept is common to all. It provides the opportunity for children to become more accepting of one another, and supplies a learning environment which is conducive to the meaningful growth and development of each child.

The survey noted some practices which have characteristics common to many successful mainstream programs. The essential components include appropriate orientation, preparation, and commitment of school administrators, regular classroom teachers and support personnel, parents, and hearing peers to the philosophy of mainstreaming.

Additionally, there is agreement that the diagnostic process (tentative, continuous, and reversible) be based on the early identification of hearing impairments and the development of listening skills through early amplification which requires appropriate and consistent use of the hearing aid.

The review of the literature illustrates that the progressive inclusion of the hearing impaired in regular school programs is being implemented at every educational level. Many professionals are in agreement that the mainstream process may have beneficial effects on hearing peers as well as on the hearing impaired through conscientious and skillful orientation, implementation, follow-up, and evaluation; followed by appropriate program modifications.

By interfacing educational programs with the many strengths provided by the interdisciplinary team as described in the literature, educational, social and cultural excellence is, indeed, attainable for the hearing impaired.

BIBLIOGRAPHY

Bitter GB, Johnston KA, Sorensen R: Integration of the Hearing Impaired: Educational Issues. University of Utah Project NEED, January, 1973

Bowling WC: Day classes for the deaf—Covina Plan. The Volta Review 69 54-57, 1967

Cole N: Hear the Wind Blow, in Northcott WH (ed): The Hearing Impaired Child in a Regular Classroom: Preschool, Elementary, and Secondary Years. Washington, D.C.: Alexander Graham Bell Association for the Deaf, 1973, pp 255-261. Also appeared in The Volta Review 73 36-41, 1971

Garrett C, Stovall EM: A Parent's Views on Integration, in Northcott WH (ed): The Hearing Impaired Child in a Regular Classroom: Preschool, Elementary, and Secondary Years. Washington, D.C.: Alexander Graham Bell Association for the Deaf, 1973, pp 248-254. Article adapted from "Parents' View on Integration." The Volta Review 74, 338-44, 1972

Harris JA: From speech delivered to the South Carolina Education Association in Columbia, 1974

Jenkins JR, Mayhall WF: Describing resource teacher programs. Exceptional Children 40: 35-36, 1973

Johnson EW: Let's Look at the Child—Not the Audiogram, in Northcott WH (ed): The Hearing Impaired Child in a Regular Classroom: Preschool, Elementary, and Secondary Years. Washington, D.C.: Alexander Graham Bell Association for the Deaf, 1973, pp 18-23. Also appeared in The Volta Review 69: 306-310, 1967

Northcott WH: The Academic Tutor and the Hearing Impaired Child, in Northcott WH (ed): The Hearing Impaired Child in a Regular Classroom: Preschool, Elementary, and Secondary Years. Washington, D.C.: Alexander Graham Bell Association for the Deaf, 1973, pp 18-23. Article adapted from "Tutoring a hearing impaired student in the elementary grades." The Volta Review 74: 432-435, 1972

Pollack D: Acoupedics: A uni-sensory approach to auditory training. The Volta Review 66: 400-409, 1964

Pollack D, Ernst M: Don't Set Limits: Expectations for Preschool Children, in Northcott WH (ed): The Hearing Impaired Child in a Regular Classroom: Preschool, Elementary, and Secondary Years. Washington, D.C.: Alexander Graham Bell Association for the Deaf, 1973, pp 156-62. Also appeared in The Volta Review 75: 359-367, 1973

Rosenthal C: Social adjustment of hearing handicapped children. The Volta Review 68: 293-297, 1966

Spidal D, Sheridan V: The child in the process: affecting his potential through life. Am, Ann Deaf 117: 520-530, 1972

Stewart J, Downs M, Pollack D: A uni-sensory program for the limited hearing child. Amer Speech Hearing Assoc 6: 5, 1964

The Volta Review: Report of Graduates, 1973

Warnke EF: Integration of hearing impaired with normal hearing students. Horgeschadigte Kinder 9: 57-59, 1972

Weinstein GW: Nursery school with a difference—Deaf and normal children in New York. Parent's Magazine, 43: 66-69, 1968

Whorton GP: The hard of hearing child: A challenge to educators. The Volta Review 68: 351-353, 1966

Perry T. Leslie

2
A Rationale for a Mainstream Education for the Hearing Impaired

Mainstream education for hearing impaired children is not new pedagogy. The statement of a mainstream rationale is not a new challenge. Rather, it is an ongoing concern. A rationale is a delineation of a philosophic position. This position may be influenced by logical presentation of fact, opinion, and a multitude of other variables.

This chapter will attempt to describe the current rationale for educational mainstreaming of hearing impaired children. The paper is entitled "*A* Rationale . . ." rather than "*The* Rationale . . ." because the author does not anticipate that this statement will stand unchanged or unchallenged in the future. As Lloyd Dunn recently stated: "Clearly special education for handicapped children is in the throes of transition. Any pronouncement at this point, . . . , is likely to be viewed in retrospect, as less than completely accurate" (Dunn, 1973, p. 5).

Hopefully information to be presented in this text and data now being collected will necessitate revision or amplification of this statement in the very near future.

As stated above, mainstream education for the hearing impaired is not new pedagogy. It has been practiced or preached for at least 20 years. In 1954, the Supreme Court of the United States proclaimed: "In these days, it is doubtful that any child may reasonably be expected to succeed in life if he is denied the opportunity of an education. Such an opportunity, where the state has undertaken to provide it, is a right which must be made available to all on equal terms" (Lippman and Goldberg, p. 1).

The interpretation of statements such as the one above result in a very wide range of service provision. Regular classes, special classes, special schools, institutions, and assorted support personnel are considered necessary, by some, for provision of the required educational opportunity. Still others interpret the statements as precluding any differentiation or classification of children. *All* children should be educated equally—equal class placement, instructional techniques, funding, etc. Some school systems point with pride to the fact that 15 percent of the school-aged population is receiving some form of special service. Still other systems proudly state that they have no school-aged children receiving special services. The interpretive differences are apparent.

What, then, is "mainstream" to mean? Webster defines mainstream as the prevailing current or direction of activity or influence. For a great many educators that definition is not inappropriate. Many are influenced simply by the prevailing direction of activity. Analysis of the trend is nonexistent.

Yet with a concerned, thinking group there would be no unanimity of definition. Again the interpretations would range from nonclassification to inclusion of all previously noted levels of service provision. Our professional literature is replete with repetitive models for service delivery (Reynolds, 1962; Deno, 1970; Dunn, 1973) and challenges to examine our classification and labelling systems (Dunn, 1968; Ross and Calvert, 1973). Suggestions have been made to "integrate," "absorb," "stream," "fuse," or "assimilate" hearing impaired children into regular classes and normal environments. For purposes of this chapter, the author has selected the most commonly presented definition of mainstreaming—"education of the hearing impaired child in as near normal an educational environment as is possible." This definition is considered necessary for reflection of a viable rationale for current educational programming.

The description of "as near normal . . . as . . . possible" does not lead to regular class placement alone. Some hearing impaired children will be fortunate enough to benefit from such a placement but there will be a need for a range of specialized services. A framework delineating the range of services is presented in Figure 2-1.

It is to be noted that the child is to be placed only as far into the cascade as is necessary and that this child is to be returned to upper levels of the cascade as soon as is feasible. There are, of course, problems associated with the cascade and some of them will be noted later in this chapter.

The chapter will now examine some of the factors that contribute to this rationale. As stated earlier, the rationale is reflective of fact and opinion or, if you will, reason where fact is not available.

Education of the hearing impaired has for two centuries, been plagued with the dearth of data related to educational programming. For the most part we have relied on reason or opinion for the development of program directions. This reliance has led to a rationale component which the author has labelled "bandwagon-support."

A Rationale for a Mainstream Education

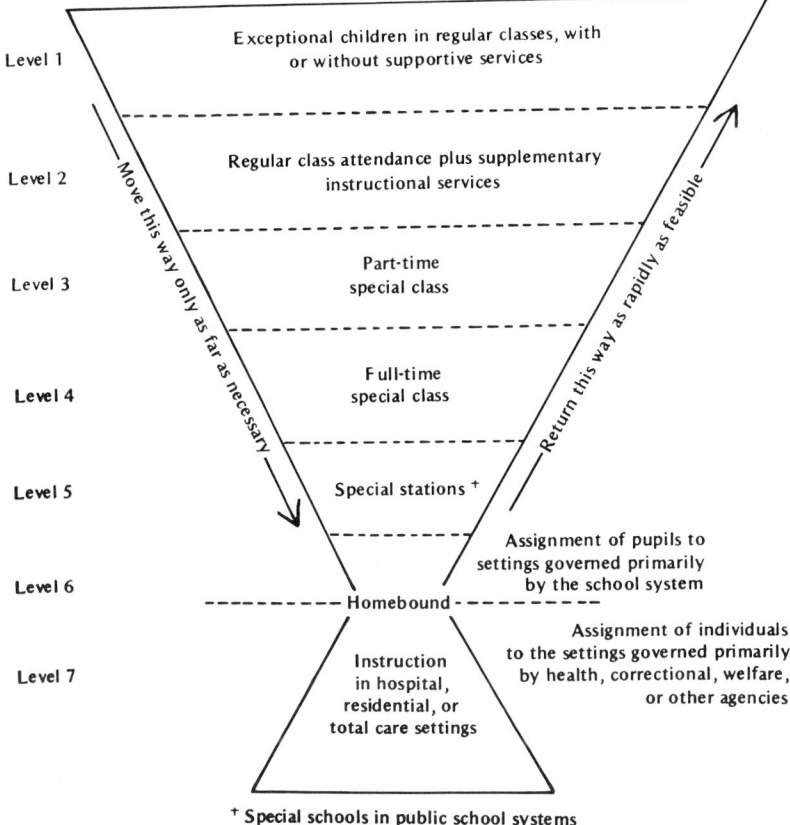

Fig. 2-1. The Cascade System of Special Education Service (DENO).

BANDWAGON-SUPPORT

Here, reference is made to the surge of popular opinion which accounts for mushrooming support for any particular methodology or practices for a particular individual or group of children. The "new" program may, for any number of reasons, meet with some success. The efforts may be applauded and given national or international recognition through professional meetings and/or journals. Other interested professionals then attempt to duplicate the program either nominally or in actual execution of similar methodologies.

Those "professionals" duplicating the program in name only appear to change little or nothing in their existing programs—with the exception of the addition of the label "mainstream." The motivation for such action is beyond the scope of this chapter. It can be noted, however, that many of the labelling group do receive reinforcements for operating programs employing "innovative" techniques.

Those professionals attempting to replicate a particular program through the bandwagon approach recognize a "successful" program and then set a target date at which time the new philosophy and methodology will be adopted in their program. These target dates vary from a day to years from the date of the decision. All of these people are involved in "spreading the word" and voicing support for the concept.

There is, then, a component in mainstreaming that relates specifically to the numbers and enthusiasm associated with the approach.

In the past some hearing impaired students were educated at all levels of the model presented in Figure 2-1 yet there was no felt need for a national symposium on the topic. It appears that the "bandwagon" people have aided in making mainstream education a real consideration for larger numbers of hearing impaired students.

Another related component in the rationale is simply labelled "dollar-support."

DOLLAR-SUPPORT

Historically, education appropriated a set amount of money for exceptional children. Each school system operating a special school or class for exceptional children was given a specified amount of money over and above the allotment for hearing children. This usually meant that the child had to be in an isolated or segregated unit. It was not uncommon for an inspector to appear and ask to see the special class *and* the children in it. If the children were in another class (temporarily or permanently) the inspector assumed that special services were not being provided and that the district was simply attempting to extract additional dollars for their schools. Programs have lost funding for this inability to produce the segregated children upon request. In some cases the inspector was correct in his assumption and, unfortunately, in others he wasn't.

Recent trends have loosened the rigidity of funding criteria. Many systems are allotted additional dollars provided it can be demonstrated that the hearing impaired student is receiving some specialized service.

Needless to say, this dollar availability has attracted a number of school systems to the mainstream model. Some systems accept the hearing impaired student and accompanying funds without providing any supportive services other than paper citation of speech therapist service.

These programs do the student and the concept of mainstreaming a disservice. However, many school systems have examined their potential for service delivery and have found that, with the available funding, they can support mainstreamed hearing impaired children within their system.

School systems are being required, in many states, to provide services for hearing impaired children or *buy* the services from agencies providing them. The costs of service provision and transportation to a school system buying services are rapidly increasing. This high cost of buying services combined with dollar availability for local service provision is resulting in many school systems developing mainstream programs for hearing impaired children.

In addition, a statement from a Lexington School study (Connor, 1972) indicated that a conservative estimate of the monetary savings to taxpayers would be $28,000 per child mainstreamed (average cost).

The funding for local mainstream programs and the estimated $28,000 savings per child contribute greatly to the growing support for mainstreaming hearing impaired children.

Another concern of many mainstream proponents is the effect of segregation. For purposes of discussion this concern is identified as "psycho-social support."

PSYCHO-SOCIAL SUPPORT

Documentation of program enrollments indicates that the majority of hearing impaired students in the U.S. attend segregated special programs (Gentile, 1972). Much of this population can be found in state residential schools. These large residential school enrollments are often reflective of the educational placement options open to parents. State governments have provided the necessary support for development of a residential treatment facility. Previous discussion indicated that support money for the hearing impaired was often difficult to acquire and maintain in school systems while the state residential facility presented a centralized, specialized service for the hearing impaired. Hence, large numbers of students were placed in the state school because it presented the most appropriate educational program available. Placement of the hearing impaired student in a segregated, often isolate, educational environment and, for many, separation from their family units created some concerns about the psycho-social development of the individual.

Goffman (1961) authored a book entitled "Asylums" wherein he described characteristics of a total institution. Goffman defined a total institution as "a place of residence and work where a large number of like-situated individuals, cut off from the wider society for an appreciable period of time, together lead an enclosed, formally administered round of life" (Goffman, p. XIII). It is recognized that Goffman developed this sociological treatise while examining a mental hospital and a prison. It is further recognized that some students in state schools do not actually maintain residence in the school. Nevertheless, there are some interesting sociological parallels to be found in these institutions.

Patients arrive at the institution with what Goffman terms

> "a 'presenting culture' derived from a 'home world'—a way of life and a round of activities taken for granted until the point of admission to the institution . . . . Whatever the stability of the . . . personal organization, it was part of a wider framework lodged in his civil environment—a round of experience that confirmed a tolerable conception of self and allowed for a set of defensive maneuvers, exercised at his own discretion, for coping with conflicts, discreditings, and failures.
>
> Now it appears that total institutions do not substitute their own unique culture for something already formed; we deal with something more restricted than acculturation or assimilation. If cultural change does occur, it has to do, perhaps, with the removal of certain behavior opportunities and with failure to keep pace with recent social changes on the outside. Thus, if the . . . stay is long, what has been called 'disculturation' may occur—that is, an 'untraining' which renders him temporarily incapable of managing certain features of daily life . . ."
> (Goffman, pp. 12, 13).

The parallels are easily drawn in residential schools for the deaf. A child does arrive with sets of defensive maneuvers and the school usually does remove certain behavior opportunities—such as interaction with hearing peers. This does lead to coping difficulties when the student is returned to the environs of the hearing. The author realizes that many residential institutions have long since recognized this problem and they are attempting to overcome this disculturation. The fact remains that most of these institutions are separated or segregated from the environment of the hearing in terms of physical plant, educational programming, and student interaction.

The preceding statements are not presented in an attempt to discredit residential programs. State schools have been filling a very real need for specialized service. The intent of the statements is to focus on the effect of child removal from his natural environment.

This consideration may be reinforced through examination of three basic adjustment patterns common to persons with impaired hearing. The adjustment patterns were suggested by Myerson (1963).

The first adjustment pattern treats the world of the normally hearing as negative. The person is clearly within the world of impaired hearing.

> "The amount of overlap or commonality with the life space of the normally hearing is slight. The valence of the overlap is simultaneously positive and negative. It is positive because some areas, like earning a living, cannot often be restricted to the psychological world of impaired hear-

ing. It is negative because a situation open equally to hearers and impaired hearers often requires the impaired hearers to function at a disadvantage. (Myerson, p. 146)

"Adjustment Pattern 1 is often called 'withdrawal' and condemned as undesirable by practically all except those who practice it. . . . Withdrawal is not necessarily an undesirable or maladjusted reaction. In many cases it is appropriate and realistic. In some degree it decreases the opportunities for varied satisfactions and gratifications. However, it also solves the problem of antagonistic overlapping role situations. (Myerson, p. 149)

Adjustment Pattern One.

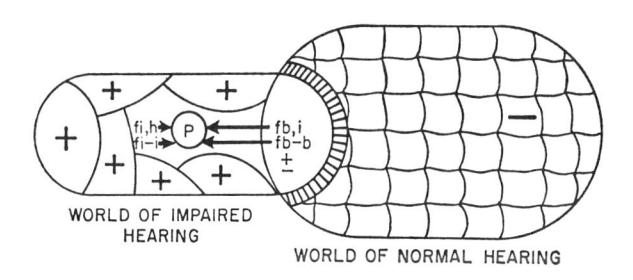

Legend: fi, h—force in world of the impaired hearing toward world of the hearing; fi - i—force in world of the impaired hearing away from the world of the impaired hearing; fb, i—force in barrier toward world of the impaired hearing; fb - b—force in barrier region away from barrier region.

From: Lee Myerson 'A Psychology of Impaired Hearing' in PSYCHOLOGY Of Exceptional Children and Youth, 2nd ed., William M. Cruickshank, (c) 1963. By permission of Prentice-Hall, Inc., Englewood Cliffs, N.J.

Adjustment Pattern Two.

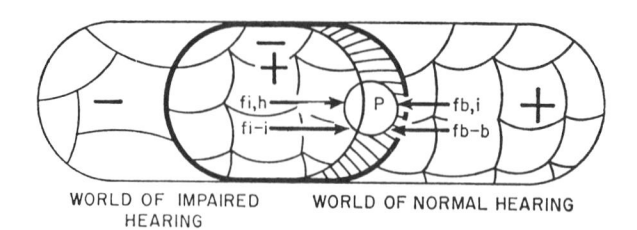

WORLD OF IMPAIRED HEARING   WORLD OF NORMAL HEARING

Legend: fi, h—force in world of the impaired hearing toward world of the hearing; fi - i—force in world of the impaired hearing away from the world of the impaired hearing; fb, i—force in barrier toward world of the impaired hearing; fb - b—force in barrier region away from barrier region.

From: Lee Myerson 'A Psychology of Impaired Hearing' in PSYCHOLOGY Of Exceptional Children and Youth, 2nd ed., William M. Cruickshank, (c) 1963. By permission of Prentice-Hall, Inc., Englewood Cliffs, N.J.

"shows the life space of a person who rejects the world of impaired hearing and aspires to the world of the normally hearing. He desires to do exactly the same things as the normally hearing and in exactly the same way. As in . . . Adjustment Pattern 1, however, the ability and social barriers to participation in the world of the normally hearing are strong. Individuals who select this adjustment pattern live on the barrier between two ways of life . . ." (Myerson, p. 147)

The hearing impaired person is unable to do all of the same things as the normally hearing in exactly the same way and he rejects the options presented by the world of the hearing impaired.

"In Adjustment Pattern 2, there are also positive and negative aspects. On the one hand, the psychological world may be larger and better differentiated. On the other hand, the person may be uncertain about the boundaries of his world, about the group to which he belongs, and about his status in the world of the normally hearing." (Myerson, p. 152)

A Rationale for a Mainstream Education

Adjustment Pattern Three.

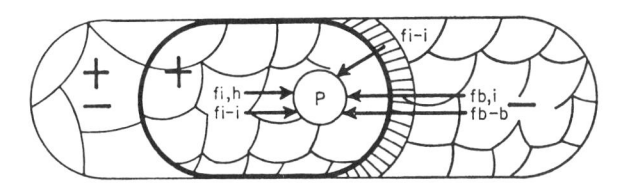

Legend: fi, h—force in world of the impaired hearing toward world of the hearing; fi - i—force in world of the impaired hearing away from the world of the impaired hearing; fb, i—force in barrier toward world of the impaired hearing; fb - b—force in barrier region away from barrier region.

From: Lee Myerson 'A Psychology of Impaired Hearing' in PSYCHOLOGY Of Exceptional Children and Youth, 2nd ed., William M. Cruickshank, (c) 1963. By permission of Prentice - Hall, Inc. Englewood Cliffs, N.J.

"is a schematic representation of the life space of a person who eagerly enters and values the large area of commonality that exists between those who have impaired hearing and those who have normal hearing. Such a person perceives himself as one who shares many behavioral areas with others. Impaired hearing is correctly perceived to be only one of his characteristics . . . (Myerson, p. 147)

Some consequences of Adjustment Pattern 3, therefore, are the following:

The person is easily able to say, 'I have impaired hearing'. He does not devalue himself or his group. Differences can be neutral. He sees the value of 'hearing behavior' as an asset, but 'impaired hearing behavior' does not affect the worth of the person. If he is placed at a disadvantage in a normally hearing world it is because of the difficulty of the task and not the incompetence of the person. He, therefore, does not blame himself or feel guilt and shame. Because he is cognitively clear about this, his behavior is flexible and not bound by anxiety. He can cognitively guide his behavior in a conscious, goal-directed, and voluntary way and describe what he is doing to others. At one stroke he frees himself from ambiguous group memberships and their conflicting group demands" (Myerson, p. 165).

The three adjustment patterns are representative of the most common adjustments made by hearing impaired persons. Each pattern is appropriate for particular individuals. It is worthy of note that segregated institutions will most likely prepare hearing impaired persons for adjustment pattern one as contact with the hearing world is minimal. Myerson points out that for "many children it is not until after they leave school that they have an opportunity to choose their own adjustment pattern" (p. 151). Myerson also notes that "maladjusting consequences of new psychological situations . . . occur in cases of impaired hearing . . . The . . . solution for the reduction of maladjustment is . . . : reduce newness" (p.145).

Attempts to mainstream hearing impaired students will result in larger numbers of pupils being placed in levels one, two, and three of the cascade of services (Fig. 2-1). These students should then have greater opportunities for reduction in newness of psychological situations involving hearing persons.

One of the major contributions to mainstream philosophy has been made by the Council for Exceptional Children (CEC). The organization has developed policy statements related to "basic commitments to education".

BASIC COMMITMENTS TO EDUCATION

"The fundamental purposes of Special Education are the same as those of regular education: the optimal development of the individual as a skillful, free, and purposeful person, able to plan and manage his own life and to reach his highest potential as an individual and as a member of society" (Lippman and Goldberg, p. 89). These goals are representative of education's respect for the integrity of each individual, whether he be impaired or not. The CEC policy statement related to this concern reads

> "The focus of all education should be the unique learning needs of the individual child, and of the child as a total functioning organism. All educators should recognize and accept the identity of fundamental purposes in both special and regular education.
>
> The purpose of special education is to enlarge the variety of educational programs for all children so that the individualization of programs may be furthered as a way of fulfilling the fundamental purposes of education for all children, whatever their needs.
>
> As advocates of the rights of all children to education, special educators affirm their professionalism" (Lippman and Goldberg, p. 90).

CEC has attempted to bring to the forefront the information that special education is not for deviant children. It is to provide a depth and variety to educational programs where the absence of special education would result in less comprehensive services and knowledges for *all* children.

One can easily see the depth and variety educators of the hearing impaired can bring to hearing as well as hearing impaired students. Knowledge of special speech and language assessment and development techniques, curricular adaptation techniques, and amplification systems, to name but a few, combined with a sensitivity toward exceptionality of individuals would certainly be of benefit in work with some hearing as well as hearing impaired students. Most important, though, are the inter- and intrapersonal effects of hearing upon hearing impaired pupils and vice versa. In order to have any student on the road to reaching his highest potential as an individual and member of society it would appear imperative that the school membership be, as nearly as possible, a representative cross-section of that society.

Review of recent special education history chronicles the development of services and professional commitments in a different direction. We were intent on working with the special child, in many instances in special settings. Our concerns were not with development of an enlarged variety of educational programs for all children. Instead, we labored for specialized programs and physical plants for our hearing impaired children.

Affirmation of the professionalism of special educators is indicative of the awareness of a role larger than provision of service to hearing impaired children alone.

Examination of basic commitments to education has provided considerable momentum for the mainstream movement for hearing impaired students.

In addition to examination of goals and commitments in special education, the CEC Policies Commission also commented on the placement of children in special school programs. The resulting CEC policy contributed to mainstream "legislation and litigation."

LEGISLATION AND LITIGATION

The policy statement reads

"Special education should be arranged for exceptional children whenever feasible to protect the stability of their home, school, and community relationships and to enhance their self-concepts. Special Education placements, particularly those involving separation from community, school and home life, should be made only after careful study and for compelling reasons.

"Within schools the placement of all children should maximize their opportunities for the best possible education. Specialized placements that are effected crudely and simply by the rejection of children from regular school situations are educationally and morally indefensible. Special Education is not and should not be used as a residual operation or catchall for children who are difficult to teach. Equally indefensible is the failure to develop needed differentiation of school programs that result in the confinement of pupils in inappropriate educational settings" (Lippman and Goldberg, p. 94).

Accountability for placement and provision of community-based programs were stressed in this policy statement. Parents and professionals applied pressure to insure that school authorities and elected government officials were aware of the needs.

Dr. Edwin Martin, Jr., Associate Commissioner for Education of the Handicapped in the U.S. Office of Education, stated

"Persons interested in education of handicapped children will work to create positive public attitudes towards the handicapped, showing the effectiveness of education and reducing the fear and ignorance which has led to discrimination; will be involved as friends of the court in the judicial process of insuring equal protection under the law for the handicapped; and will work with legislators and administrators to develop effective programming for each child" (Exceptional Children, March, 1972).

CEC continued in its efforts and developed a model law for the education of seven million handicapped children.

The model law was developed to allow states to examine their own laws, policies, and services in light of a standard acceptable for the education of all handicapped children. This evaluative tool pointed out the need for compulsory school attendance for all children and specification of services provided for handicapped children. Included in this model law was service provision for handicapped persons extending from birth to 21 years of age. Mechanisms for implementation of service provision were also provided. Many states have examined their legislation and modifications have been made. The modifications range from minor changes to the Tennessee efforts which adopted, virtually intact, the model legislation. To date there are a minimum of 30 states with legislative provisions for permissive or mandatory service delivery to hearing impaired persons between the ages of 1 and 21 years (Hanners, 1974).

Establishment of laws alone does not ensure program implementation. Parents, educators and other professional workers are "operating in a new arena: the courts. Litigation is not a substitute for all previous forms of social action; it is, rather, a major addition to the armamentarium of those who would obtain more effective services for the handicapped" (Lippman and Goldberg, p. 2).

We have had support in our quest from the executive and legislative branches of government and we are now experiencing reinforcements from the judiciary.

One suit of great importance in special education is *Mills vs the Board of Education of the District of Columbia*. The decision in this case "provided that all handicapped children . . . have an equal right to education. Also, the *Mills* case is considered 'a final and irrevocable determination of plaintiffs' constitutional rights" (Mann, p. 1).

> "The *Mills* decision mandates too that the handicapped be provided a regular public school assignment or with alternatives at public expense and with constitutionally adequate hearings. Thus each child of school age must be provided ' . . . a free and suitable publicly-supported education regardless of the degree of the child's mental, physical or emotional disability or impairment . . .' (Abeson, 1973, p. 3).

> "In other words, the excuse of insufficient funds is not adequate reason to exclude these children from their right to an education" (Mann, p. 2).

The court's decision is clear. Hearing impaired children have the right to a mainstream education—regardless of expense.

The challenge before us is to see that the child's rights and the law are not ignored or violated. In addition, *we* must be prepared to provide the services.

The author feels compelled to discuss professional accountability at this point. We, along with parents and other professionals, continue to demand that the hearing impaired child be educated in as near normal a situation as possible. It is in order for educators to examine preparation. Are we certified to work with hearing as well as hearing impaired children? Have we identified the parameters of placement? That is, do we understand which variables contribute to successful performance in a regular classroom? Should specialized individual services be provided the hearing impaired child prior to integration with hearing children; if so, for how long? Are we able to define cognitive and affective growths in children? How do we determine the success or failure of a particular placement? The list of questions could fill a book. Obviously, mainstreaming is not an educational panacea.

School systems are being held accountable in the courts. The next logical step would be to have educators accountable for their front line delivery system decisions.

The chapters to follow will be most helpful in answering some of the immediate concerns.

SUMMARY

Discussion has centered on five major components in the rationale for a mainstream education. Obviously, some are more important than others.

The bandwagon supporters are helpful in the sense of numbers alone. They are, however, a potential problem as their support is hollow. These people don't really understand what mainstreaming involves and they should be educated quickly if they are to become a positive force in the mainstream movement.

Financial support is also a positive-negative component. Increased dollar availability enables development of services needed but it also attracts some money vultures. We must continually examine the expenditures vs. services rendered ledgers.

One of the largest and more positive components is the basic commitment to education. Stress is placed on the recognition of individual difference of all children. Achievement of the educational goals involves special education as *a part of* the regular system in order to provide a greater depth and variety of experiences for *all* children. Special educators have worked with a very few exceptional children rather than all individuals.

The component creating the most rapid developments toward achievement of mainstreaming is the support of the judicial and legislative branches of government. Official recognition of the exceptional child's right to an education in as near normal a situation as possible is now recorded in the courts and a majority of state legislations. We have the precedents to ensure service delivery to any hearing impaired child in the United States.

In the author's opinion, the most important component in the rationale is the psycho-social consideration of the hearing impaired child. The recognition that preparation for societal life necessitates the development of a hearing impaired person's integrity and identity within that society is long overdue and welcome.

BIBLIOGRAPHY

Connor L: That the Deaf May Speak. Paper presented at Madison Association for the Deaf annual banquet, Madison, Wisconsin, Spring, 1972

Deno E: The Cascade System of Special Education Service in Northcott WH (ed) The Hearing Impaired Child in a Regular Classroom. A.G. Bell Assn. for the Deaf, Washington, D.C., p. 6, 1973

Dunn L: The Normalization of Special Education. Inaugural lecture, Laycock Memorial Lectureship, University of Saskatchewan, Saskatoon, Saskatchewan, Canada, November, 1973

Dunn L: Special education for the mildly retarded—Is much of it justifiable? Exceptional Children, 1968

Gentile A: Special Report from the Office of Demographic Studies, Gallaudet College National Survey of State Identification Audiometry Programs and Special Educational Services for Hearing Impaired Children and Youth, United States, Washington, D.C., 1972

Goffman E: Asylums. Anchor Books, Doubleday and Company, Inc., Garden City, New York, 1961

Hanners B: A Model Service Delivery System for Audiologic Management of Young Hearing Impaired Children, paper presented at ASHA Convention, Las Vegas, Nev., Nov. 8, 1974

Lippman L, Goldberg I: Right to Education. Teachers College Press, Columbia University, New York, 1973

Martin E: Individualism and behaviorism as future trends in educating handicapped children. Exceptional Children, 1972

Mann P: Mainstream Special Education. Proceedings of the University of Miami Conference on Special Education in the Great Cities, Council for Exceptional Children, 1974

Myerson L: A psychology of impaired hearing, in Cruickshank W (ed): Psychology of Exceptional Children and Youth. Prentice-Hall, Inc., Englewood Cliffs, N.J., 1963

Reynolds MC: A framework for considering some issues in special education. Exceptional Children, 1962

Ross M, Calbert DR: The semantics of deafness, in Northcott WH (ed): The Hearing Impaired Child in a Regular Classroom, A.G. Bell Association, Washington, D.C., 1973

Derek A. Sanders

3

Residual Hearing—The Yeast of Communication

The title of this chapter was selected for two reasons. Firstly, it illustrates the concepts to which I shall draw your attention and, I hope, does so in a sufficiently novel manner as to cause you to recall them by the title. It was also selected because, contrary to what one might otherwise expect, the process to which it refers is a rather slow, but nevertheless, necessary one.

Yeast serves as a leavening agent in the baking process just, as I wish to suggest, the use of residual hearing serves as a leavening agent in the development of communication processes. A leavening agent is defined by Webster's New World Dictionary (1970) as "any influence spreading through something and working on it to bring about a *gradual* change." Residual hearing, or the effective use of it, serves, therefore, to provide a catalytic action. You may recall from your school chemistry lessons that a catalyst is any substance which acts as the stimulus in bringing about, or hastening, a result.

Perhaps the most limiting element in the exploitation of the potential resources of residual hearing is our concept of the role which it can play in the growth of communicative abilities. I believe that our limited thinking arises from two factors. Firstly, those of us in the field of speech and hearing have been trained to think within the framework of a clinical model. This is particularly true when we consider the effects of deafness. Most of the concern in audiology, until recently, has been concentrated upon the diagnosis of the problem, thus attention has been focused upon the hearing that has been lost. We speak of "hearing loss," "hearing deficit," and/or "hearing impairment." These terms place emphasis upon what is *not* present, upon the extent of the deviation from the norm. From a diagnostic point of view this is an appropriate attitude. However from the point of view of the educator or rehabilitation worker, such an approach is not only inappropriate, it is counter productive. Our concern is not with what is absent, since there is presently no way that we can recover that. Our concern is, rather, with an accurate definition of the resources which remain, and the identification for each child or adult, of the most effective procedures for exploiting those resources.

A second limiting factor in the maximal use of residual hearing arises from the narrowness of our view of the processes involved. We tend to exhibit symptoms of tunnel vision when we approach the task of making maximal use of residual hearing.

Let me risk an heretical statement for an audiologist, and state that as educators or rehabilitation audiologists we really are not concerned with hearing per se at all. The diagnostic audiologist is concerned with hearing for it is his task to define, as accurately as possible, the sensory capability of the auditory system. Such definition requires measures of sensitivity, temporal resolving power and channel capacity. *The education or rehabilitation specialist has as his or her task the management of perceptual and learning strategies in the child.* It is true that the auditory system will play an important role in the educational plan. It is, nevertheless, in terms of its role in the far more comprehensive process of total perception, that we must consider it. If we confine our thinking about hearing to the processing of sensations, which is the rightful concern of the psychoacoustician, we will necessarily exclude from our training programs those children whose hearing deficit is so severe as to preclude their ability to perceive speech through the auditory system alone.

If on the other hand we direct our attention to the perceptual process then we are no longer concerned with hearing as an end in itself, but as a means to an end.

THE PERCEPTUAL PROCESS

Let us briefly consider the nature of the perceptual process. Garner (1966) has stated

"*To perceive is an active process,* one in which the perceiver participates fully. The perceiver does not passively receive information about his environment; rather, he actively perceives his environment. Nor does he simply impose his organization on an otherwise unstructured world—the world is structured. But he does select the structure to which he will attend and react, and he even provides the missing structure on occasion" (p. 11).

The first point I would like to make then is that *perception is an active rather than a passive process.* As such it is not simply determined by the degree of hearing sensitivity present but is a function of the readiness and effectiveness of the individual's perceptual system to search out, and focus in upon, relevant sound patterns.

I want to emphasize most strongly that such a viewpoint makes it impossible to use a pure tone audiogram as an indicator of a child's actual or potential effectiveness in processing spoken language. An audiogram is, at best, an indication of sensory capability for processing pure tones. *It is a measure of end organ function.* It is *not* a measure of the perceptual processing competence involved in the transformation of sensory stimuli into the patterns of coded information which comprise phrases and sentences.

There is at present no way in which we can change the sensitivity of the damaged hair cells of the organ of Corti. It is however worthwhile noting that in experimental animals the efferent fibres of the auditory system have been shown to be capable of exerting a tuning effect even down to the level of the auditory nerve (Desmedt, 1960, 1962). Certainly efferent motor fibres are known to be able to control the flow of afferent impulses, either enhancing or decreasing responses of neuron groups. As Abbs and Sussman (1971) have stated

> "This process acts to enhance differences and reduce confusion at the periphery and at higher stations by the inhibition of one nerve cell by another without specific central control" (p. 25).

There would therefore seem to be neurophysiological evidence to support the probable existence of an auditory system which can be tuned by the brain to give preferential treatment to those patterns of stimuli sought, while inhibiting the processing of irrelevant patterns. This means then that the effective utilization of sound is heavily influenced by the readiness of the auditory perceptual system to process it. To clarify the concept I suggest that we use the term *expectancy,* instead of readiness. Thus, to repeat our statement in a slightly different form—*the effectiveness with which a sound stimulus is processed by the auditory system is directly related to its expectancy of that stimulus.*

I am saying, therefore, that we are not dealing with an all-or-none situation. Except in rare cases of total hearing deficiency, it is not a question of whether a sound is heard or not heard, but whether the expectancy of the system is sufficiently appropriate to permit the percept of an object event or idea to be evoked by less than the total sound stimulus.

What is this expectancy? How is it generated? Expectancy can only be generated when structure is present. It arises from the experience gained from repeated exposure to orderly patterns. As Garner (1966) stated, it is not necessary to impose structure upon the world, the world is structured. The emphasis is, therefore, upon the identification of a structure or pattern; the differentiation of one pattern from another. This necessitates learning, for a pattern is generated as a function of the interrelationship between the component parts. This interrelationship results in an envelope, the shape of which is determined by its contents. The envelope is equivalent to the gestalt or wholeness of the pattern.

If we are familiar with the envelope we will not need to know each and everyone of its contents. Knowing only some of them will frequently be sufficient to permit us to generate a picture of the envelope by simply linking the key component measures. How many you will need to know will, of course, depend upon your familiarity with the pattern. The greater its familiarity the less you need to process in order to identify it. In other words the greater your expectancy the less you are dependent upon an analysis of the stimulus pattern. A second factor is of course the degree of similarity between the given pattern and others resembling it.

What I am speaking about is of course the processing of information. *Information* is an appropriate concept to introduce at this point for it refers in this context to the value of each of the contents of the envelope, rather than to the meaningful whole. If you are able to predict the presence of a particular component you barely need to process it; its information value is low for it does not tell you anything you did not already know. It merely confirms your prediction.

It should be apparent from this that *your need for the stimulus is inversely related to your ability to predict it*. This is not, as I said, a situation of "now you hear it now you don't" for if I can increase your familiarity with the stimulus pattern, the ease and rapidity with which you will identify it will increase accordingly. This holds true for envelopes which encompass a phoneme, a morpheme, a word, phrase or sentence. Even a whole idea can be conceived as being recreated by the listener in this way.

THE EFFECT OF HEARING DEFICIT ON THE PERCEPTUAL PROCESS

Let me now try to relate this to the problem confronting the hearing impaired child. He is suffering from the effect of the hearing deficiency which deprives him of sufficient auditory information necessary to identify the auditory stimulus. As a result he is not naturally exposed to the acoustic structure of his environment, neither to environmental noises nor to speech sound patterns. In many instances the deprivation will be severe, in other less handicapped children, the deficit will result in the failure to receive parts of the potential auditory information. His opportunities to deduce the rules by which we generate speech will be seriously limited.

Note that the emphasis is not on the acquisition of language as an additive function, but as a *generative* function. If you are to generate something you must be familiar with the rules before you can use the system. The growing infant spends the first year or more receiving and processing, with increasing complexity and accuracy, the acoustic signals of speech. Not until he is into his second year does he have a sufficient understanding of the generative rules of language to begin to make them work for him. Not for a further two years will he have mastered all the grammatical forms of adult spoken language.

The irony of the situation in which the hearing impaired child finds himself is that the rules which his brain must deduce, if he is to learn to process language, can only be deduced naturally through the auditory pathway. That pathway, however, is not functioning efficiently. Furthermore, as I will later explain, the effectiveness with which he can process the acoustic information, and his dependency upon it, are both related to language competency.

The problem, therefore, is how to recover as much as possible of the leavening effect of residual hearing. We know that unless we are able to utilize residual hearing communication processes cannot develop in the same manner as occurs in a normal hearing child. This means that the child will develop communicative strategies which are inappropriate to the processing of speech communication. A system in its early stages of development possesses a high degree of flexibility, or "plasticity" as Lenneberg (1967) calls it. This is essential because its evolution is determined not only by genetic endowment, but also by feedback concerning its effectiveness in the task of need satisfaction. It is important to realize that neither one of these two factors alone determines the evolution of the system. It is the interaction of genetic coding and environmental influences which molds the structure. As Church (1961) has stressed, ontogenetic evolution stands in a circular feedback relationship to experience.

The congenitally hearing impaired child stands in double jeopardy. He is born with a deficient auditory structure which also serves to seriously reduce the capacity of the environment to act upon him. This limits the learning of the language rules which are so important in facilitating the processes of translating the acoustic signals of speech.

We must further add to the problem the fact that, as the system develops, it progressively loses its plasticity, reducing its capacity for change. Again let me remind you that we are talking not about hearing, not even about auditory perception, but about the complete communication system. This involves not only the use and pattern of integration of sensory systems, but also the processes of perceptualization, conceptualization and language processing.

Each of these processes involve the systems capacity and efficiency in the utilization of information. I have stated that perception involves the identification of patterns or structures of information. Information, I explained, is not in itself meaningful, but is analogous to the ingredients of a cake. The dependency of the cook upon the recipe, using the same analogy, will be inversely related to his familiarity with it. The process of baking the cake is a sequential one in which each step is dependent upon each previous step. The pattern or sequence of steps which the cook follows is itself indicative of the cake he is baking. If you are familiar with the recipe, the first few steps will simply serve to identify which recipe the cook is using, after which you should be able to take over and complete the task yourself without reference to the recipe because you are able to predict the steps still to be completed. If, on the other hand, you are unfamiliar with the recipe you will have to read each step from first to last if you are to complete the process.

When we consider the child with a hearing deficit, we find a similar situation. A speaker generates a spoken language code according to a set of well defined linguistic rules, the nature of which we have only recently begun to understand. Despite our conscious ignorance of these rules, our efficient use of speech is testimonial to our subconscious knowledge of them. Rules, when followed, result in structure, structure in turn represents ordered probabilities for each component. Familiarity with the probable relationships of each component to all other possible components, and of each sequence to all other possible sequences, makes it possible to predict the emerging pattern before all the information is in; a process normally referred to as *closure*. In communication, closure may occur at any level of language processing from phonemic to semantic. The ability to complete early closure is therefore dependent upon a knowledge of the rules or constraints operating on the speaker generating the speech signal. Familiarity with these rules permits you to generate the envelope of the pattern from less than the full total of components.

Our interest lies, not in what the hearing impaired child is able to hear (though such information is valuable in planning lessons) but in what he is able to perceive. I have tried to show that what he is able to perceive is as much a function of his expectancies or predictions as it is a function of his hearing.

Since this is the case it is necessary for you to realize, that our criterion for the measure of auditory function must be communicative behavior not pure tone audiometry.

This requires yet another concession on your part. If communicative behavior is the criterion, we cannot, in all fairness, judge a child's *capacity* to communicate orally until he has acquired the basic rules by which communication is made possible. To fail to concede this point would be like judging the effectiveness of the yeast immediately after it has been added. Even responses to pure tone stimuli not uncommonly improve after a child learns to use residual hearing.

Auditory behavior therefore is learned behavior, learned either in a natural manner or as a result of the management of environmental exposure. Communication training, of which auditory training is a major component, is concerned with the management of environmental exposure in order to enhance the auditory learning process.

Before we examine the implications of these ideas it seems appropriate to summarize them for you:

I have suggested that auditory perception and auditory sensation are two related but different processes; that the level of auditory perception is not exclusively dependent upon auditory sensitivity. To better describe our concern I used the term "sensory capabilities" which I borrowed from a text title (Stark, 1974). I stressed that we must direct our attention not to peripheral hearing, but to the actual and potential auditory abilities of the child, not to the hearing itself but to the effect which it can have upon the development of the communicative abilities of the child.

In my discussion I have stressed the active nature of the perceptual process, which involves the participation of the organism. I explained that in doing this the sensory system is actively postured or oriented in a manner most likely to be appropriate to the reception of the incoming sound pattern. This posturing is based upon expectancies generated internally on the basis of subconscious knowledge of the linguistic system. I tried to show how expectancies reduced dependency upon the acoustic signal, turning the process of listening into one of sampling key components, probably just the stressed syllables (Martin, 1972). Such expectancies permit the perception of the whole pattern, the envelope, on the basis of a confirmation of these key landmarks. This process is equally valid at all levels of language patterning from phonemic to semantic.

When considering the hearing impaired child, I stressed the double jeopardy in which he is placed. The peripheral deficit, unless compensated for, reduces the child's exposure to the examples of naturally occuring everyday speech from which language rules are developmentally deduced. This in turn results in a limiting of the process of developing expectancy which increases the child's dependency upon the very system which is deficient.

I impressed upon you the urgency of intervening in this situation before the natural plasticity of the system hardens before the aberrant communication system develops such inertia that all the training in the world will not shift it significantly.

Finally, I emphasized that auditory behavior, listening as opposed to hearing, is learned behavior.

THE ROLE OF RESIDUAL HEARING IN TRAINING THE HEARING HANDICAPPED CHILD

In our assessment of the hearing impaired child's auditory learning potential we have leaned heavily on the audiogram as a predictive tool. While it is not denied that a relationship exists between pure tone audiometric thresholds and speech intelligibility, the function is not a linear one

(Boothroyd, 1974). Unfortunately this fact has often been overlooked. There has been a tendency to equate audiometric deafness to functional deafness. Too often this has resulted in the labelling of a child as "deaf", with all its semantic overtones, on the basis of the audiogram. Ross and Calvert (1973) have cautioned us about the dangers of this labelling process. The child who is identified as "deaf" is frequently received by teachers who hold low expectations for his maximal use of residual hearing. A climate is created in which the role of the auditory system in communication and learning is deemphasized. The child learns to function according to the limited auditory behavior patterns characteristic of a deaf child, confirming the original assumption.

Functional deafness need not be a natural corollary of audiometric deafness, although we are not justified in assuming at this time that every hearing impaired child is capable of learning through auditory input alone. Not every child will be able to depend exclusively upon auditory learning for the acquisition of speech, language, and conceptual function. I believe it is our responsibility to ensure that each child is provided with a system of communication which permits him to develop maximally as a human being. For some children, insisting on a purely auditory/oral system will seriously limit both their conceptual development and their ability to communicate with others. For other children only an auditory/oral approach can fully meet their needs. To politicize the issue, to make decisions for individualized children on the basis of a generalized political philosophy is to me abhorrent. Decisions must be made in the best interest of the child not to support and justify a particular opinion you may hold!

It must be recognized that in the case of some children audiometric deafness and functional auditory behavior concur even after intensive auditory/oral training. The moral commitment which we must make is to demonstrate clearly that we have made every effort possible to exploit residual hearing to a maximum. The issue of whether, for the child with little demonstrable residual hearing, this should be done using an auditory approach, as advocated by Pollack (1970), or using a modified auditory/oral-manual approach as advocated by Furth (1966, 1971), needs to be faced.

The problem which confronts educators concerns how to identify a teaching/learning model of communication which is valid for an individual hearing impaired child. Even if we reject the either/or choice between the auditory/oral model and the manual models of finger spelling and signing, and elect an approach based upon a continuum model ranging from a purely auditory unisensory approach to a purely manual approach, we still need criteria for placing a child within the continuum. We lack a definitive understanding of the factors involved in sensory learning even when the information across modalities is compatible. When the information patterning in the two or more channels used for sensory input is governed by different genera-

Residual Hearing—The Yeast of Communication

tive rules as occurs, for example, in the simultaneous presentation of speech and sign language, it way well be that an inhibitory factor operates. We simply do not know enough about how children learn to understand the implications of auditory deficit for the teaching of hearing impaired children. Thus the responsibility for identifying an appropriate teaching approach for a given child still lies heavily on the shoulders of the teacher. Commitment to a given philosophy or model is not sufficient. What the teacher needs is to be able to make realistic predictions about which particular method might be most appropriate for a particular child. We need to know which parameters are important in reaching this decision.

Because of the critical nature of the first year of life in the processes of language and concept acquisition it is of great importance to make an assessment of which teaching approach to take as early as possible. An interesting approach to early assessment of a child's potential for auditory learning has been outlined by Downs (1974). While the criteria she uses are still at a rather gross stage, they afford a potential for refinement. Downs has identified a number of weighted factors which she believes may aid in the identification of those children for whom a purely auditory/oral approach is counter indicated. Downs has checked the usefulness of her system by assessing it by those children, now grown, for whom she feels she made what proved to be an incorrect judgment when they were small. I recommend that we encourage this type of approach to our problem. I believe in the past our assessment of the potential which a child has for the development of auditory/oral communication has been affected by the unreality of the political climate which insisted that no child should be provided with any alternative to auditory/oral education. The many failures we experienced placed the whole system in jeopardy. Many teachers lost their confidence in the auditory/oral appraoch with the result that in fewer and fewer instances was a total commitment made to the maximal exploitation of residual hearing. Yet such total commitment is essential to success. It is our philosophy, our conviction of its correctness, and the vigor with which we pursue its goals, that for many children ensures that residual hearing plays a major role in the development of communication skills. We must not assume that functional deafness is inevitable, yet it is necessary to be realistic concerning those children who after a period of intensive observation and evaluation give no indication of being affected in any way by amplified sound.

Downs (1974) feels that some 20 percent to 40 percent of children with what we call severe to profound hearing losses are in the category that precludes successful auditory input. It is essential to identify these children as early as possible for as Downs says,

> "To expect that children with no effective auditory input will learn adequate language through speech reading alone is a folly that we must not perpetuate."

For these children an alternative system of complete language input must be provided. This, Downs points out, is requisite if the biological language readiness period of the first two years of life is to be maximally operative. That a complete system of manual communication such as the Seeing Essential English (1973) system used in conjunction with traditional methods of communication training, does not hinder learning has been attested to by Schlesinger and Meadow (1973). This however does not obviate the fact that for children with sufficient residual hearing language is best learned by the auditory/oral method. It is with this group that we must make maximal efforts to capitalize on the potential auditory abilities. The reason I have considered those with little or no residual hearing is because I feel that a total commitment to an auditory/oral approach can be made with conviction only if we first identify the children with whom we have every reason to presume that we can and will be successful. With this latter group, the effective use of amplification coupled with a pragmatically designed program of language stimulation can result in achievements which will belie the audiogram.

If we are to prevent functional deafness from arising from audiometric deafness we must ensure that

Amplification is Provided as Soon as a Hearing Impairment of Peripheral Origin is Diagnosed

The earlier we achieve this the less likelihood there will be that the child comes to us with a language handicap. The optimal language learning period (0-2 years) can then be capitalized upon before the language and communication system begins to be laid down in nonauditory/oral patterns which become increasingly difficult to shift as the child grows older. Only through appropriate amplification can this be achieved.

Amplification is Optimally Functioning at All Times During the Child's Waking Day

It is totally inadequate to assume that because a child is wearing his aid it is necessarily functioning. A daily check of the aid should be made when the child arrives at school. The child should be taught the criteria by which he can make his or her own assessment of the performance of the aid. Any reported change in the child's communicative behavior should lead you to suspect the performance of the aid. Audiological evaluations and informal evaluation of communicative abilities should always include a comparison of aided and unaided performance with and without visual cues.

The Child is Given Repeated Exposure to the Auditory Pattern of all New Language Concepts

This means that the child must be asked to listen to several presentations of the sound of the word phrase or sentence being learned without visual cues. He must be encouraged to close his eyes and listen with his whole self. The auditory pattern should then be integrated with the visual speech pattern and then with the written form. Then the auditory pattern should again be isolated and presented several times.

Emphasis Be Given to Both Segmental and Suprasegmental Components of Speech

Increasing evidence is appearing in the literature (Martin, 1972; Robinson and Solomon, 1974) to support the claim that stress and rhythm play a far more important role in speech processing and perception than we have previously believed. We must therefore train the child to listen for, to evaluate, and to discriminate stress and intonational patterns relative to the semantics of the message.

The Major Unit With Which We Work be the Sentence and Not the Word

"The ordinary vehicle for reference is a sentence not a word" (Whorf, 1956, p. 258). Spoken language does not consist of a series of words threaded on a string of syntax like so many beads. It is a complex pattern of interactions between particular sounds, between particular words, and between particular phrases. The particular pattern of these relationships at each level is in itself highly informative. If the child is to learn to take advantage of this information he must be taught in units which expose him to it.

Lesson Materials Always Be Drawn Directly From, and Be Relevant to, A Child's Experience and Needs

Unless the child is motivated by need, the auditory pattern of the need related spoken message will have little meaning to him. Naturally occurring daily needs provide the basis of listening training. For the school child scholastic demands create a pressing need. Therefore preparatory and review lessons related to classroom subjects should be the major source of training materials.

The Reception, Discrimination, and Perception of Speech Sound Patterns be Simultaneously Related to the Speech Production of Those Sounds (Phonemes, Words, and Phrases)

Speech perception and speech production are two aspects of a single process (Halle and Stevens, 1959; Berry, 1969; Liberman, Mattingly, and Turvey, 1972). It is critical therefore to relate in the child's mind the sound pattern received and the manner of its production. This process will contribute to the correctness of perception.

Auditory Stimulation Always be a Component Part of Language Instruction

This brings us back to our initial statement, namely that auditory stimulation is the leavening agent in the process of the development of language skills, the yeast of communication. Auditory stimulation if not intimately related to the greater language environment of the thought or idea, will prove of little value. Auditory stimulation is a tool used to facilitate the growth of communication. It has no other justification.

In conclusion I would like to quote Freedle and Carroll (1972) who, in reflecting on language comprehension and acquisition, state

> "The individual's knowledge of the lexicon, grammar, and semantics of a language develops only gradually, even though some sort of "basic" competence is normally achieved at a fairly early age. Therefore, a child's comprehension of a verbal message is inevitably constrained, to a large extent, by his level of competence with respect to the vocabulary and syntax of the message." ". . . . . there is evidence that language competence develops only as the individual is exposed, over long periods of time, to increasingly difficult materials; somehow the individual is able to use this material as a basis for increasing not only his general knowledge and understanding, but also his basic linguistic competence. To a degree, the material itself can teach him new lexical items, new meanings, and new and complex syntactical constructions. But he can also be helped by instruction in understanding, by use of the dictionary, and by discussion of the content" (p. 360).

The authors are writing about the normal hearing child. Their comments illustrate how critical language is to thought and they point out that to some extent it is self generative. Yet even the hearing child benefits from instruction. How much more crucial that instruction is to the hearing impaired child.

The maximal use of residual hearing is about building language and communication skills. Since oral language is our major means of communication the auditory system provides the channel for language acquisition and for the monitoring of speech production. Hearing impairment reduces channel capacity. Unless we take major steps to keep the auditory perceptual system functioning, many children with the capacity to use residual hearing will grow up to be functionally deaf children. The term "deaf" defines a communicative behavioral pattern. For some children an alternative pattern is not achievable despite our best efforts. For most, however, functional deafness is not the inevitable result of audiometric deafness. We have been charged with the responsibility of ensuring that every child who has the potential also has the opportunity to remain in the mainstream of our society. Only with our help and our unwavering conviction that it can be done will this challenge be met.

BIBLIOGRAPHY

Abbs JH, Sussman HM: Neurophysiological features and speech perception. A discussion of theoretical implications. J. Speech Hearing Res. 14; 23-36, 1971

Berry MF: Language Disorders of Children. Appleton-Century-Crofts, New York, 1959

Boothroyd A: Effect of level of hearing loss upon speech intelligibility sensory capabilities in normal and hearing-impaired children, Discussion: Relation of speech perception and production to assessments of auditory function, in Stark R (ed): Sensory Capabilities of Hearing Impaired Children. Baltimore, University Park Press, 1974, pp 41-89

Calvert D, Ross M: The semantics of deafness, in Northcott WH (ed): The Hearing Impaired Child in a Regular Classroom, The Alexander Graham Bell Assoc. for the Deaf, Inc., Washington, D.C., 1973

Church J: Language and the Discovery of Reality, New York: Random House, Inc., 1961

Desmedt JE: Auditory evoked potentials from cochlea to cortex as influenced by activation of the efferent olivo-cochlear bundle. J. Acoust. Soc. Amer., 34: 1478-1496, 1962

Downs M: The Deafness Management Quotient. Hearing and Speech News, 21: 1974

Freedle RO, Carroll JB: Language comprehension and the acquisition of knowledge: reflections, in Freedle RO, Carroll JB (eds): Language Comprehension and the Acquisition of Knowledge, New York, Wiley, 1972

Furth HG: Thinking Without Language, New York, Free Press, 1966

Furth HG: Linguistic deficiency and thinking: research with deaf subjects, Psychol. Bull. 76: 58-72, 1971

Garner WR: To perceive is to know, Amer. Psychol. 21: 11-19, 1966

Halle M, Stevens KN: Analysis by Synthesis, in Wathen-Dunn W, Woods LE (eds): Proceedings of the Seminar on Speech Compression and Processing, Vol. 2. AFCRC-TR-59-198 U.S.A.F. Camb. Res. Ctr. 1959, Paper D7

Lenneberg EH: Biological Foundations of Language, New York, Wiley, 1967

Liberman AM, Mattingly IG, Turvey MT: Language codes and memory codes, in Melton AW, Martin E (eds): Coding Processes in Human Memory, Washington, D.C., V.H. Winston and Sons, 1972

Martin JG: Rhythmical heirarchical versus serial structure in speech and other behavior. Psychol. Rev. 6: 487-509, 1972

Pollack D: Educational Audiology for the Limited Hearing Infant, Springfield, Illinois, Charles C. Thomas, 1970

Robinson GM, Solomon DJ: Rhythm is processed by the speech hemisphere. J. Exp. Psychol. 102: 508-511, 1974

Sanders DA: Aural Rehabilitation, Englewood Cliffs, N.J., Prentice-Hall, Inc. 1971

Schlesinger H, Meadow K: Sound and Sign: Childhood Deafness and Mental Health, University of California Press, 1973

Seeing Essential English. Hearing and Speech News, Nov/Dec, 1973

Stark RE (ed), Sensory Capabilities of Hearing-Impaired Children, University Park Press, Baltimore, 1974

Whorf BL: Selected writings, in Carroll JB (ed): Language Thought and Reality. Cambridge, Mass., MIT Press, 1956

Barbara A. Hanners

4

The Audiologist As Educator: The Ultimate Hearing Aide

A cursory review of the literature of the last few years reveals a firm commitment to early identification and intervention to ameliorate the effects of handicapping conditions in children. A considerable amount of money, federal and local, has been expended on model early intervention programs. Some 30 states now have mandatory or permissive legislation for services to handicapped children in the vital years between birth and three. Early intervention programs for hearing impaired children have been in the vanguard of this movement in the United States for more than 20 years. Yet, audiologists, who should have been leading the way as a professional group interested in the welfare of young hearing impaired children, have been comparatively silent. Training institutions have prepared audiologists to test hearing, but primarily the hearing of cooperative people who understand some language. Testing the hearing of young children who have yet to develop language presents a different challenge. A recent survey will be reported here which suggests that some if not many audiologists are not meeting the challenge offered by early intervention systems. The survey suggested some of the inadequacies of the present methods of service delivery and audiologic management. We will then examine some of the ways in which the skills of audiologists can be utilized to improve services to hearing impaired children, and we will draw some implications from the changes suggested.

PRESENT STATE OF THE ART

When an adult goes to a hearing and speech center requesting that he be fitted with a hearing aid, the audiologist makes certain routine measurements.

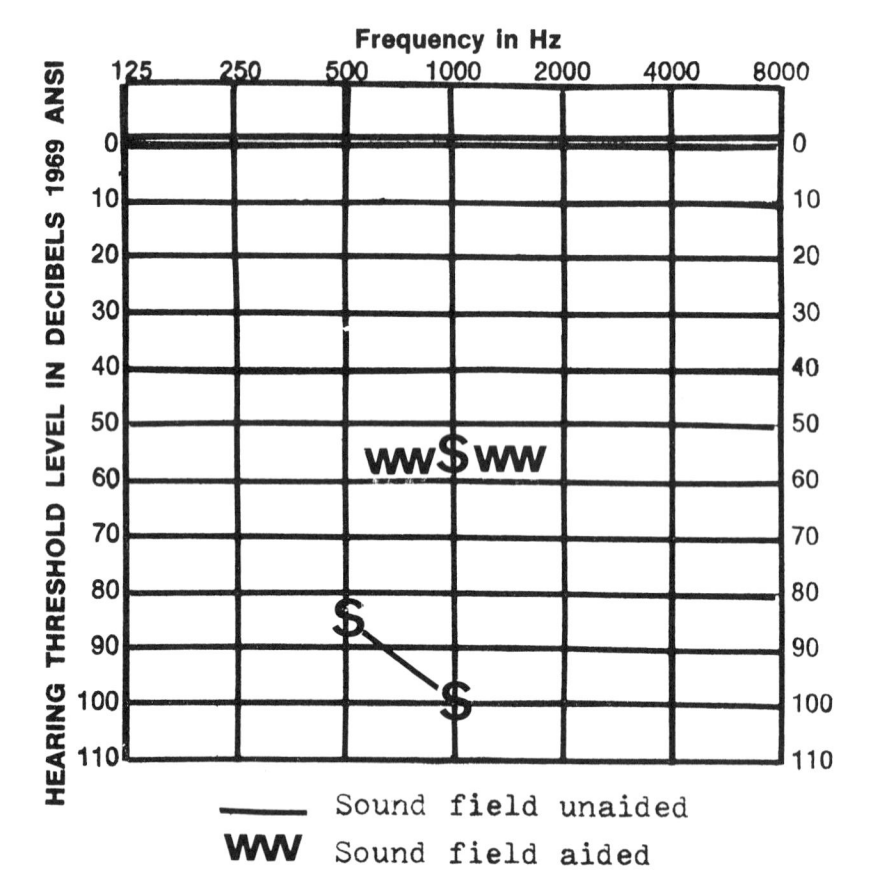

Fig. 4-1. JRC Age: 2/3 Audiogram No. 1 Date: 1-73.
Recommendations:
1. Body-worn aid with Y-cord
2. John Tracy Clinic Course
3. Preschool Program
4. Re-evaluation in this clinic in one year.

The person's hearing thresholds for pure tones by both air-conducted and bone-conducted signals are assessed, and these measures are made for each ear. The client's thresholds for hearing speech and his ability to understand speech when comfortably loud are measured, in conditions of both quiet and noise. Then begins a painstaking repetition of some of the measures for each of several hearing aids, followed by an evaluation of the person's tolerance for amplification. Some centers arrange for a period of trial use of an aid before a purchase is recommended. Most audiologists as careful, competent clinicians would not consider the recommendation of a hearing aid for an adult with

The Audiologist as Educator

less information than outlined here. Conversely, recommendations for hearing aids for young children are sometimes made on the basis of much less information. Indeed, it is difficult and time-consuming to obtain extensive information on a child's hearing. As a result, recommendations of hearing aids for children often made on the basis of sound-field audiograms, with no indication of individual ear responses or responses to bone-conducted signals. Such hearing aid recommendations are made on inadequate information, despite the difficulties encountered in obtaining additional data. A survey of early intervention programs in the spring of 1974 suggested that hearing aid recommendations based on inadequate information are distressingly frequent.

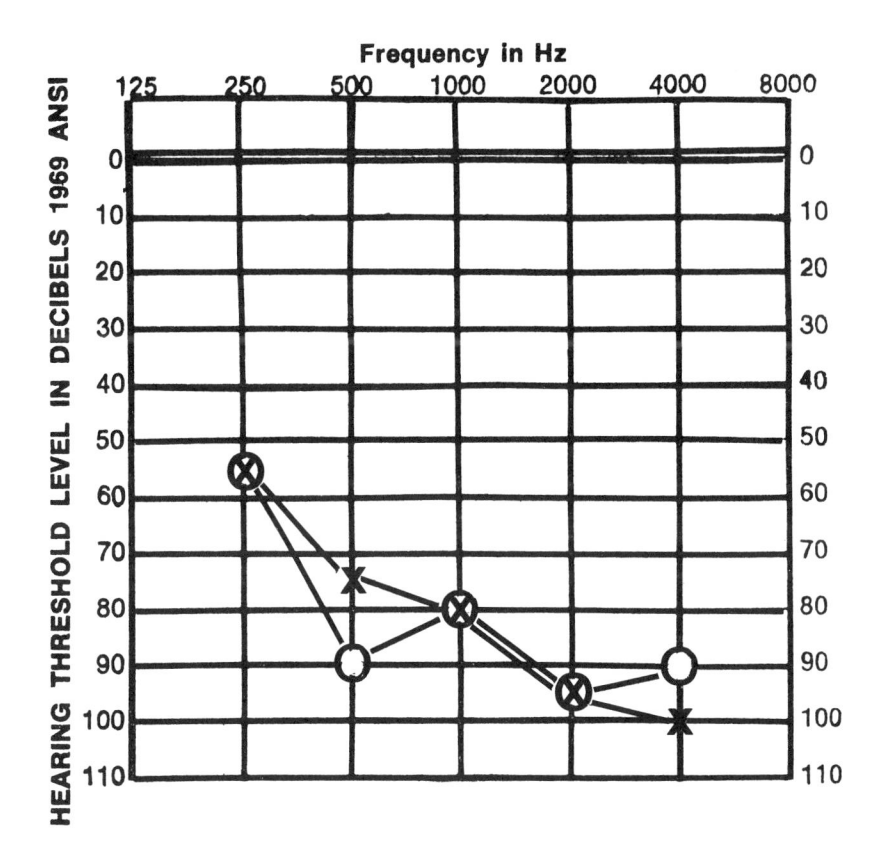

Fig. 4-2. JRC Age: 3/10 Audiogram No. 2 Date: 8-74 ". . . it is felt that J-- does so well with his body aid, it would be foolish to recommend binaural aids at this time. When he is evaluated again in one year, binaural aids will be reconsidered" (from audiologist's report).

The survey included 17 unsystematically selected early intervention programs for hearing impaired children in 10 states. Six of the 17 programs use the "total communication" approach to teaching language and the program directors expressed firm commitments to maximal use of residual hearing through appropriate amplification. The remaining 11 programs expressed similar commitments and reported the use of an auditory-oral approach to language development. All 17 program directors indicated concern and distress about the audiologic management available to them in their communities. They reported a variety of individual cases which demonstrated these difficulties. Five of these cases are presented here as examples of the present state of audiologic management.

Subject JRC was two years, three months of age when first diagnosed as hearing impaired. On the basis of one visit and sound-field testing, the recommendations included the fitting of a body-worn hearing aid with a Y-cord, which is not true binaural amplification, enrollment in a preschool, and re-evaluation in one year. The parent, who was functionally illiterate, was advised to subscribe to the John Tracy Clinic Correspondence Course. There is no information about which, if either is the better ear, and no attempt was made to test responses to bone conducted signals. Impedance audiometry was not available in this center. Consequently, there is no information about possible conductive elements in the hearing impairment.

Twenty months later, JRC returned to the center for his second audiogram. His preschool had requested that consideration be given to binaural amplification. The audiologist assumed that binaural amplification could only be provided by ear-level hearing aids, and declared such a notion to be "foolish." Once again, there was no attempt to test hearing by bone conduction. When questioned by the early intervention teacher about bone conduction hearing testing, the audiologist stated that threshold levels and configurations indicated a sensorineural impairment, and it was not thought necessary to take the required additional time for bone conduction testing. JRC had a history of ear infections, but, according to the audiologist, the effect of a conductive impairment would be minimal because of the child's "high thresholds." One must question if the child, three years, ten months of age on the day of the test, yielded true threshold responses. If JRC's audiogram represents the levels at which he ceased listening, his true thresholds might be somewhat better than indicated. The difficulties encountered in testing the hearing of young children frequently relate to the child's inability or unwillingness to attend to minimal signals, particularly those near his threshold of hearing for a particular signal. Therefore, the possibility of a conductive element should not be lightly dismissed.

FTR, a severely involved child, difficult to test, was first seen by the audiologist at three years, two months of age. Electroencephlographic audiometry resulted in this audiogram, with "presumed thresholds" extrapo-

The Audiologist as Educator

[Audiogram chart: Frequency in Hz (125–8000) vs Hearing Threshold Level in Decibels 1969 ANSI (0–110). Stimulus presented to both ears.]

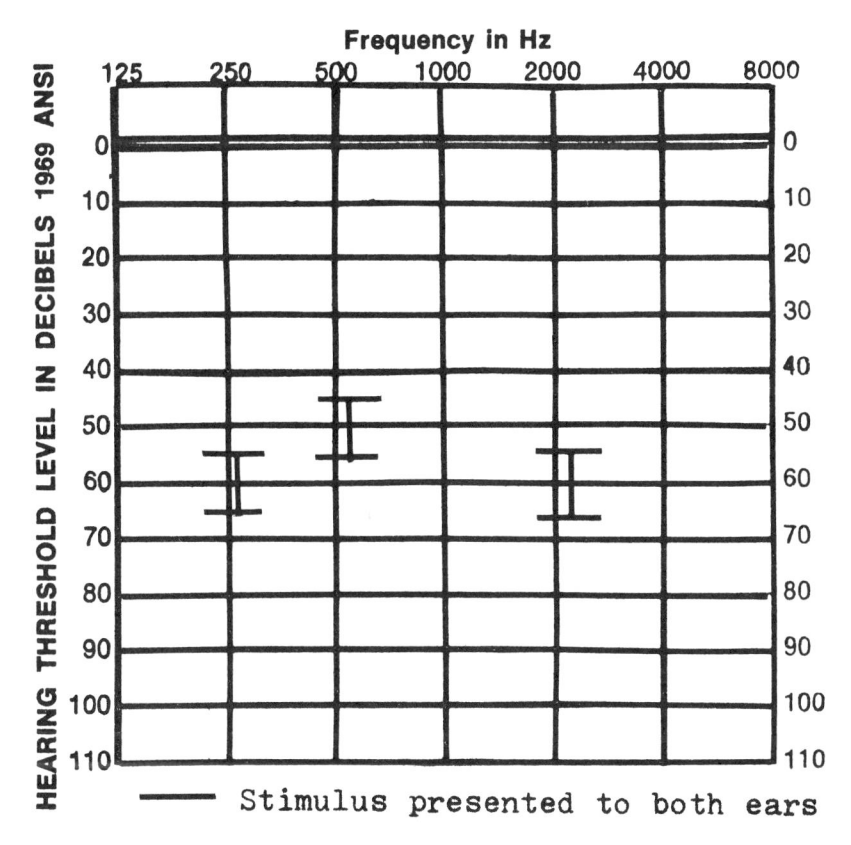

Fig. 4-3. FTR Age: 3/2 Audiogram No. 1 Date: 6-72. Audiogram is reproduced as received.
Recommendations: "Presumed hearing thresholds are shown on the audiogram. Tone presentations under EEG ranged between 70 and 90dB." No sedative was used. An ear level hearing aid was fitted to the right ear on a trial basis.

lated from tone presentation levels of 70 to 90 dB. These signals were presented to both ears simultaneously. An ear level aid was fitted on a trial basis. The preschool reported that the child responded consistently to minimal auditory stimuli without his hearing aids. FTR's second visit to the audiologist 10 months later yielded the audiogram in Figure 4-4 again based on EEG results.

The child was referred for otologic examination, which was negative. A second ear level aid was recommended for the left ear. The preschool continued to report responses to unamplified minimal auditory stimuli and that the child often turned off his hearing aids. In January, 1974, FTR flushed both hearing aids down the toilet. The audiologist recommended that the

58   Barbara A. Hanners

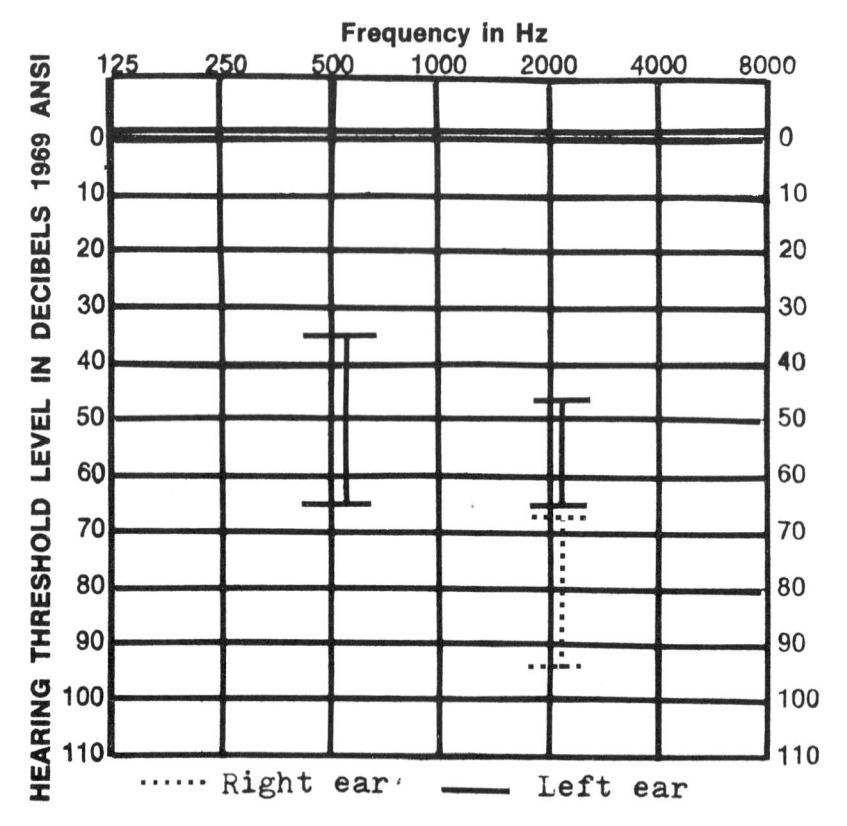

······ Right ear   ——— Left ear

Fig. 4-4. FTR Age: 4/0 Audiogram No. 2 Date: 4-73.
EEG with Seconal. Tones presented monaurally in ranges of 70-110 dB.
"Presumed thresholds" shown above.

   No attempt was made to test responses to bond-conducted stimuli. Child was
referred for otologic evaluation. A second ear level aid was recommended for the left
ear. Re-evaluation six months later after aids were lost resulted in a recommendation
for the purchase of two more aids.

family purchase two more hearing aids, which they did. The preschool sent
the audiologist a video tape of the child responding to auditory stimuli without amplification, and an evaluation was scheduled. That test by behavioral
audiometry in March, yielded the audiogram in Figure 4-5. The audiologist
concluded that the child had hearing within normal limits. The hearing aids
were removed by the parents.
   While the audiologist is the expert, or should be, in measurement of
hearing, parents and teachers observe the child daily in a variety of meaningful listening situations. Observations of the child's listening behavior in those

The Audiologist as Educator

situations can be organized by the audiologist, even when it is impossible for him to personally document the observations. Teachers may often provide valuable insight into the child's responses to meaningful environmental stimuli. Such information is lost when the audiologist does not seek it or use it when presented.

BCF's hearing was first evaluated when the child was two years, five months of age. Only testing by bone conduction was attempted, with right mastoid placement, at three frequencies, without masking. See Figure 4-6. Responses to signals presented only by bone conduction reveal little about possible responses to air-conducted signals. Unmasked bone-conducted signals similarly reveal little about which ear, if either, is less impaired.

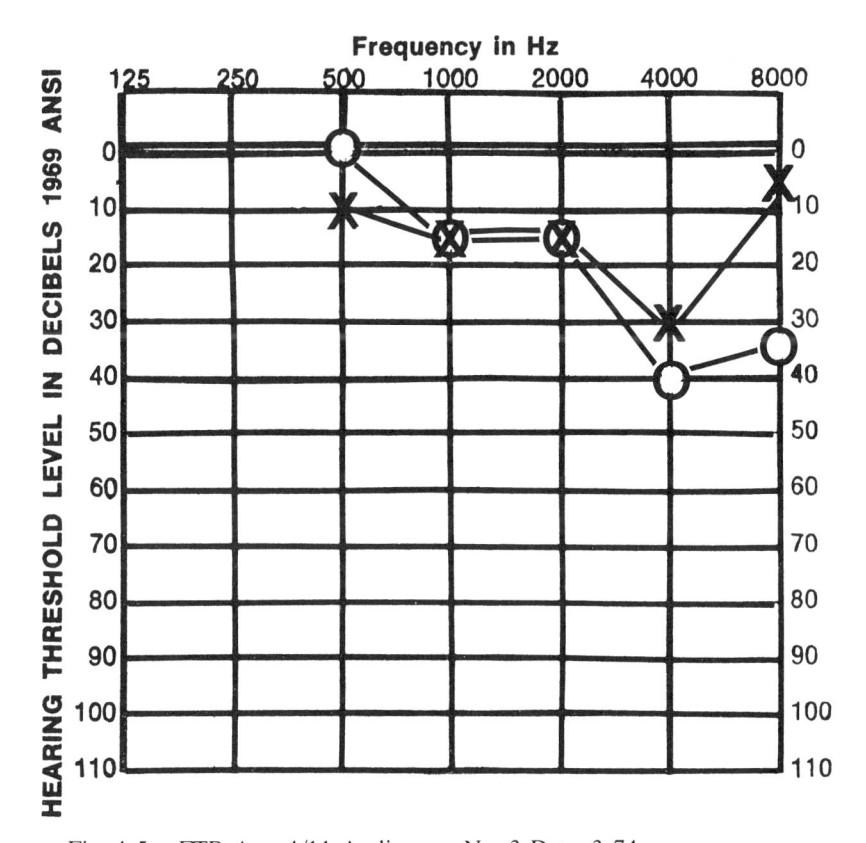

Fig. 4-5. FTR Age: 4/11 Audiogram No. 3 Date: 3-74.
Child was tested using conditioned observed response audiometry.
His responses were consistent.
Results indicated that the child had hearing with normal limits.
No comment or suggestion was made about the second set of hearing aids.

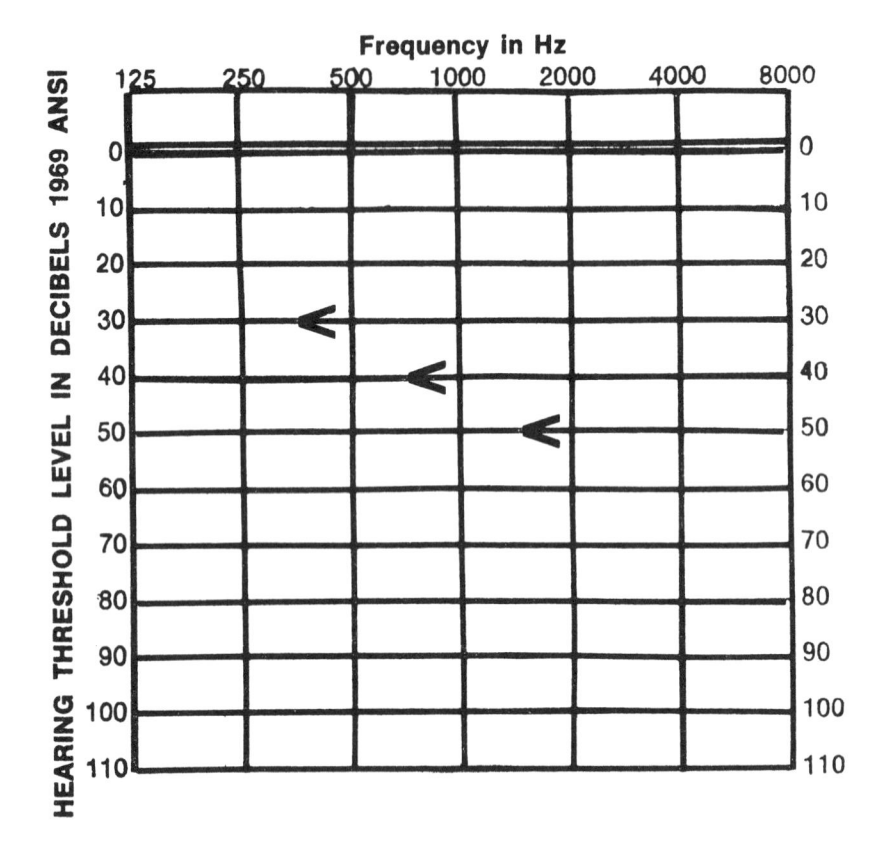

Fig. 4-6. BCF Age: 2/5 Audiogram No. 1 Date: 2-72.
Visit Record, B. C. F.
- 2-72   Initial Audiogram
- 3-72   Hearing aid loaned to child
- 3-72   Hearing aid check
- 4-72   Hearing aid check
- 6-72   Two aids recommended
- 10-72   Second aid delivered
- 2-73   Aid check, speech awareness
- 4-73   Air conduction only, aided speech awareness
- 1-74   Air and bone conduction
          Otologic referral followed.

On the basis of the limited information in Fig. 4-6, an ear level hearing aid was recommended for use. Five visits to the audiologist were noted over the next eight months, but no audiometric tests of hearing function were administered during those visits. See Figure 4-6 for a list of the visits. Aided speech awareness levels were tested for the first time 12 months after the ini-

The Audiologist as Educator

tial evaluation. The preschool reported that the child responded to some sounds without his aids, and that he often had earaches. In April, 1973, air conduction testing showed the results indicated in Figure 4-7. No attempt was made to test hearing by bone conduction, although the child was reported to be cooperative. The preschool teacher reported inconsistent responses to auditory stimuli in the classroom, responses which seemed to vary from day to day.

In January, 1974, two years after the initial audiogram, a routine re-test yielded the result shown in Figure 4-8.

The audiologist became concerned about the air-bone gap shown in the audiogram and referred the child for otologic examination, which in that center meant a 20-foot trip down the hall. The examination revealed "chronic

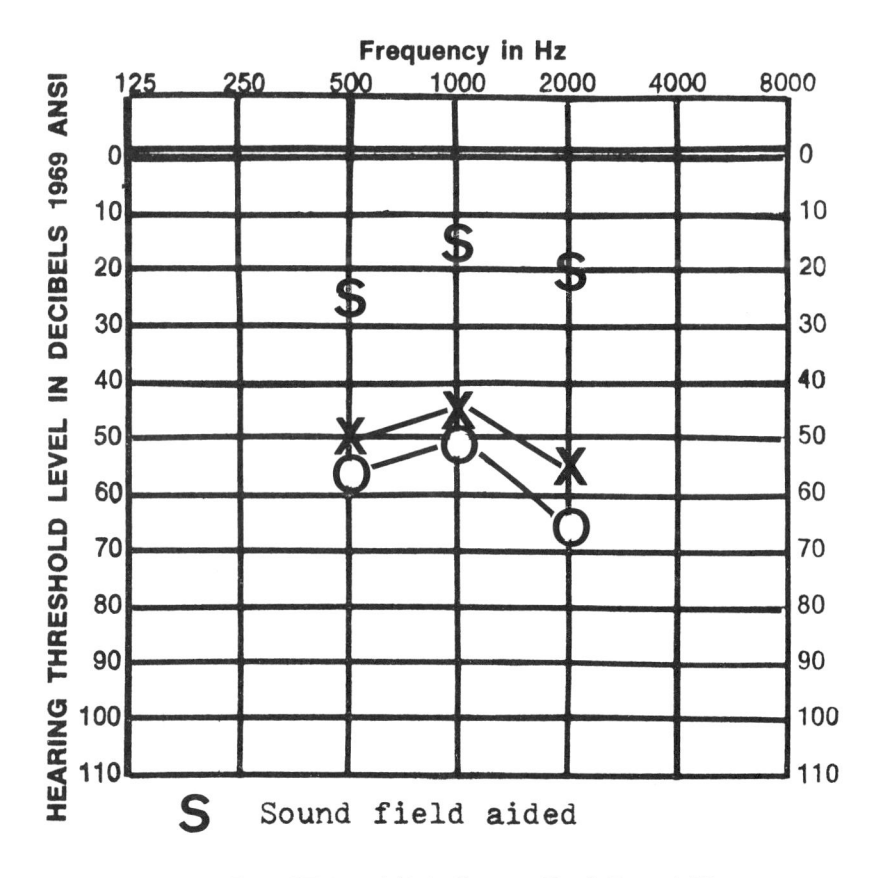

Fig. 4-7. BCF Age: 3/7 Audiogram No. 2 Date: 4-73.

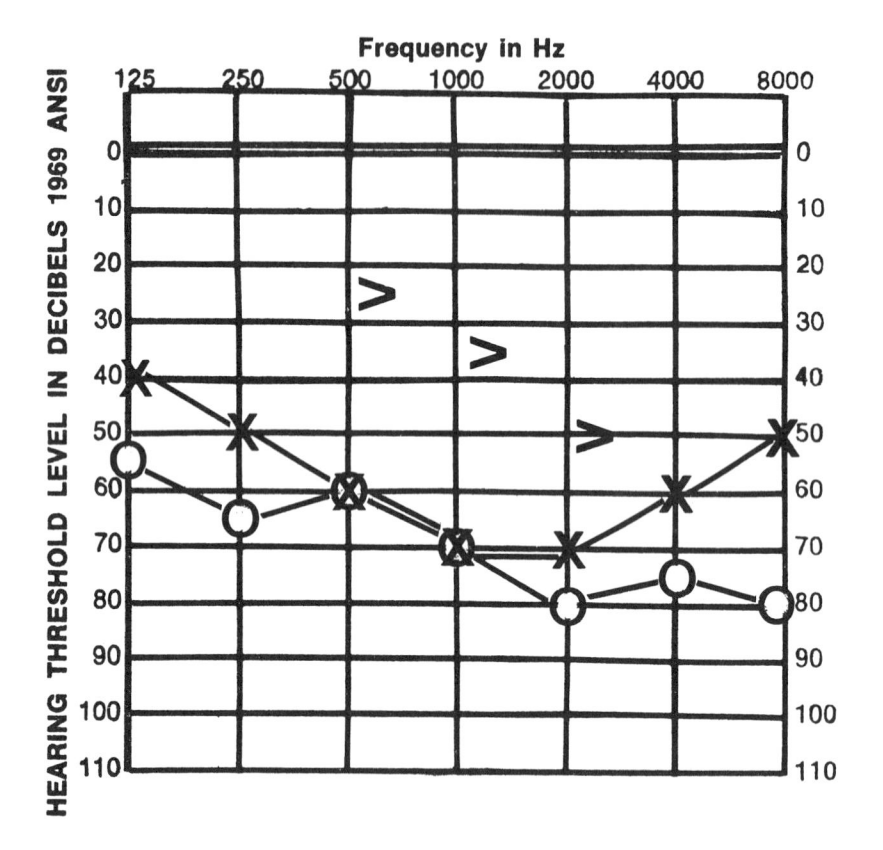

Fig. 4-8. BCF Age: 4/4 Audiogram No. 3 Date: 1-74.

otitis media" which had caused "substantial damage to both tympanic membranes." If we compare BCF's first audiogram with the one which showed the air-bone discrepancy for the first time, we see that they are not exceedingly discrepant audiometrically, but they are two years apart in time. See Figure 4-9. Impedance audiometry was not available in this center, but otologic consultation was readily available.

ERM was seen for his first audiogram at two years, five months of age, with the result indicated in Figure 4-10.

The audiologist stated that ". . . wearable amplification is essential for this child to develop language . . . ." Recommendations included a hearing aid, a preschool program "when old enough;" the parent was advised to

The Audiologist as Educator 63

subscribe to the John Tracy Clinic correspondence course, and re-evaluation was scheduled in one year. The preschool enrolled the child, only to find that the hearing aid had been stolen from the family's residence. Before the child could be rescheduled, it was noted that his responses in class were not those of a hearing impaired child, and he demonstrated some language development, although it was not appropriate for his chronological age.

Sixteen months later, when the child, the audiologist, and the family managed to come together once more, the child's audiogram revealed an air-bone gap, suggesting a conductive component in the hearing impairment. See Figure 4-11.

The audiologist immediately recommended an otologic examination. Medical treatment resulted in hearing within normal limits for this child, who fortunately never wore the prescribed hearing aid. Medical referral and treat-

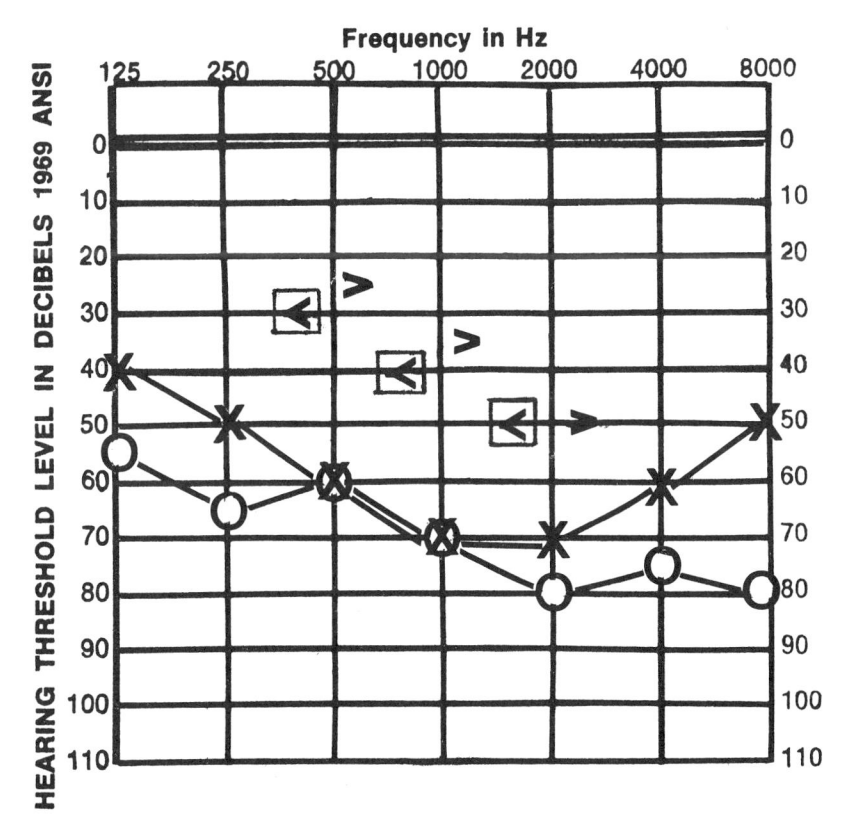

Fig. 4-9. BCF Audiograms 1, 3 Dates: (1) 2-72 (3) 1-74. Responses from Audiogram No. 1 are shown in squares.

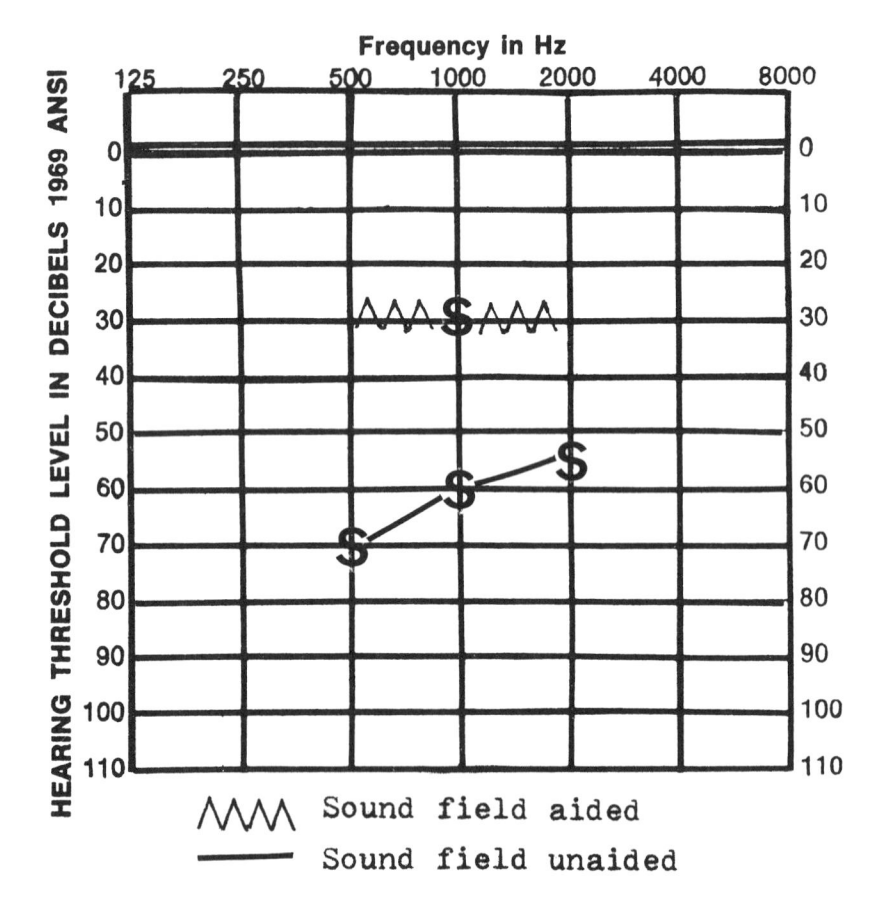

Fig. 4-10. ERM Age: 2/5 Audiogram No. 1 Date: 10-71.
Recommendations:
1. ". . . wearable amplification is essential for this child to develop language. . ."
2. Preschool program when old enough
3. John Tracy Clinic Course
4. Re-evaluation in this clinic in one year.

ment was delayed in part by the long duration between initial evaluation and the first followup visit. The delay was the result of several factors, including parental failure to keep appointments and a busy hearing clinic schedule.

KMB was two years, one month of age when his hearing was evaluated for the first time. The early intervention program was sent the audiogram in Figure 4-12 with a letter of referral. The recommendations of the audiologist included the comment that the child was "too young to determine specific

The Audiologist as Educator 65

monaural thresholds." However, a body-worn hearing aid with a Y-cord was recommended, along with the John Tracy Clinic course, enrollment in a preschool and re-evaluation in six months.

The preschool requested that some consideration be given to binaural hearing aids as that was the school's preference, whenever the recommendation was suitable. Obviously, additional information was needed prior to such a recommendation. The school requested a re-evaluation as soon as possible. Eleven months later when the child returned to the audiologist, the audiogram had the configuration shown in Figure 4-13. No attempt was made to test frequencies other than those noted.

The audiologist's report stated that "only the right ear should receive amplification as . . . it is felt that sound is not yet a meaningful stimuli (sic)

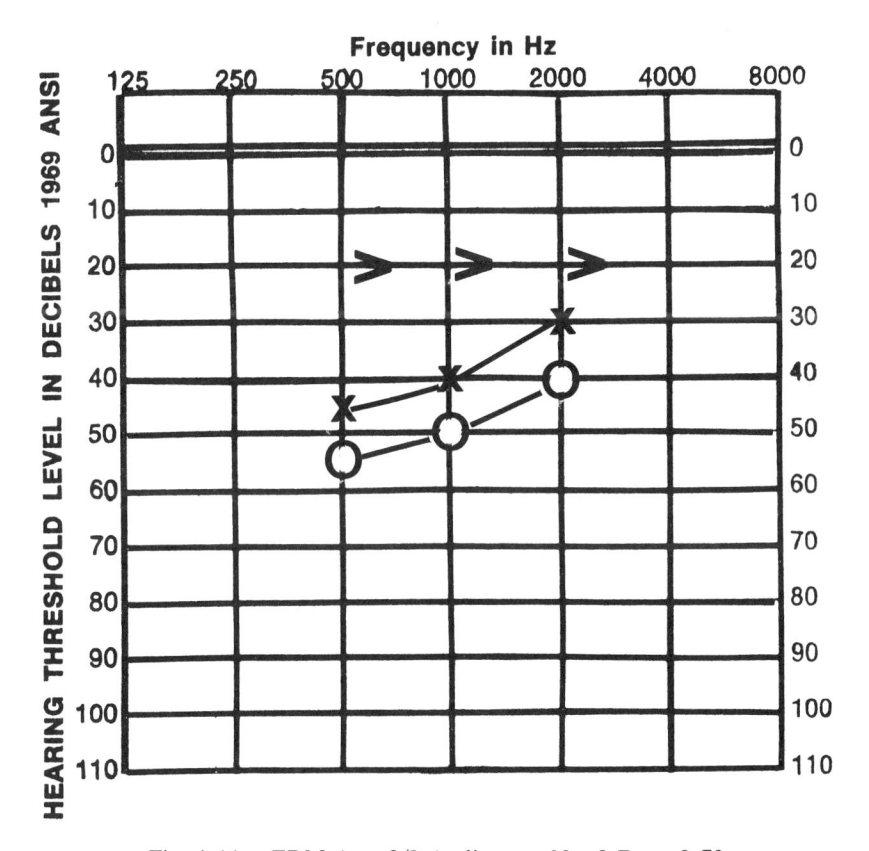

Fig. 4-11. ERM Age: 3/9 Audiogram No. 2 Date: 2-73.
Recommendations:
1. Otologic referral
2. Re-evaluation in six months

66   Barbara A. Hanners

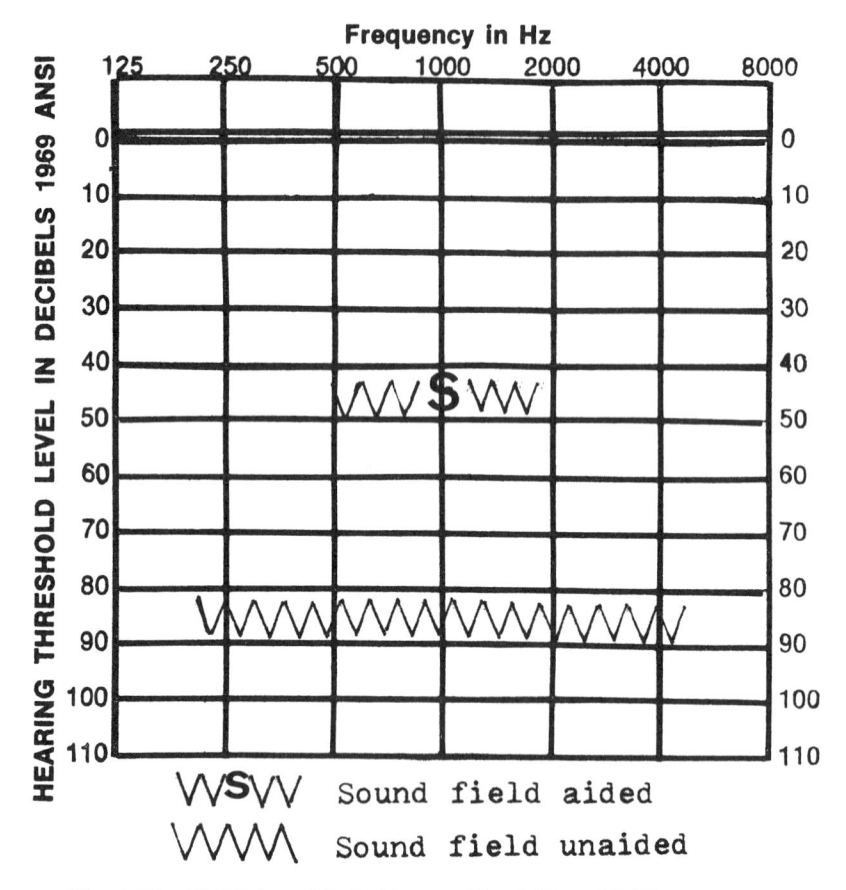

[Audiogram chart: Frequency in Hz (125–8000) vs. Hearing Threshold Level in Decibels 1969 ANSI (0–110). Sound field aided (S) marked around 45 dB at 500–2000 Hz. Sound field unaided marked around 85–90 dB across frequencies.]

WSW   Sound field aided
WWW   Sound field unaided

Fig. 4-12. KMB Age: 2/1 Audiogram No. 1 Date: 10-72.
Audiogram is reproduced as received
Child was ". . . too young to determine specific monaural thresholds."
Recommendations:
1. Body-worn hearing aid with Y-cord.
2. John Tracy Clinic Course
3. Enrollment in preschool when old enough
4. Re-evaluation in four to six months

to this child." The report concluded with the note that the audiologist's "philosophy has not leaned to binaural amplification." The philosophy of the early intervention program in this case was subverted by the audiologist on whom they were dependent for audiologic management, but who in his turn had no direct responsibility for the child's educational program. The audiologist apparently overlooked or did not subscribe to the possibility suggested by the preschool teacher; that is, the child might require amplification in order for sound to be meaningful to him.

The Audiologist as Educator 67

In all five cases, the audiologists were experienced clinicians, holding the Certificate of Clinical Competence in Audiology of the American Speech and Hearing Association; they were licensed in their respective states; the clinics in which they worked were approved by ASHA's professional services board. Their actions were neither unprofessional nor unethical, according to present

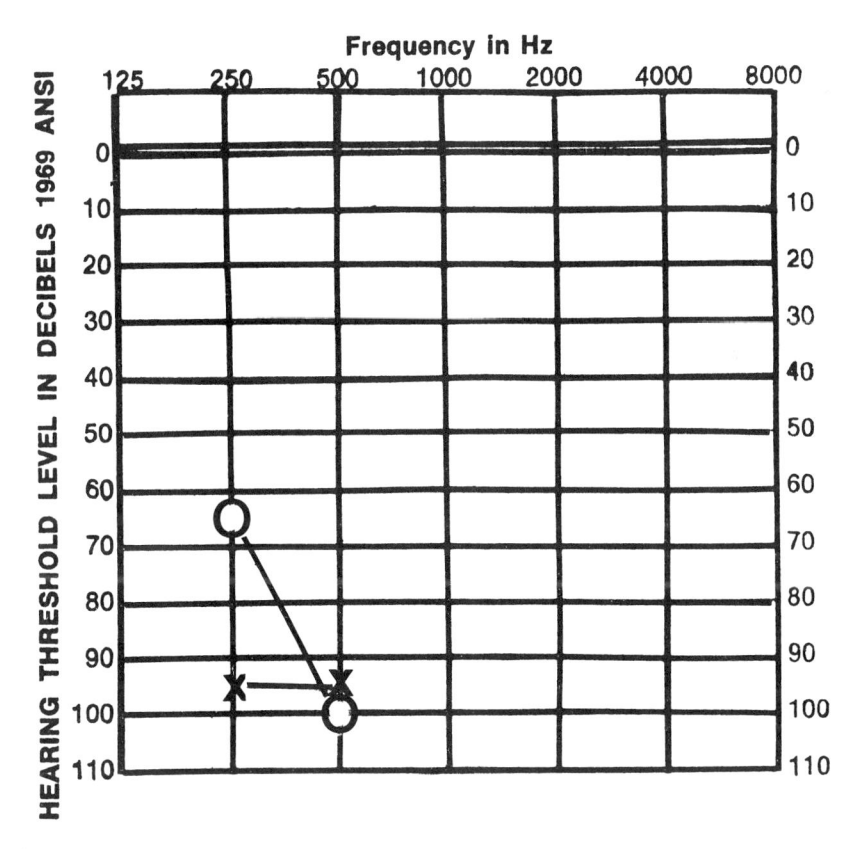

Fig. 4-13. KMB Age: 3/0 Audiogram No. 2 Date: 9-73.
Recommendations:
Only the right ear should receive amplification as . . . "it is felt that sound is not yet a meaningful stimuli (sic) to this child." "Our philosophy has not leaned to binaural amplification."

standards and practice. None of the audiologists were incompetent or careless. In most if not all cases, they were prevented by circumstances or custom from obtaining the information required, and from providing the management necessary for young hearing impaired children.

Responses to the survey suggested that the average amount of time spent with the child actually under test in a sound treated room was approximately

30 minutes. The time a child spends in such a situation depends upon his attention span, and the examiner's skill in utilizing the span maximally. One would not expect a young child to be cooperative for long periods, and about half an hour would be a reasonable estimate of his attention to the task of audiometric testing. Consequently, it is necessary to test young children several times, perhaps even to train them for the task, and to do so with as little delay as possible to meet the constraints of early intervention. The cases cited here suggest that important decisions regarding amplification and even school placement may have been based on a single half hour exploration of hearing behavior. At least two audiologists quoted in the survey, when reporting audiograms similar to that in Figure 4-12, stated that the children in question were "too deaf to learn language orally," and the children were referred to manual language classes. To make a decision of this magnitude on the basis of one visit to a test booth is inconsiderate if not incautious. The recommendation of amplification on the basis of testing in the sound field, as in Figure 4-12, places the child's residual hearing in some potential jeopardy, as Muir (1974) pointed out. Yet, some hearing and speech centers have scheduling constraints which prevent the audiologist from seeing a preschool child every day or so for two or three weeks or more in order to obtain adequate information about his hearing behavior with and without amplification. The routine of such visits might be difficult for the family to arrange as well. Young children are difficult to test; time, patience and skill are required. Hearing and speech clinics may not be routinely capable of schedule adjustments required for the testing of young children.

Unfortunately, the results of the survey reported here suggest that the practices similar to those described are wide-spread if not common. The consequence is poor audiologic management of hearing impaired children, at a time when early intervention programs are demanding cooperation and assistance. The cases cited here exemplify the problems faced by early intervention programs when they do not have an audiologist as a contributing member of the staff. The seventeen programs reported other problems as well; that present procedures of audiologic management are unsystematic and fragmented; that there are excessive delays between identification and initiation of service and between audiologic evaluations and follow-up visits.

No Systematic Identification

The 17 communities represented in the survey apparently have no systematic approaches to identification, initial diagnosis and referral. In one city, for example, there were four different agencies responsible for screening the hearing of young children, each of which had its own techniques, procedures, and referral routines. There was no speech and hearing center in the city and children were referred as far as 500 miles for audiologic evaluations.

The Audiologist as Educator

The early intervention program dealt with five different audiologists, each with his own notion of audiologic management. Another program in the survey reported that the local audiologist referred all hearing impaired children to all three of the early intervention programs in the city. While this approach is diplomatic, it also served to confuse parents. At least two children in that city were found to be receiving on-going services from two of the early intervention programs, for which the state health department paid the bills.

Fragmented Services

Audiological services in the surveyed communities tended to be fragmented. The 17 early intervention programs trained parents to teach their children in the years 0 to 3, with a preschool component as a second step in the hierarchy. Audiologic diagnosis and management were available only through administratively and geographically separate facilities. Parents and children were thus denied the guidance which can best be provided by an audiologist; management and help in the utilization of residual hearing. The most common complaint of the 17 programs was that audiologists frequently made decisions regarding management without consultation and on occasion in contradiction of the early intervention programs. Several of the auditory-oral programs, for example, reported that they preferred the use of binaural hearing aids for bilateral hearing impairments, whenever appropriate. The directors of the programs were dismayed when local audiologists refused to consider binaural recommendations, citing a variety of reasons, few of them related to the child's hearing. By refusing to even consider binaural amplification, the audiologists were inadvertently exerting control over the early intervention programs, preventing them from applying their skills in what they felt to be the most effective manner.

Delays in Service

All programs surveyed reported excessive delays between identification and initiation of service. These programs reported delays of 20 months or more, vital months in the lives of congenitally or prelingually hearing impaired children. There were additional delays of several months between the audiologist's initial evaluation and the first routine follow-up visit. The most frequently reported interval was 12 months.

MODEL SYSTEM

If we are to provide adequate services for hearing impaired children through early intervention programs, then we must organize our service delivery system and the audiologist must be a member of the service team at every step in that system. As important as vision is to any child, hearing is the vital sense for learning language. It is even more important that the hearing impaired child have the maximum possible benefit of his residual hearing, no matter how minimal, and the child must learn to use his hearing. The audiologist is the "resident expert" in hearing, its measurement, and its utilization through appropriate amplification. There are a number of ways in which the audiologist can be useful in the systematic delivery of service to hearing impaired children. Some of them are presented here for consideration, within the framework of a model service delivery system.

Organized Early Identification

Whatever the community resources may be for early intervention, there should be an organized mechanism for referral of young children who fail hearing screening tests, whose hearing is suspect or at risk. Such programs may vary widely from community to community, but the audiologist can and should provide guidance to agencies responsible for identification. Some federally funded demonstration programs have developed active early identification systems and this information is available in our current literature.

Organized Early Intervention

Early intervention programs provide guidance and management in the early years of a hearing impaired child's life. The audiologist should be a fully functioning member of the program staff, providing continuing diagnosis, audiologic management, and monitoring of amplification. Detailed management is necessary, for example, to detect variations in hearing which may occur as a result of middle ear pathology. Osberger and Danaher (1974) have presented some evidence that temporary conductive pathologies can alter significantly the residual hearing of severely impaired adults. When conductive components were superimposed on already extant sensorineural impairments, students in the Osberger and Danaher study reported noticible changes in their hearing, which were documented audiometrically. It seems reasonable to assume that similar alterations of hearing function can occur in very young children, who show some susceptibility to middle ear pathology. With an audiologist available within a program, hearing could be checked daily, if necessary.

Hearing aids and amplification systems should be tested daily. While the audiologist may not be directly responsible for daily testing of hearing aids, he can supervise teacher aides or volunteers who perform such duties, and he can be responsible for a selection of hearing aids available to lend to children whose own aids are sent away for repair. In a recent study, Northcott (1971) asked 12 experts in education of the hearing impaired to rank in order of importance 77 competencies required by teachers of such children. The most important competency was judged to be the "ability to provide appropriate auditory and linguistic stimulation." Ranked twenty-third was "knowledge and understanding of the function and utilization of group and individual hearing aids." Yet it is obvious that the most inspired teacher or parent cannot overcome the disadvantage of an undetected dead battery or broken receiver cord. The audiologist can actively insure that the probability of such occurrences is reduced to a minimum.

Preschool Programs

Preschool programs for children ranging in age from approximately three to six years of age provide another step in the system. Here again the audiologist can provide continuing assessment and monitoring of the child's hearing, its amplification, and the child's use of both. Jones (1973) suggested that the audiologist can serve as a liason between clinics and preschools. These services are best provided when the audiologist is a contributing member of the preschool staff.

School Programs

School programs have similar needs for audiologic services. Hearing impaired children do not outgrow their needs for either amplification or audiologic management. School administrators, however, may not yet be aware of the unique contributions the audiologist can make to a program for hearing impaired children. The audiologist on the other hand may not yet be ready to fulfill such a role.

Consistent, Continuous Audiologic Management

In a model service delivery system, the audiologist has a primary role to play at every level, providing detailed management of residual hearing. Ventry (1965), Pollack (1970), Ling (1971), Fuller (1971), Hanners (1973), and Jones (1973) have all suggested that the audiologist is a vital member of any program for hearing impaired children. The results of the informal survey reported here suggested that audiologists are not now assuming those responsibilities, and they may not be properly prepared to do so.

If we are to prepare audiologists for participation in systematic service delivery to young hearing impaired children, we must make some changes in our thinking. These changes at the least should include training programs and possibly certification requirements; changes in staffing patterns; and changes in funding sources.

Changes in Training

Our training institutions are committed to preparing clinical audiologists who meet the certification requirements of our professional association, which include supervised practicum. The burden of providing opportunities for practicum with very young children will fall on the training institution. Early intervention programs can provide that practicum, even though they may not be university-affiliated programs. Such arrangements, however, are not made overnight or without effort.

The American Speech and Hearing Association's present certification standards are probably broad enough to permit the inclusion of a subspecialty in audiology, and this possibility should be explored. At the moment, however, there seems to be little movement in the direction of preparing audiologists to work within early intervention programs. Unfortunately, few training institutions are providing either appropriate coursework or practicum.

Changes in Staffing Patterns

If the audiologist is to be a member of the service delivery team for hearing impaired children, administrators must add another job description to their planning. Directors of early intervention programs in this study reported that they did not initially employ audiologists because of the availability of clinical services in their communities, or at least nearby. Some of the programs have revised their plans, primarily because of the management demonstrated in this survey. Some of the programs have employed audiologists who received considerable in-service training. Public school administrators should be encouraged to consider hiring appropriately prepared audiologists for services to hearing impaired children, even as audiologists should be encouraged to consider such employment.

Changes in Funding Patterns

The clinical audiologist employed in a hearing and speech center can normally expect to earn at least a portion of his salary in fees charged for his services. An audiologist in an early intervention program will see a restricted number of children annually, and fees may be insufficient to cover salary. As a consequence, it may be necessary to find funds which are separate from a fee-structure to support the audiologist and the equipment he needs. All early intervention is costly, and an audiologist will make such services even more so, but the benefits demonstrated by federally funded programs, especially those in the First Chance Network (Handicapped Children's Early Education Program), make the expense of early intervention appear worthwhile.

This chapter has presented an informal survey of early intervention programs for hearing impaired children, the results of which suggested that current practices in audiologic management of these children may be inadequate to meet their needs. It has been suggested that the audiologist should be a well-prepared integral member of the service delivery system for hearing impaired children, from identification through the school years, a concept which appeared in our literature at least nine years ago. Implications of the initiation of a model service delivery system were drawn. On the basis of present trends, it appears that early intervention programs for hearing impaired children are now upon us, and audiologists should be there, too, as the "ultimate hearing aides."

BIBLIOGRAPHY

Fuller CW: The audiological diagnosis of deafness. In Hicks D. (ed): Proceedings of National Forum IV: Medical Aspects of Deafness. Washington, D.C. Council of Organizations Serving the Deaf, 63-66, 1971

Hanners BA: The role of audiologic management in the development of language by severely hearing impaired children. Paper presented to the annual convention of the Academy of Rehabilitation Audiology, Detroit, Michigan, October 12, 1973

Jones BL: The audiologist in the educational environment. The Volta Review 76: 545-550, 1973

Ling D: The hearing impaired preschooler: A family responsibility. Hearing and Speech News. 39, 8-13, 1971

Muir PP: Deaf education. The Volta Review 76: 88-92, 1974

Northcott WH: Competencies Needed by Teachers of Hearing Impaired Infants-Birth to Three Years of Age-And Their Parents. Ph.D. Dissertation, University of Minneapolis, Minnesota, 1971

Osberger MJ, Danaher EM: Temporary conductive loss in students with severe sensorineural deafness. The Volta Review 76: 52-56, 1974

Pollack D: Educational Audiology for the Limited Hearing Infant. Springfield, Illinois, Charles C. Thomas, Publisher, 1970

Ventry IM (ed): Audiology and Education of the Deaf. Washington, D.C. Joint Committee on Audiology and Education of the Deaf, 1965

Ruth R. Green

5
Psycho-Social Aspects of Mainstreaming for the Child and Family

The New York League for the Hard of Hearing is a nonprofit, multidisciplinary rehabilitation agency, founded in 1910 by four deaf men attempting to help one another find employment. Today, this type of activity might be considered a self-help group. In 1910, and probably up through the early 1950s, the population served by the League could be classified as hard of hearing. With the advent of transistor hearing aids and the development of more powerful amplification, probably close to half of the population served at the League during the past quarter of a century are audiologically deaf. Because of early intervention and intensive communication therapy, these people are helped to develop skills which enable them to function as hard of hearing individuals in the normal world. Mainstreaming has become a 1970s concept but at the League, mainstreaming has been at the root of our philosophy since 1910.

In 1973, 18,757 individuals and families were served by the agency. Included as part of our program are otological, audiological, communication therapy, psychological, social work, rehabilitation, and public education services for children and adults, spanning the cradle to the grave. At the League, mainstreaming means giving the individual the skills to function in the world at large.

Now, let us look at the psychological and social implications of mainstreaming, or being part of the hearing world. There is general agreement in the literature on physical disability which indicates the problem of the handicapped is physical, and also social and psychological. Gordon Allport, the well-known psychologist, has pointed out that physique is one of the three principal raw materials of personality. It is apparent that physique is as much a psychological problem as it is physical. If normal variations in physique, such as being tall or short, handsome or ugly, are important factors in personality formation, clearly the pathological variations known as physical disability are likely to be even more important. The movies and comics, for example, learned early that one of the easiest ways to characterize an adult as a villain was to cripple the person. Witness the old story of "The Hunchback of Notre Dame." On a more sophisticated level, Time magazine which cuts thousands of words from each issue, recognizes the significance attached to physique by printing the physical characteristics of persons in the news.

The attitude of society toward atypical physique has varied from the Greek view of "a sound mind in a sound body" with its negative implications of crooked body, crooked mind, crooked personality, to the widely held "overcompensation" theory. This theory implies that the adjustment process necessary to come to terms with life after severe illness or physical disability, makes a person superior and capable of achievement which otherwise might have been beyond his grasp. Similar variation is found in religious doctrine, from the Old Testament conception of disability as punishment for sin, to the New Testament view of salvation through suffering.

A hearing loss is a variation in the degree of hearing ability and this is often associated with negative values. These negative values have been considered in three ways by psychologist, Lee Meyerson.

1. Negative values imposed by society
2. Negative values imposed by the person himself or herself
3. Negative values imposed by the disability

The negative values imposed by society, even for minor variations, are obvious. Newspapers and television are full of advertisements on how to become slimmer, or look younger. For more extreme deviations, society tends to impose positive restrictions. A child with a severe hearing impairment may not be permitted to attend regular school, an adult may not serve in the nation's armed forces, and finding employment may be difficult. Social distance in personal areas may be equally great.

The negative values imposed by the hearing impaired person upon himself or herself stem from the regard in which he or she is held by the community. Low self-esteem is intensified because hearing impaired persons may have had normal hearing and may have been part of the majority group holding the majority judgment. Consequently, they devalue their own self-image with their own previously formed attitudes or in the case of children, by the learned attitudes of the parents. When these attitudes persist, the hearing impaired person has an emotional involvement, as well as a hearing impairment.

The negative values imposed by the hearing loss may be created because of the inability to reach simple, universally achieved goals. The hearing impaired person doesn't feel inferior because he or she can't appreciate good music, but because he or she cannot communicate easily. Failure may be experienced which may be translated into "I am a failure." The hearing impaired person may often have to ask for help in order to reach a goal—for example, the hearing impaired person may need to have someone use the telephone for him or her in order to make an appointment. Because of this, he or she may have to expose personal areas of his or her life, feel dependent and accept from others a lowered status.

The ultimate adjustment of the hearing impaired person is influenced by the reaction of the community and family. No two of us feel alike towards a particular person whether he or she is hearing impaired or not. There are many variables that determine the interpersonal relationships between people. Most vividly influencing one's attitude is the relationship to and the investment of emotion in the person concerned. If this person is a member of one's immediate family, the attitude is very different from that felt towards a stranger.

Emotional feelings are not only expressed by word of mouth, but more importantly by facial expression and behavior. One of the basic facts that has been learned in the study of personality is that we may be more influenced by another person's attitudes or feelings than by his or her words or actions. In a close relationship, real feelings are communicated automatically in many other ways than by what is said.

A common reaction of normal hearing people to a hearing impaired person is "he or she is different" and this may engender feelings of pity, over solicitousness, annoyance, sympathy, or curiosity. These feelings may be beyond what a person will admit or often beyond his own understanding.

The ultimate social adjustment for a person who loses his hearing as an adult is different from that of the child. From infancy until the age of 6, a child's world is that of his parents and family circle. The child's acceptance of himself or herself and his or her hearing loss and the ultimate social adjustment will very much depend on the parents' attitudes and degree of acceptance of the hearing disability.

Parents are key figures in a child's growth and adjustment. When parents learn that their child has a hearing impairment, various reactions or combination of reactions take place, from acceptance to unwillingness to accept, guilt, rejection, overprotection, etc. These reactions vary in degree and intensity.

Parents usually have an image of what they expect their child to be like when he or she is born. Almost all parents must make some adjustment because the image they projected is usually somewhat distorted—a girl is born rather than a boy, a brown-haired, brown-eyed baby rather than a blue-eyed blond. Parents of hearing impaired children are called upon to make additional adjustments. Early in the child's life parents may realize that something is wrong, but they may not know what. Thus, they may experience a period of confusion, anxiety and guilt. Finally, a diagnosis is made. It would be strange if parents were to find out that something was wrong with their child and they felt good about it. The kinds of reactions parents have when they learn something is wrong are natural and to be expected. It is only when feelings of disappointment, anxiety, rejection, etc. are permitted to grow unchecked that they develop into troublesome feelings and attitudes. Once the diagnosis is made and a program is evolved, parents become better able to accept the fact of a loss of hearing because they know they are doing something positive about their problem. However, I think it is unfair for us to try to reassure parents with, "Don't worry, everything will be OK," because almost never is everything always OK for all parents. Parents need to be helped to understand that there will be problems and frustrations. There is also a need for trained people to help the parents and the children cope with their feelings and frustrations.

Hearing impaired children have much in common with all children. It must be remembered that they are children first and hearing impaired children second. Like all children, they want to love and be loved; to please and to avoid displeasing; they want to learn and to play. Parents of hearing impaired children have much in common with all parents. All parents worry about their children, their development, their future, their place in the world. Parents of normal hearing children, as well as parents of hearing impaired children are concerned about the psychological and social adjustments of their children. Parents of normal hearing children often search for something definitive to account for their child's adjustment problem. Parents of hearing impaired children may lay the blame on the hearing impairment.

When parental feelings are permitted to grow unchecked, they can provide psychological and social adjustment problems for their children. For example, take parents who see their child as not being able, not being capable because at seven the child cannot communicate easily. The parents in their over solicitousness and underlying rejective attitudes then don't permit the child to ride a bicycle or go to school alone. This behavior may create psychological, as well as social problems. The child will translate this inability into: I cannot do what others are doing; I am a failure. These perceptions and feelings, if permitted to grow unchecked, will develop into psychological and social adjustment problems.

It is important for a hearing impaired child to be diagnosed at a young age or as soon as the problem is observed and for the parents to obtain supportive counseling and direction as early as possible. Counseling will assist the parents in handling their feelings and help them help their child grow socially, emotionally, and psychologically. Parents need to be helped to develop realistic goals and expectations for their child. Because the child doesn't talk doesn't mean he or she is not able or capable.

Involving the child in his or her early years into a normal milieu (nursery school, play group, Headstart) helps the child in a variety of ways. The child, early in his or her life, is able to learn that he or she can manage without a parent present. The child is able to see that he or she can compete with other children, and in some areas be more successful. The child learns early in life to make adjustments and accommodations for his or her hearing loss. The child learns to be open about the hearing problem because the family is open about it.

It is not unusual for a young hearing impaired child mainstreamed into a normal hearing nursery school program to stay on the sidelines for a period of time, to be cautious in his or her first attempts at socialization, to judge the situation, to size it up visually so as to know how to behave appropriately.

This may often be the child's first awareness of his or her differences. As the child becomes familiar with the routines, understands what is expected, has built up a trust, he or she begins to participate in the activities and begins to develop social skills. The child quickly becomes aware of what he or she can do—sometimes better than the other children, and develops positive strokes for himself or herself.

It is easier to structure a positive mainstream situation for a child of three than for a child of thirteen. Little children are very accepting of differences. In general, nursery schools are supportive. This can provide a hearing impaired child with a positive first experience into the world at large which can provide the basis for future experiences. The child must be given the opportunity to develop a strong ego concept. He or she must see himself or herself as someone who can do things. All children have certain strengths and it is the parents' and educators' responsibility to develop the strengths and to help the youngster become aware of his or her ability rather than his or her disability.

Let me tell you about one of the youngsters at the League with a profound hearing loss who was in a nursery school program. She had very limited language, but had made a satisfactory adjustment during her first year at school. When she was four, she learned to tie bows on her shoes, on her hood, etc. Soon she was tying bows for all the members of her class. Amy was able to perceive her own strengths and adequacies, she was developing her ego strengths which would promote her adjustment in the hearing world.

Given the normal model, given the chance to emulate a peer group, given realistic expectations, hearing impaired children can develop social skills as adequately as their hearing peers. This was indicated in a study done by Thomas Lawrenson in 1963. He investigated the social maturity of three different groups of girls, two with profound hearing impairments and one group of institutionalized girls with normal hearing. The object of the study was to compare the level of social maturity of a group of girls with profound hearing losses attending a school for the deaf, a group of profoundly hearing impaired girls attending regular schools in their community and a group of girls in an orphanage. Of the three groups, the girls with profound hearing losses attending regular schools scored significantly higher on the Vineland Social Maturity Scale than either of the other two groups.

This doesn't mean that in the early years environmental manipulation may not be needed, but this is part of the educational process. What do I mean by environmental manipulation? Environmental manipulation is using the environment—home, school, church, etc.—to provide beneficial experiences for the hearing impaired child in order to help develop social skills and social maturity.

It may be necessary to invite other children to the home; to enroll the child in Boy Scouts or Girl Scouts; to expose the child to appropriate social situations; to manipulate the environment to help the hearing impaired child grow socially and psychologically. Social maturity is a learned behavior and this learning experience needs to begin early in the life of a hearing impaired child. Even for the child who for a variety of reasons may not be able to be mainstreamed for educational purposes, there is a need to find ways to expose the child to hearing peers outside the educational institute.

Recently, Edna S. Levine, a well-known psychologist, conducted an investigation of personality patterns in the deaf by means of the Hand Test. Eighty-three young adult subjects with profound hearing losses were selected for investigation on the basis of a number of control criteria involving deafness, schooling, health, and other disabilities with level of linguistic competence as the independent variable and as indicated by reading level and written communication. The three principal experimental groups were described by Levine as "1) exceptional; 2) typical deaf with linguistic level equivalent to 6th grade; and 3) marginal deaf with an average linguistic level equivalent to 1st to 2nd grade. In addition to these linguistically divergent groups, a group of deaf psychiatric in-patients was included in the study mainly as a check on the discriminatory abilities of the Hand Test with the deaf." The results of this study show "that there are wide divergencies in personality patterns among the deaf and that psychiatric integrity tends to correlate with the presence of sufficient linguistic capability to effect the reality inputs necessary for wholesale development and adjustment. Although some overlap occurs among the groups, the basic characterizing patterns are as follows:

1. Marginal Deaf—characterized by a rigid, compulsive, pathologically weak personality pattern with inefficient perseveration on rudimentary action tendencies.
2. Typical Deaf—characterized by a tendency toward compulsivity and some perseverative activity but with an otherwise reasonably intact pattern which permits such persons to engage in many of the activities of the non-deaf.
3. Exceptional—characterized by personality patterns indistinguishable from the Hand patterns of the nonpathological, non-deaf population.

4. Psychiatric—characterized by an inability to establish meaningful, organized interpersonal, environmental relationships" (Levine and Wagner, 1974).

It should be noted that the population that was included in the "exceptional group" by Levine were those young adults with profound hearing loss who had been educated in hearing schools. At the League we have found that, when a profoundly hearing impaired person is mainstreamed, and the levels of expectation are the same as they may be for hearing peers, their personality patterns reflect that of their hearing peers.

The results of Levine's study indicate that linguistic competence is related to personality development. It has been our experience at the League that mainstream education assists in developing linguistic competence. The hearing impaired person has the need to be understood and to understand and this is important in helping to develop linguistic skill and personality organization.

At this point let us examine the effects of mainstreaming on the family. In general, the parents should view the child as a child, limited in hearing but able to participate and be part of the normal hearing world. How the family sees the child will affect the child's self-perception. The hearing loss is only one of the child's characteristics. The parental demands and expectations should be similar to those for the hearing peer group in areas not related to language. This will be related to the self-perceptions developed by the child.

The composition of the self picture is a complex one made up of a variety of characteristics that define the psychological identity. The child develops a notion about his or her own body, abilities, etc., which in part are learned by leads given to him or her by others. If the handicap becomes pervasive for the family, and everything is related to the handicap, the child's self-concept development will be strongly affected by how he or she is viewed by his or her family and those surrounding him or her. If realistic expectations are set and opportunities are given to the child to develop and utilize his or her abilities, there is a better chance for the development of positive ego strengths.

Very often the views of educators of the deaf have been that integration into a normal hearing school (mainstreaming the child) depends upon the child's social maturity and academic achievement. My experience has shown that social maturity and academic achievement depend on integration. When the child lives in a "special world" which caters to his or her special needs and which is protective, the child has a difficult time adjusting to the demands of the normal world and often lives at the peripheral edges.

Perhaps the best way to illustrate this is to give you a case history of a League client.

NEW YORK LEAGUE FOR THE HARD OF HEARING
71 West 23rd Street
New York, New York 10010
Watkins 4-3230

Name J Birthdate ______ Date ______

Address ______ Phone ______

Tester ______ Audiometer Dahlberg Standard ANSI Reliability Good

PURE TONE AUDIOGRAM
Frequency in cycles per second

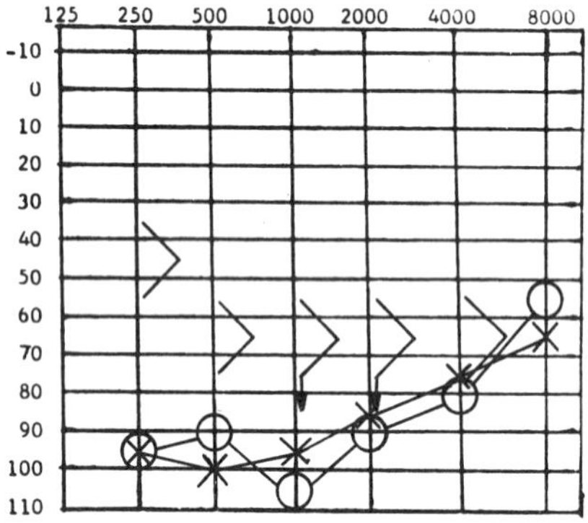

Audiogram Code

Ear	Unmasked	Masked	Unmasked	Masked	Color	No Response
R	O–O	△–△	<	◁	Red	♀
L	X–X	□–□	>	▷	Blue	X
Soundfield pure tone threshold ~						

SITE OF LESION TESTING

SISI
Freq
RE
LE

TONE DECAY
Freq.
RE
LE

BEKESY
RE
LE

ABLB

OTHER

PURE TONE AVERAGE

	Air Right	Air Left	Bone Right	Bone Left
Three Freq.	dB 95	dB 97	dB	dB
Two Freq.	dB 92	dB 97	dB	dB

SPEECH HEARING TESTS

	Ear	SAT	SRT	SP.DISCRIM SCORE	MCL	UCL
Right Ear		75 dB	85 dB	0 % at 90 dB	90 dB	95 dB
Left Ear		70 dB	85 dB	8 % at 95 dB	90 dB	dB
Soundfield		70 dB	CNT dB	CNT % at dB	dB	dB
Aids 1.		dB	dB	% at dB	dB	dB
2.		dB	dB	% at dB	dB	dB
3.		dB	dB	% at dB	dB	dB

Fig. 5-1. J's audiogram.

J, twenty-two, was born congenitally deaf, a profound hearing loss. (See Fig. 5-1) Her hearing loss was first diagnosed at age three and she was fitted with amplification and received intensive communication therapy until she was graduated from high school. She always attended normal hearing public schools. J is a graduate of a four year college in Connecticut with a degree in accounting.

I asked J to think in retrospect concerning how she felt about being part of the mainstream. She said, "Being in a regular school made me feel like a normal person, it helped me to be accepted, made me no different from others."

J had some social problems in high school which she did not encounter at college. In college she was away from home for the first time, away from the academic and emotional support her family had given her. In spite of this, she felt she had fewer social problems because her classmates were open to people and their individual needs.

Psycho-Social Aspects of Mainstreaming for the Child and Family

I asked J what would have happened if she went to a school for the deaf and she said, "I wouldn't have had an identity as a normal person and the transition would have been more difficult." Mrs. C., J's mother, when questioned about the psychological implications of mainstreaming indicated that, "It was a great support to see her as normal as possible." This is typical of the response repeated by hearing impaired young adults who have been "mainstreamed" and by their families.

The following dialogue is a transcript of a taped interview with another young woman who has a profound hearing loss (see Fig. 5-2), uses amplification and has been educated in normal hearing schools. She had the benefit of intensive early communication therapy, tutorial help, strong parental support, and ongoing counseling for her and her family.

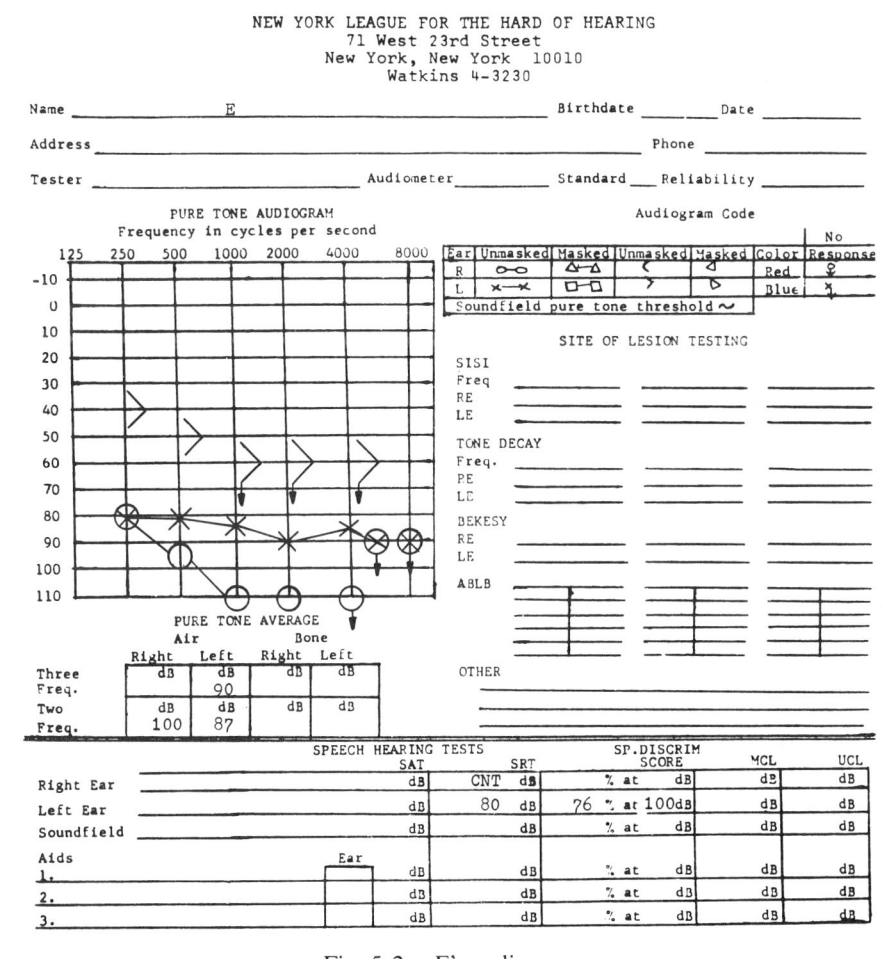

Fig. 5-2. E's audiogram.

Interviewer: Where did you go to School?

E: My whole education was based in a normal hearing school. I graduated from Springfield College in Springfield, Massachusetts with honors. I got my Bachelor's degree from there and then from there I went on to Teachers College at Columbia University in New York City and I went for my Masters in therapeutic recreation and now I have just received my Masters of Science.

Interviewer: What are you doing now?

E: Now I am working in a nursing home as a recreation director. I have a hundred patients to deal with.

Interviewer: Are you married?

E: Yes, I am very happily married. I have been married two and a half years to a normal hearing person.

Interviewer: What were some of the problems you faced in being in a normal hearing school?

E: One of my biggest problems being in a normal hearing school were first the teachers used to speak to the blackboard instead of face to face to the class and I always missed out because her back would be turned to me and I could never get anything she was saying. Also, another problem was with the teachers. Some of them used to walk around the classroom and I felt I needed to be in a swivel chair to follow their conversations. When I was young in elementary school years and also even in junior high, the kids used to make fun of me. They could never understand why I used to wear what they used to call a button in my ear and I realize now that they were never educated—they were just ignorant and their parents should of taught them not to make fun of me but now I have overcome that problem.

Interviewer: What did you see as the advantages?

E: The advantages of going to a normal hearing school first were that I never had to use sign language. I was literally forced to speak to people and I do not regret it at all today because now I have been able to speak not just to the teachers, or to the peers, but also to everybody around me now. My association with peers and teachers was meaningful in that it created a rapport and understanding between us.

Interviewer: Do you think you had more problems because you went to regular hearing schools or that it helped you in your adjustment to the world at large?

E: I don't think I had more problems but rather it helped me adjust to the world at large. It gave me an incentive to speak as normally as everyone else. Also, being in the business world today, I had to learn to compete with normal hearing people and to have them accept me as an equal. In one instance while I was being interviewed for a job, the interviewer honestly told me that despite my qualifications he felt that I could not handle the job because of many telephone calls I would have to deal with. Although I am capable of using the telephone, this interviewer never gave me the opportunity to prove myself.

Interviewer: Is there anything else you would like to say?

E: Yes, I would like to say that from personal experiences I truly recommend that every hard of hearing person be given the opportunity to go to a normal hearing school today. It would not only create a better understanding, but it will also help educate the public to the needs of the hearing impaired.

E and J are representative of many profoundly hearing impaired people who have had the advantages of mainstreaming.

In summary, it should be noted that the League's experience has shown that early identification, early appropriate amplification, early intensive communication therapy, intensive supportive tutorial help, and early involvement in the normal hearing world contribute to assisting the child toward self development. Parents are key figures in this process and in helping the child maximize his or her potential. These factors contribute to developing linguistic competence which has been shown to relate to social maturation and psychological well-being.

As there is no one psychology of the deaf, hearing impaired children given the opportunity will reflect the adjustments, the problems, the feelings of all children.

BIBLIOGRAPHY

Allport G: Personality: A Psychological Interpretation. New York, Holt, 1937

Cruickshank W: Psychology of Exceptional Children and Youth. 2nd ed, Englewood Cliffs, N.J., Prentice-Hall, pp. 118-192, 1963

Crum C: The normality of deaf children. Volta Review, 63:231-233, 1961

Green R: Counseling parents of the hearing impaired. Highlights 52:18-19, Spring 1972

Green R: Integration—A philosophy of expectation. Highlights 52:10-12, Spring, 1973

Green R: The hard of hearing child at home. Highlights 50:5-7, Winter, 1971, Lawrenson TJ: An investigation into the social maturity of two different groups of girls with profound impaired hearing and a group of institutional girls with normal hearing. Dissertation Abstracts 24:7 1964

Levine ES: The Psychology of Deafness. New York, Columbia University Press, 1960

Levine ES: Lisa and Her Soundless World. New York, Human Science Press, 1974

Levine ES, Wagner EE: Personality patterns of deaf persons: An interpretation based on research with the Hand Test. Perceptual and Motor Skills, Monograph Supplement 4, 39:1974

McDonald ET: Understand Those Feelings. Pittsburgh, Pa., Stanwix House, Inc., 1962

McGee DI: The benefits of educating deaf children with hearing children. Teaching Exceptional Children 2:133-137, 1970

Ronnei E: Tim and His Hearing Aid. Washington, D.C., Alexander Graham Bell Association for the Deaf, 1965

Rosenthal C: Social adjustment of hearing impaired children. Volta Review, 68:293-297, 1960

Schlesinger H, Meadow KP: Development of maturity in deaf children. Exceptional Children 38:461-467, 1972

Worthington AM: Psychological implications of integration of deaf children with hearing children. Amer Ann Deaf 103:467-472, 1958

Wright BA: Physical Disability—A Psychological Approach. New York, Harper Bros., 1960

Grant B. Bitter

6
Maximum Cultural Involvement For The Hearing Impaired: Environment Impact

DATELINE: U.S.A. 1974—ENVIRONMENTAL CRISIS!

On the rise "children's liberation movement" *U.S. News and World Report,* August 5, 1974, pp. 42-44) which considers that 68 million Americans under 18 years of age are the nation's "most oppressed minority." Is democracy for children? To hire a lawyer, to sue parents, to sue the school, to choose a guardian, to leave school—are among the issues!

For the 5th year in a row, divorces in America are at an all time high (*U.S. News and World Report,* April 22, 1974, pp. 43-45). Last year 913,000 couples (one for every four marriages) were divorced in the U.S. By the end of 1975, predictions are that a million marriages will dissolve. What are the social, emotional, psychological impacts on children?

Self-inflicted deaths in America during 1973 claimed 24,440 persons according to the official record (*U.S. News and World Report,* July 1, 1974, pp. 47-48). Unofficially, the estimate would be much higher, probably placing suicide as number 4 or 5 on the list for causes of death—What a loss of potential human energy!

The United States Department of Health, Education and Welfare reports (HEW, Reports on Alcoholism, 1974) that alcoholism, and alcohol-related problems cost the United States economy $25 billion every year (Americans spend nearly $22 billion in the consumption of alcohol); liquor costs America nearly $10 billion a year in lost production of goods and services; $8 billion in health and medical care; $6.5

billion in motor vehicle accidents (alcohol plays a major role in 28,000 highway deaths each year); $640 million in alcohol programs and research; $500,000 in criminal justice proceedings; $2.2 billion in welfare payments; $4.5 billion in fire losses and $135 million in Social Service costs.

According to the *U.S. News and World Report* (June 24, 1974), damage and destruction to schools in the United States during the 1972-1973 school year was one-half billion dollars ($10.87 for each student).

Why 1.4 million Americans can't read or write is a major worry in a nation that spends 60 billion dollars a year on one of the world's leading systems of education (*U.S. News and World Report,* August 19, 1974, pp. 37-40).

Educators across the United States are taking a new look, often a disillusioned one, at the "New Math" and the "New English" that were supposed to revolutionize classroom learning during the past 15 years (*U.S. News and World Report,* May 20, 1974, pp. 65-66). Now it isn't only "Why can't Johnny read?" it's "Why can't Johnny add?"

In looking at a profile of America's adult handicapped, one out of every three persons, or about 11,265,000 Americans, ages 16-64 are physically or mentally handicapped (*U.S. News and World Report,* July 22, 1974).

In education, compared with the population at large, more of the nation's handicapped failed to complete the eighth grade, 22 percent compared with 14 percent for the total United States.

In income, 21 percent of these persons were living below the poverty level. In jobs about 42 percent of them were employed. Under pressure of militancy, litigation, and advocacy, government, business, and industry are making bold moves to bring a fresh hope, and a better life for these people in bringing them into the mainstream of the nation's environment, socially, educationally, and economically.

Mainstreaming exceptional children—or preventing unmainstreaming children—is a major issue of 1974.

How special should Special Education be is a growing issue.

What are the relationships of regular and special education is another concern; can they interface more effectively? Should they merge?

Teacher education practices is a mounting issue—*quality, quantity,* curriculum for whom and for what are serious concerns.

Equal rights—*advocacy, litigation, accountability, reverse discrimination,* competency-based education, *educational options* is "a call to arms" which will hopefully guarantee children a more positive and acceptable future.

Considering the present economic crisis—and a probable cutback in the funding of special programs, what will be the effects on children?

Considering the apparent and alarming decline of the moral and spiritual fibre of the American family, what remedial techniques are needed?

Will the courts be dictating educational policy and practices if educators do not rise up to meet the contemporary educational crisis?

Obviously, the choices that professionals and parents make in the interest of quality education for children is of singular importance.

Indeed, this volume can serve as a catalyst from which there might emerge new hope, new ideas, a resurgence of energy and strength to teach language, to teach speech, to develop residual hearing, to utilize more effectively all aspects of the environment for children with hearing differences in helping them be and become functional participants in society, better equipped to make the world a more meaningful place in which to live.

Whither do we go? What decisions ought we make? What is the value of crisis? What is the value of options? Of opinions?

John Stewart Mill observed

"If all mankind minus one were of one opinion, and only one person were of the contrary opinion, mankind would be no more justified in silencing that one person, than he, if he had the power, would be justified in silencing mankind. Were an opinion a personal possession of no value except to the owner, if to be obstructed in the enjoyment of it were simply a private matter, it would make some difference whether the injury was inflicted only on a few persons or on many. But the peculiar evil of silencing the expression of an opinion is that it is robbing the human race; posterity as well as the existing generation; those who dissent from the opinion still more than those who hold it. If the opinion is right, they are deprived of the opportunity of exchanging error for truth; if wrong, they lose what is almost as great a benefit, the clearer perception and livelier impression of truth, produced by its collision with error" (Kerber, 1964).

As noted in the datelines, 1974, momentous times are upon us. Giant political and social forces are in contention for world-wide control of mankind. Ideological struggles confront us daily. Political, sociological, and educational panaceas are offered for mass consumption. A frustrating feeling of economic, political, and social bankruptcy is all too apparent on the horizon. These conditions pose imminent danger, either through the homogenizing of our society which diminishes sensitivity to human need and human value through apathy to critical social and educational issues ("The I don't care" or "I don't want to get involved" attitudes), or to the chaotic disruptive forces which would erode any degree of political, social, and educational progress.

While the basic ideals of democracy are being challenged, they are also being reaffirmed as we are moving with accelerated momentum toward human rights, equality of education, and social and educational accountability.

It would appear then that as opinions clash, as social and educational systems are challenged and questioned; as truth and error do collide, "clearer perceptions and livelier impressions of truth" will emerge.

Kipling put it this way.

> It is not learning, grace nor gear,
> Nor easy meat nor drink,
> But bitter pinch of pain or fear
> That makes creation think.

The phenomenon of crisis seems to bring great numbers of people together for a common cause. Out of crisis comes better hearing aids, better radar, more durable mattresses and comfortable homes, at least for some. However, there does appear to be a significant ecological unbalance created by the hand and mind of man in his quest for security, superiority, and comfort. Indeed, the environment has been both abused and used by some to restrict, control and even prevent human life from being and becoming, and fulfilling destiny.

Scientists, educators, specialists, the clergy, political leaders, parents, indeed, all of us would be remiss if we were unwilling to accept some responsibility for the contemporary social, political and educational dilemma that confronts us. Through the social, political and educational "sins of commission or omission"—the making of inappropriate decisions, or making no decisions at all; through the apathy of convenience, or by other means, we have not utilized the environment around us as effectively as we might have done to reduce human suffering and enhance human dignity.

Indeed, none of us are immune from this social and educational malady. Unfortunate results can accrue when human beings resist and/or reject new ways or are slow to modify traditional approaches that might enhance the social and educational achievement of mankind.

An example of such stratification might be best described by the ironic witticism, "Some people die at thirty and are not buried until seventy." Putting it another way; sad indeed is the condition of that man who, when his wife tells him to pull his stomach in, thinks he already has.

Erich Fromm (1966) described the obstacles to human achievements in this manner.

A man sits in front of a bad television program and does not know that he is bored; he reads of Viet Cong casualties in the newspaper and does not recall the teaching of his religion; he learns of the dangers of nuclear holocaust and does not feel fear; he joins the rat race of commerce, where personal worth is measured in terms of market values, and is not aware of his anxiety. Ulcers speak louder than the mind.

Theologians and philosophers have been saying for a century that God is dead, but what we confront now is the possibility that man is dead, transformed into a thing, a producer, a consumer, an idolator of other things.

Because the ancients have stolen my thoughts, I make no attempt to convince you the ideas presented regarding an ecological model are new ones, but are offered rather as a reaffirmation of, and adherence to those basic principles and laws of human contact and conduct which are always central to individual and/or group achievement and progress.

The motivating philosophy underlying this environmental approach to human development and relationships is based on the simple premise that children who have hearing differences have the right to dignity, individuality, independence, and uniqueness, and are entitled to full participating citizenship in the culture. The term used to define and describe this process and goal is called Maximum Cultural Involvement.

The parameters of the environment encompassed in the Maximum Cultural Involvement point of view consists of the *family*, the *community*, the *church*, and the *school*. It is believed that the extent to which hearing impaired children become full participating members of their culture is in direct proportion to the degree that they are accepted by their families, their communities (their peers and others), their churches, and their schools.

The Maximum Cultural Involvement philosophy is based on the premise that from the moment of birth, the infant begins a lifelong quest for satisfying, meaningful relationships with other human beings. These intricate and complex *inter*relationships and *inter*actions determine to a great extent what kind of social being he is and will become.

The implementation of this cultural model (Bitter, 1973) enhances the development of positive self-concept, personal resiliency, competent educational skills, social adequacy, and emotional stability in the forming of sensible, realistic, and meaningful personal goals. It permits the maximum utilization of the environment by hearing impaired children in becoming and being self-reliant, productive human beings. It produces achievement through a wholesome, dynamic process of cultural continuity.

Note the powerful implications of each dimension in the child's environment.

THE FAMILY

The family (grandparents, cousins, parents, siblings, etc.) is the first laboratory in which the hearing impaired child discovers and experiences the meaning and purpose of life. From these initial contacts within the family constellation, he learns to accept or reject, to love or hate, to aspire or despair, to serve or be served, to develop responsibility or irresponsibility, to become meaningfully independent or tragically dependent. Indeed, the family establishes his commitment to life. It is, therefore, imperative that each member be encouraged to assist in providing a stimulating teaching-learning environment for him which will have far reaching and longlasting impact.

Living at home supplies the invaluable experiences of wholesome family interaction. It allows hearing impaired children to share in the fun, the pain, the laughter, the pleasures, the conversations, the responsibilities and the confrontations of family give and take. Furthermore, it adds a functional opportunity for the meaningful use of auditory/oral skills in the world of important people.

THE SCHOOL

Involvement in the neighborhood school where and when feasible provides the opportunity for the hearing impaired child to model after hearing peers. It offers a stimulating teaching-learning situation in which the child can flourish socially and academically. The atmosphere of the regular school offers the reciprocal exchanges of experiences which can increase tolerance, acceptance, personal resiliency, self-confidence, meaningful development of language and auditory skills which have functional meaning. It is possible that in this environment, hearing impaired children can be freed from a negative social image of deafness and unnecessary dependency.

Obviously the world of the regular school can be frustrating and limiting, too, for the hearing impaired child, if legislators, educators, parents, support personnel, the church, and the community have not done "their homework." The rewards are great, however, for the interdisciplinary team that works untiringly to mainstream children where feasible, and to prevent segregation from ever happening at all when and where possible.

THE CHURCH

The church is capable of assisting also, in bringing about cultural excellence. The survival of civilization does not depend wholly on technological and scientific achievements. The computer might not save mankind from catastrophic demise. The development and use of devasting weapons of war are only continuing to contribute to increased human misery and destruction among contemporary societies.

Faith, prayer, religious worship in its divergent forms offer a source of genuine and growing love for life and others. These spiritual experiences may enhance self-esteem and self-renewal; they may give more purpose to living.

The involvement of the hearing impaired child with his parents, brothers and sisters, peers, church leaders and teachers within the spiritual community, permits him to obtain invaluable experience in developing acceptable social conduct, desirable values, and positive attitudes in dealing constructively with reality, wherein he finds more satisfaction in giving than receiving and in having a greater capacity to love. Genuine spiritual involvement can be inseparably linked to one's total life experience. It becomes a vibrant, vital source of energy in the developing and enlarging of the inner self.

THE COMMUNITY

To be active participants in the neighborhood and community prevents hearing impaired children from being and becoming social isolates and truly culturally disadvantaged, for it is through positive interaction with friends and neighbors that they continue to generate self-enhancement, confidence, and a favorable impression on other people. It is from this miniworld that they may gain the poise, the grace, the integrity to face the larger world in which they must be able to function effectively under the pressures required in a highly competitive society, particularly in the world of work.

Through the constant and positive interplay of meaningful interaction with the world, the limitations of the disability which severe to profound hearing differences may impose are minimized or removed; the limitations which the individual imposes on himself, such as self-pity, are eliminated; the restrictions which society thrusts upon him through stereotypes and labels are dispelled; and most importantly, the kind of limitations which the individual imposes on society through unnecessary dependency are removed.

It should be readily apparent that the conservation of human resources and their appropriate utilization can be best implemented when there is a common, cooperative effort on the part of the family, the school, the church, and the community to provide meaningful, maximum services for children, including the child with limited hearing.

Inasmuch as great emphasis is being placed on early childhood education and intervention, it seems appropriate to consider some of the implications which are significant in the teaching-learning environment of children. This information is frequently helpful in establishing and/or maintaining educational programs for children at any age.

Through the years the research has been consistently definitive concerning the importance of the environment of the home, child growth and development patterns and school age entry. Following, is a brief review of the literature (Phi Delta Kappan, 1972) regarding

1. Early and late school entrance
2. Neurophysiological research, including brain changes which affect vision, hearing, and cognition
3. Maternal deprivation
4. Family attitudes toward children, and comparisons between the home and the school as alternatives for early childhood development

Consider first the research on *early and late school entry.* Successful educational progress is determined, many scholars tell us, by the child's ability to read.

Smith (1966) reported that "Dozens of investigations indicate that reading maturation accompanies physical growth, mental growth, emotional and social maturity, experiential background, and language development."

Olsen (1947) indicated that "Children of the same age and the same grade level were found to differ by as much as four or five years in their maturation and task readiness."

This leads us to ask the questions: When is the child really ready for school? Does he have sufficient maturity to sustain learning? What is the psychological, emotional, intellectual impact on the early starters as compared to late starters?

Early childhood development studies (Keister, 1941; Carroll, 1964; Halliwell and Stein, 1964) concerning retention of learning at most all grade levels and socioeconomic status levels tend to agree that later entrants impressively excelled those children who had an early start.

Gesell and Ilg (1946) determined that school tasks, i.e., reading, writing, and arithmetic depend upon motor skills which are governed by the same rate of growth which control creeping, walking, and grasping.

In reference to *neurophysiology and cognition,* the research is impressively convincing in regard to the timing of stages when children are ready to think, organize facts, and retain learning without any serious damage or strain. Numerous neurophysiological studies indicate significant changes in brain patterns, occur between the ages of seven and eleven. This had led some scholars and researchers to question the use of formal academic instruction before the age of seven. Some findings indicate that the child's brain is not fully insulated or completely developed until after seven years of age or later. (Phi Delta Kappan, 1972)

Overton (1972) suggested that Piaget's findings agree with the research of the neurologists. He stated that

"The changes from the preoperational to concrete operational periods (2 to 7 years and 7 to 11 years) of childhood finds the very young child involved in direct perception relationships with a minimum of reasoning. So this child relates quantity to shape and form of objects, but if the shape or form is changed, he is confused. He must also change the quantity. For instance, they cannot understand how a low, wide glass can hold as much water as a tall, narrow one. It is not until he is seven or eight or later that he becomes a full 'reasonable' creature. As he goes through this transition, he begins to reason."

The impact of the home in developing positive self-concepts, emotional stability and the like as a primary base for later stability in cognition was reported by Fisher (1951).

"Psychologists have demonstrated that a normal child commencing his education in adolescence can soon reach the same point of progress he would have achieved by starting to school at five or six years of age. I have often thought that if a child could be assured a wholesome home life and proper physical development, this might be the answer to a growing problem of inadequate classroom space and shortage of qualified teachers—and the instinctive reluctance of all of us to hand over tax dollars for anything that doesn't fire bullets."

Husen (1967) concluded that a strong negative correlation existed between early school entry age and attitude toward school. Elkind (1969) found no support for "the claims of the lastingness of preschool instruction."

In reference to *visual maturity,* findings (Kappan, 1972) indicate that the child's visual system is highly similar to those of his brain. It is reported that

"The processing of visual stimuli in the brain traces the same electrical path as do the impulses involved with cognitive activity that occur between the thalmus and the cortex. Therefore, if these connections are not completed in their development, the visual signals are not interpreted correctly."

Strang (1964) reported that when children cannot adjust to the difficulties and discomforts of tasks requiring clear vision, they give up reading.

Cole (1938) indicated not more than 10 percent of five-year olds can see any difference between "d" and "b" or "p" and "q." Such confusions may not be avoided until children are at least eight years old.

In regard to auditory maturity, Cole (1938) reported further "if the child has normal six-year old ears he will still be unable to distinguish consistently between the sounds of 'g' and 'k' and 'm' and 'n', 'p' and 'b' or any other pair of related sounds."

With respect to *maternal deprivation,* the literature indicates if a child is taken from home for early schooling or remains at home without love from the very important people in his life, there may be mental and emotional problems which affect his learning; motivation and behavior. The "disturbances of attachment from too little loving can continue for a short period of time or might become permanent" (Bowlby, 1969).

Mother's attitudes are of greatest importance in the child's growth and development. Bowlby's (1969) studies

> "Make it plain that when deprived of maternal care, the child's development is almost always retarded—physically, intellectually, and socially—and that symptoms of physical and mental illness may appear . . . and that some children are gravely damaged for life."

It is reconginzed that under certain conditions, e.g., severe physical or psychological disabilities, and severe economic stress, children may be removed from their home environment. Nonetheless, the evidence points toward maternal deprivation and early schooling as primary reasons for a variety of physical and behavioral problems in children. Even though special education services are required for many children, research suggests programs should be provided as close to the family as possible.

As participators, opinion-makers, developers, implementors of programs for the hearing impaired, may we assess our personal, professional, and/or parental state of being by asking a series of reflective interrogations as follows.

In the zeal to help the language deprived, hearing impaired child "catch up" with his hearing peers or to even get him in "the ball park," and prepare him for the world; in the enthusiasm to see that he uses his residual hearing effectively in the hope that he can become a socially, academically, vocationally well-adjusted human being, it is critical that his appropriate growth and development crescendos are not violated. Is the learning environment consistent with his neuro-physiological abilities? Is it compatible with his psychological, intellectual, social, and emotional needs?

Is the criteria for identification, diagnosis, prescription, and evaluation of children, based on the needs of each individual and his family? Are the sources and resources available in the natural environment being utilized effectively? Is the diagnostic process tentative, continuous, and reversible? Are there some children diagnosed as deaf and then programmed to be deaf the rest of their lives?

Is it easier to meet the needs of a special child in a special class with other special children, using a special curriculum and giving him a special label and then sending him out with a special tag one day to meet the realities of the world?

Maximum Cultural Involvement for the Hearing Impaired

Be mindful that instruction is more than pouring in information according to the following ritual.

> Ram it in cram it in!
> Students' heads are hollow!
> Ram it in jam it in!
> There's more of the same to follow.

Does curriculum preparation include experiences for critical, reflective thinking, inquiry, exploration, creativity, independence, and intellectual integrity?

Is instruction relevant? Values are taught either explicitly or implicitly when knowledge and skills are taught. Are grades used diagnostically or punitively?

Students often think of school as a prison; what can we do to get them out? Children are required by law to attend school. Is the curriculum worth it?

On the basis of research findings, and the example of some excellent contemporary programs and practices and, considering the reservoir of expertise available to help us to utilize the environment more effectively, the following recommendations are offered for consideration in utilizing the environment for continuing progress in mainstreaming hearing impaired children.

1. Mobilizing all community resources to help families help themselves to meet crisis and overcome the obstacles inherent to handicapping conditions and disabilities. This means more adequate parent-child educational programs with itinerant services; allowing parents to participate in the functions of the interdisciplinary team decisions, and providing more meaningful services within local school districts, including both teachers and supportive personnel to meet the special needs of children.
2. Implementing preservice and inservice programs to assist the professional personnel in implementing mainstream processes.
3. Reducing teacher/student ratios to more effectively accommodate children with diverse differences.
4. Implementing more competent identification, diagnostic and placement practices which provide a continuum of services for children. (Do not establish a dangerous precedent of merely placing hearing impaired children in the regular classroom without thorough orientation and preparation of the regular school personnel, the parents, and the hearing impaired child and his peers for mainstreaming.)
5. Minimizing and/or removing institutional necessity through a "readiness" attitude on the part of all professionals who deal with hearing impaired children. If institutional programs are selected as an option, as opposed to regular class placement, every effort should be made to provide

an environment which parallels the natural environment of the child as much as possible (reverse mainstreaming, foster placement, minifamily experiences in the dorms, local community, and church involvement with responsible hearing peers and adults). *Remember the goal is to remove and/or minimize social, educational, vocational, and personal dependency.*
6. Expediting the modification of teacher-education programs on a non-categorical continuum to prepare teachers to more adequately meet the needs of children in a variety of educational settings.
7. Modifying all elementary, high school, and university curricula to include substantive content dealing with more adequate preparation for parenthood, child growth and development, and how to cope with disabilities.
8. Considering a curricula for life whereby alternatives for education could be obtained exclusive of the classroom, or at least modify our present curricula to make "life the classroom" with indulgence in the classroom per se as only one facet of education.
9. Continuing research on the neuro-physiological, and psychosociological developments of children which will assist further in the appropriate modification of the environment to meet their needs.

Active participation of all of those persons who constitute the whole environment of the child—including the family, the community, the church, and the school—in accomplishing educational and social goals is both realistic and relevant for contemporary and futuristic societies. It can maximize cultural excellence and achievement for all children.

Such an ambitious plan has international possibilities, for when human beings have common purposes, they tend to forget or minimize the differences that downgrade and destroy. It may help us to "beat our guns into pruning shears and plowshares."

The impact can have far-reaching and long lasting results, indeed. It might in fact bring about the "gentle generation"—or the Age of Dignity.

In being or becoming models of authenticity through our personal commitments to cultural excellence, may the words of David Hume exemplify our actions:

Among well-bred people,
Contempt is controlled; authority
concealed, and attention is given to
each in its turn.
An easy stream of conversation is
maintained without eagerness for bickering,
or without any air of superiority.

May the influence we have on others be so effective in impact on them that they think of us as the kind of people who were described by Helen Keller.

"There are red-letter days in our lives when we meet people who thrill us like a fine poem whose handshake is brimfull of unspoken sympathy and whose sweet rich natures impart to our eager, impatient spirits a wonderful restfulness which, in its essence is divine . . . Perhaps we never saw them before and they may never cross our life's path again; but the influence of their calm, mellow nature is a libation poured upon our discontent, and we feel its healing touch, as the sea feels the mountain stream freshening its brine."

That "healing touch" can be exemplified by "good works" in employing the dynamics of the environment through maximum cultural involvement to assist those with limited hearing find continuing purpose in using their residual hearing, and oral and written language—from birth until death in control of their environment in maintaining productive citizenship; continuing self-fulfillment, and in giving service to their fellowmen.

Good luck in this endeavor; good luck, you know, is the crossroads of opportunity and preparedness.

BIBLIOGRAPHY

Bitter GB, Mears E: Facilitating the integration of hearing impaired children into public school classes. The Volta Review 75: 13-22, 1973

Bowlby: Attachment and Loss. Vol. 1. New York, Attachment Basic Books, 1969

Carroll M: Academic Achievement and Adjustment of Underage and Overage Third-graders. 290, 1964

Cole L: The Improvement of Reading, with Special References to Remedial Instruction. New York, Farrar and Rinehart, Inc., 1938

Elkind D: Piagetian and psychometric conceptions of intelligence. Harvard Ed Rev. 319-37, 1969

Fromm E: New York Times, A report of an address to the 43rd annual meeting of the American Orthopsychiatric Association in San Francisco, April 17, 1966

Fisher T, Hawley S: A Few Buttons Missing. Philadelphia, J.B. Lippincott Company, 13-14, 1951

Gesell A, Ilg FL: The Child from Five to Ten. New York, Harper and Brothers, 388-89, 1946

Halliwell J W, Stein B W: A Comparison of the Achievement of Early and Late Starters in Reading Related and Non-Reading Related Areas in Fourth and Fifth Grades. Elementary English 631-639, 1964

Husen T: International Study of Achievement in Mathematics, Vol. II. Uppsala: Almquist and Wiksells, 1967

Keister BU: Reading skills acquired by five-year old children. Elementary School J 587-596, 1941

Kerber A, Smith W (eds): Educational Issues In a Changing Society. Detroit, Wayne State University Press, 202, 1964

Kipling R: The Benefactors. Stanza 3, in Bartlett's Familiar Quotations.

Olson, WG: NEA J 502-503, 1947

Overton WF: Piaget's Theory of Intellectual Development and Progressive Education, in the Yearbook of the Association for Supervision and Curriculum Development, 1972, Washington, D.C. The Association, pp. 95-103, 1972

Phi Delta Kappan. Early Childhood Education For All. 615-621, 1972

Smith NB: Early Reading: Viewpoints, In Rasmussen M (ed): Early Childhood Crucial Year for Learning. Washington, D.C. Association for Childhood Education International, 61-62, 1966

Strang R, Diagnostic Teaching of Reading. New York, McGraw Hill, 164-165, 1964

Mark Ross

7

Assessment of the Hearing Impaired Prior to Mainstreaming

I'm going to take the liberty of interpreting the title of this chapter in my own fashion and proceed in my own idiosyncratic way. As I understand the common use of the term "mainstreaming" it means that a child should be educated alongside his normal hearing peers. This is a laudatory goal, and I agree with it. What is often left unsaid, however, is the explicit recognition that every child is not a candidate for full mainstreaming; that there are, and should be, degrees of mainstreaming; and that this is an individual matter which has to be individually considered, with appropriate alternatives for every child depending upon his capabilities and potential, and the competencies, commitment, and sensitivities of the specific "mainstream" educational setting. In my judgment, almost every hearing impaired child can profit from some educational and social interactions with normal hearing children in a normal school setting. This is a far cry, however, from the belief that every hearing impaired child can be completely and socially absorbed in the "mainstream" educational setting.

I like the distinction frequently made by my colleague, Dr. Winnifred Northcott, between "assimilation" and "integration." "Assimilation," is the hearing impaired child's ability to function and profit from the normal school environment, much as his normal hearing peers do—although certainly some supportive help is not precluded. "Integration," on the other hand, is the physical presence of a hearing impaired child in a normal school setting. Occasionally, I see references which imply that we have succeeded in "mainstreaming" a child as evidenced by his integrated placement. I should like to emphasize that the physical presence of a child in a normal class is not, by itself, any indicator of success in any academic or behavioral dimension.

We are, I'm sure, a little too critical and objective in our thinking to make the claim that every hearing impaired child can be fully "mainstreamed." I think it important, however, that we do explicitly recognize the reality confronting our children in the educational mainstream, or else I'm afraid that we will be reaping the all-too-familiar harvest of educational problems, speech and language incompetencies, social isolation, and shattered expectations. Davis (1974) from the University of Iowa reported on a study in which she administered the Boehm Test of Basic Concepts to 24 hard-of-hearing children. This is a test which consists of 50 picture displays which represent verbal concepts selected from basic kindergarten, first, and second grade material, and which are considered necessary for understanding instructions and verbal directions issued by teachers in these grades. She found that 75 percent of the hard-of-hearing children (with losses between 35 and 70 dB in the better ear) scored at or below the tenth percentile compared to a comparable group of normal hearing children, and that furthermore, the older hearing impaired children did not seem to do any better than the younger ones. She did find a difference between the children with the less and more severe hearing losses, which I'll discuss in more detail in a moment. Remember, I'm not talking about "deaf" children, but hard-of-hearing children who were either completely or partially mainstreamed. These are fairly typical findings and they replicate a number of similar previous studies using hard-of-hearing children as subjects (Young and McConnell, 1957; Kodman, 1963; Steer et al, 1961; Quigley and Thomure, 1968; Hine, 1970). We cannot and must not ignore such findings in our efforts to "normalize" the educational exposure of our children. On the other hand we certainly should not throw up our hands in despair either. I know of some other work, in Texas and Michigan (Rister, 1974; Paul, 1974), which shows that a significant percentage of hearing impaired children can function quite normally in a mainstream setting. There's a great deal we can do, if we but confront the facts.

One of the facts is that a whole series of educational alternatives must be made available to our children. Leslie in Figure 2-1 presented a model which provides a cascade of educational alternatives. Ross in chapter 18 details a model service delivery system. The models visualize a sequential progression, from a fully self-contained setting to a fully mainstreamed placement. We have developed this concept at the Willie Ross School in which we have organized a number of educational alternatives for our children, ranging from a parent-infant program, mainstreamed nursery and kindergarten, a multiple handicapped program, a fully integrated program serviced by an itinerant teacher, resource rooms in regular schools, and a total communication program in another regular school.

The other fact we must confront is that the key to such differential placements is a comprehensive and continuing assessment, of *both* the child and the

Assessment of the Hearing Impaired Prior to Mainstreaming

school setting, which is where, perhaps, I should have started this chapter in the first place.

The first, and maybe the most important piece of information of all, is the sadly misunderstood old standby: measures of hearing acuity as established by a pure-tone audiometer. All of us have seen so many exceptions to this generality, however, that it seems somewhat in disrepute. We all

Table 7-1.
Summary of Speech, Hearing and Language Assessments and Achievement in June 1973

	Willie Ross School		Resource		Integration	
Age	8.7		8.7		8.5	
Hearing Level (Better Ear)	96.7 dB		82.7 dB		76.3 dB	
WIPI	Audit.	Comb.	Audit.	Comb.	Audit.	Comb.
	29%	64%	66%	81%	74%	94%
Peabody	Oral	Read	Oral	Read	Oral	Read
	3.2 yr	3.9 yr	4.1 yr	4.4 yr	5.0 yr	
Presch. Lang. Scale	Recept.	Express.	Recept.	Express.	Recept.	Express.
	3.26 yr	2.84 yr	5.56 yr	5.19 yr	6.17 yr	6.34 yr
Goldman-Fristoe	46%		67%		86%	
RISA						
% Correct	29%		56%		82%	
*Intelligibility	1.8		3.3		5.1	
*Voice Quality	2.9		2.8		5.2	
*Rhythm	2.6		2.6		4.9	
*Stanford Achievement						
Word Reading	1.8 G.E,		2.2 G.E.		2.5 G.E.	
Para. Meaning	1.7 G.E.		1.8 G.E.		2.4 G.E.	
Vocabulary	1.3 G.E.		1.3 G.E.		1.5 G.E.	
Spelling	1.6 G.E.		2.1 G.E.		3.0 G.E.	
Word Study Skill	1.4 G.E.		1.8 G.E.		2.4 G.E.	
Arithmetic	1.4 G.E.		1.6 G.E.		2.2 G.E.	

*Subjective rating scale from 1 (poorest) to 7 (best).
**Grade Equivalent (G.E.) scores at 1.5 and below may represent chance scores.

know children with severe or profound hearing losses who appear to be doing beautifully in public schools, and others with mild or moderate losses who are doing horribly. We should, therefore, keep in mind that we *are* talking about generalities, but that, as a generality, the single best predictor of a hearing impaired child's performance *is* the degree of hearing loss. The statement should not really be too surprising: after all these children are handicapped precisely because they do have a hearing loss, and it requires no great leap of logic to conclude that the degree of their handicap must bear *some* relationship to the degree of hearing loss they manifest.

I'd like to share with you some of the evidence which supports this generalization. Table 7-1 shows some of our results which we collected in June 1973. We collected these data as part of our regular yearly evaluation. Notice that the children in the self-contained classes at the Willie Ross School had an average loss of 97 dB; that the children in our resource room had an average loss of 83 dB; and that the children in the fully mainstreamed program, who had all previously been students at the school, had an average loss of 76 dB. We didn't plan it this way; we just evaluated the children as they were. Notice, too, that every other dimension follows the same progression, with the children with the best hearing doing best in all the measured dimensions. I should point out that the achievement tests of grade equivalence of 1.3, 1.4, and 1.5, can represent chance scores on this test.

In Table 7-2, I have excerpted some results from a larger study by Dr. David Luterman from Emerson College, as well as quoted from some of his conclusions. As you can see, he found, with a retrospective analysis, the same kind of results we found, namely that the children in the mainstream setting had more hearing.

In Table 7-3, we find results of a study completed by Quigley and Thomure in 1968. Again, as you can see, as the degree of hearing loss increases, so does the degree of academic retardation. The surprising aspect of

Table 7-2.
Educational Placement And Hearing Level*

	Integrated	Self-contained
Hearing Level	90 dB	106 dB
Conclusions:	"Significant relationship between hearing level in better ear and educational placement. It appears that hearing level is the single, most important factor in determining educational placement and, therefore, perhaps success in an auditory approach, as long as we maintain the criterion of integration as a measure of success."	

*From: Luterman DM: A comparison of language skills of hearing impaired children in a visual oral method and auditory/oral method. Emerson College, Boston, 1974

these results is the effect even mild losses can have upon academic performance, when one looks at the group data. (Just as an aside, can one consider the children who are three years behind in academic achievement to be successfully mainstreamed? Certainly one criteria of a successful mainstream placement is just this: academic performance.)

Table 7-3.
Differences Between Expected Performance and Actual Performance of the Subjects on Various Subtests of the Stanford Achievement Test***

Hearing Threshold Level (Better Ear)	N	IQ	Word Meaning	Paragraph Meaning	Language	Subtest Average
-10 to 14 dB	59	105.14	-1.04	-0.47	-0.78	-0.73
15 to 29 dB	37	100.81	-1.40	-0.86	-1.16	-1.11
27 to 40 dB	6	103.50	-3.48	-1.78	-1.95	-2.31
41 to 55 dB	9	97.89	-3.84	-2.54	-2.93	-3.08
56 to 70 dB	5	92.40	-2.78	-2.20	-3.52	-2.87
Total Group	116	102.56	-1.66	-0.90	-1.30	-1.25

*Expected Grade Placement in School (N=116) M, 6.90; sd, 2,63. Actual Grade Placement in School (N=116) M, 5.78; sd, 2.61.

**From: Quigley SP, Thomure RE: Some effects of hearing impairment upon school performance. Institute for Research on Exceptional Children, University of Illinois, 1968

I don't want to be guilty of overkill, so I'll just mention several other studies which support the conclusion that the performance of hearing impaired children is related to their degree of hearing loss. Edna Monsees, who at the time was at the Children's Hearing and Speech Center in Washington, did a major study of several years duration in which she related a number of variables to the language performance of hearing impaired children. She found the hearing loss variable a highly significant predictor of language achievement. I related the same variable to speech discrimination scores and found similar results (Ross et al, 1972). Erber from the Central Institute for the Deaf, Boothroyd from Clarke School for the Deaf, and Levitt from the City University of New York, using Lexington School for the Deaf students, all found significant relationships between degree of hearing loss and measures of speech production and speech perception (reported in Stark, 1974).

In my judgment, it is this latter relationship, that between degree of hearing loss and speech production and perception, which is the most significant for our purposes here today. I can think of no more important predictor of successful mainstreaming than the ability to communicate effectively with normal hearing individuals, and by that I mean both the ability to speak intelligibly and to comprehend most normal conversation under normal environmental circumstances. Certainly, other factors play an important role. For example, in our own work, we have found that the elementary school age hearing impaired child, who is three or more years behind his normal hearing peers on standardized language tests, is not apt to be successfully "assimilated" completely, regardless of communication skills, though he can still benefit from a transitional room placement in a regular school. And some children with poor communication skills but advanced social capacities can sometimes make amazing personal compensations. Nevertheless, if one visualizes "mainstreaming" as the ultimate goal, then the ability to engage in effective, relatively effortless, oral communication is, in my judgment, the single most important predictive criterion.

The next logical question to ask at this point is, how is this assessment made? How do we evaluate the oral communication skills of our hearing impaired children? What tools do we use? What standards do we apply? And are the judgments we make valid? That is, do they indeed predict successful assimilation in a mainstream setting?

These questions, it seems to me, go to the heart of our concern. I wish we had some good answers. Unfortunately, we do not. All of us, I think, make these judgments using our own personal standards, based on our experiences, perceptions, and philosophy. We do our best, but it is often not good enough. Frankly, I think it rather a disgraceful commentary on our profession to find that after all this time we still do not have a standardized, nationally accepted method of assessing the speech production and speech perception of hearing impaired children. We all seem to go our own way in making these evaluations, thereby compounding the communication problems of hearing impaired children by our own inability to communicate with each other. What I'd like to briefly cover now is how we attempt at the Willie Ross School to answer the questions I raised above. I recognize that I am presenting no absolute truths.

We use several of the speech tests which have been standardized on normal hearing children, such as the Goldman-Fristoe and the Fisher-Logeman tests. We use a test we are developing at the Willie Ross School composed of brief sentences within which multiple choice words are embedded. We have used the Hudgin's technique of having normal listeners score word lists recorded by the children. We have thought about the sentence lists developed by Marjorie Magner at Clarke School and the five point rating scale developed at the National Technical Institute for the Deaf. Our teachers and speech pathologists rate the communication skills of their children, and we are always most receptive to learning how others approach this same problem. In the final analysis, however, though all this information is helpful and will be more so in the future, we do what all of us here probably do: we draw on our experience and background to make the best judgment we can.

Because of the nature of our program, we are fortunate in not having to make irrevocable decisions. In our resource program, we are able to evaluate a child's total adjustment in a regular class, and if he appears ready, then we recommend the mainstream program. Our itinerant teachers follow the child in his local school to assess whether the placement is appropriate. To make this assessment, the itinerent teacher spends a full school day accompanying the child to all of his classes. She observes his responses to classroom instruction and to conversation from other children; she judges how intelligible others find his speech; she evaluates his past and present classroom performance; she consults with all the relevant school personnel; and either administers or requests standardized tests of academic performance and language achievement. Assessment, as we view it, is an on-going process and our recommendations regarding educational placement cannot depend upon any single test or diagnostic session. The most valid assessment we can possibly make is a critical and continuing observation of the child himself in the mainstream setting. *I can't emphasize this too much; we must build into our educational programs a formal system of educational alternatives and we must simultaneously provide the mechanisms for this critical and continual observation.*

It is not only the child who must be assessed, but also the school and classroom into which he is to be placed. The regular teachers have to be prepared to receive our children. They must understand that our children frequently leave a sheltered, small class, individualized environment and that they may initially have difficulty adjusting to the apparently chaotic, bustling, and competitive world of the normal school. Expectations and standards may be set too high, or more often, too low. Severe communication problems are often overlooked, as long as the child is not disruptive. Our children are often socially promoted, and simply passed on from grade to grade, with a resigned acceptance of the children's poor accomplishments. Most regular teachers *are* sincerely interested in helping our children; we owe them, and our children, the obligation to support their efforts with an organized, regularly scheduled orientation and follow-up program.

In summary then, mainstreaming as an objective must entail more than the physical presence of a hearing impaired child in a regular school setting. He must be there for a purpose, and that purpose must be demonstrated superior academic and personal performance than that achievable in a special school or class setting. Based on our assessment of a child's residual hearing, communication skills, and personal qualities, there must be an array of educational alternatives available for them. The pinnacle—complete assimilation in our regular schools and in our society—can and should be reached by many, but it should not be done at the expense of devaluing the magnificent accomplishments of many other hearing impaired children who have not reached this particular pinnacle through no fault of their own.

BIBLIOGRAPHY

Davis J: Performance of young hearing-impaired children on a test of basic concepts. J Speech Hear Res 17: 342-351, 1974

Deno EN: Council for Exceptional Children. Bulletin, Exceptional Children, 39: 495, 1973

Hine WD: The attainments of children with partial hearing. Teacher Deaf 68: 129-135, 1970

Kodman F: Educational status of hard of hearing children in the classroom. J Speech Hear Dis 28: 297-299, 1963

Paul RL, Young B: The hard of hearing child in the regular classroom. ESEA Title III Project. Oakland Schools, Pontiac, Michigan, 1974

Quigley SP, Thomure RE: Some effects of hearing-impairment upon school performance. Institute of Research on Exceptional Children, University of Illinois, Urbana, 1968

Rister A: A follow-through study of pre-school hearing handicapped children, Speech and Hearing Institute, Health Science Center, Houston, Texas, 1974

Ross M, Kessler ME, Phillips ME, Lerman JW: Visual, auditory, and combined presentations of the WIPI test to hearing-impaired children. The Volta Review 74: 90-96, 1972

Stark RE (ed): Sensory capabilities of hearing-impaired children. Baltimore, Md., University Park Press, 1974

Steer JD, Hanley TD, Spuehler HE, Barnes NS, Burk KW, Williams WG: The Behavioral and academic implications of hearing losses among elementary school children. Purdue Research Foundation Project Number P.U. 0240, 1961

Young D, McConnell F: Retardation of vocabulary development in hard of hearing children. Exceptional Children 23: 368-370, 1957

SECTION II

Mainstream Problems and Practices

Winifred H. Northcott

8

Mainstreaming the Preprimary Hearing Impaired Child, 0-6: Practices. . . . . Progress. . . . . . Problems

This is the decade of the rights of the infant and preschool child who is at risk or high risk for educational failure in essential life tasks upon reaching school age. Edwin Martin (1974) has focused attention upon the need to develop a publicly supported delivery system of services to these children and their parents, relegating private agencies to the role of subcontractors to the local school district offering early childhood education services based on a "zero reject" concept.

In recognition of the fact that certain children enter the primary grades at a position below parity in competition with their classmates, the Bureau of Education for the Handicapped, U.S. Office of Education, has identified early childhood education for the handicapped as one of its top priorities for attention and has expanded allocation of funds as "seed money" for action among local education agencies, community agencies and state departments of education.

The literature today furnishes the retrieval terms which describe the characteristics of direct service programs for this population from birth to six years of age, and the social and political climate in which they are flourishing. They include

Tax supported
Least restrictive environment
Principle of normalization
Appropriate education
Individualized educational prescription
Multidisciplinary team
Parent involvement

The National Advisory Committee on Education of the Deaf in its 1973 Annual Report to U.S. Commissioner of Education, John R. Ottina (*Basic Education Rights,* 1973) considered that there are basic rights to which all deaf persons are entitled, including

> "Early educational programs for deaf infants and their families, which should be available as soon as a hearing loss is established."
>
> "Educational placement of a deaf child ranging from the neighborhood school to special classes, special schools and/or residential schools."

An examination of the topic at hand, practices. . . progress. . . problems relating to the placement of preprimary hearing impaired children in regular nursery school, day care or Head Start programs must be considered as imbedded in the description of a total system of delivery of services to the hearing impaired child, birth-6 years, and his family.

The premise is that the first level of intervention is a parent oriented, home centered program in recognition that the center of learning for any young child is in his home and parents are the first natural and informal teachers. Group educational experience in a regular nursery school or day care program with nonhandicapped peers, around the age of 36 months, is an integral component (but only one) of a comprehensive program for the hearing impaired child, from birth to around the age of 3-1/2, and his family in the United States today. The full range of services includes

> Parent counseling, guidance and parent education
> Parent teaching (guided experiences in a home living center or family domicile)
> Integrated group educational experience (nonhandicapped peers)
> Self contained class (if appropriate)
> Individual instruction: child (auditory, linguistic)
> Site visitation; inservice training (staff: integrated program, community based agency)

Each of these dimensions of educational service is related to the notion of the match between potential and performance, ensuring minimum disparity among the child's. 1—chronological age; 2—listening age (commencing the day the child is fitted with a hearing aid and full time usage begins; 3—developmental age; 4—linguistic age; 5—congruity between home and school activities and goals for the child.

This is also the decade of the rights of parents of a hearing impaired (deaf or hard of hearing) child and the author advances a bill of rights to describe them, which has only the credibility of internal consistency with the philosophy and publications to her name.

A BILL OF RIGHTS FOR EVERY PARENT OF A HEARING IMPAIRED (DEAF OR HARD OF HEARING) CHILD

The right to:

AN INTACT FAMILY	1.	Availability of a regional public school program (0-21 years) permitting home care and active parent/school interaction as a preferred alternative to residential school placement.
ACCESSIBILITY TO SCHOOL SUPPORT SERVICES	2.	A program of continuing parent guidance, counseling and education as an integral component of an accessible comprehensive educational program for a hearing impaired child from birth or as soon as the diagnosis of hearing loss is established, to age twenty-one.
PARTICIPATORY MANAGEMENT	3.	Participation with school personnel in the major decisions affecting the development of an individualized educational program for your child, including educational setting and choice of method of communication for instructional purposes during the school day.
SCHOOL RECORDS	4.	Examination and challenge of the content of official and documentary school records for your child, giving written consent before any information is released to third parties.
CONCERTED ACTION	5.	Organization for the purpose of orderly and constructive action leading to initiation, improvement and expansion of educational programs stressing individualization of services.
ACCOUNTABILITY	6.	Evidence from school authorities (measurable/demonstrable) of your child's continuing progress in essential life skills: intelligible speech; academic and vocational education; inner-directed personal/social behavior; motivation to learn.

The underlying assumption, in terms of this chapter, is that parents have chosen an auditory/oral method of initial communication with their child.

While mainstreaming of young hearing impaired children in regular nursery schools is an accepted fact today (McConnell, 1974; Kirkman, 1974; Northcott, 1973; 1971; Kennedy, 1974) the degree of assimilation is the imponderable (Watson, 1973).

An open-ended list of critical variables to examine would include 1. the population being served 2. funding patterns 3. curricular models 4. support services (Parents; child; general educators in early childhood education programs)

Definitions: Antics with Semantics

The term *hearing impaired* has been identified (Wilson, Ross, Calvert, 1974) in a study involving college students who were "naive in the area of speech pathology and audiology" as the least stigmatizing term as far as prediction of interpersonal effectiveness, speech and language skills are concerned. The authors pointed out that the terms *deaf* and *hard of hearing* connote differing problems with differing affect and that since the category *deaf* is a more functional than physiological one, it is difficult to apply in the instance of a young child.

The entire preprimary years are diagnostic ones in the broad sense of supplying clearer answers to the pertinent questions, "What does the child hear?" and "What can he do?" The child's teachers serve as primary and functional psychoeducational diagnosticians, checking their observations against the full reports and shared conversations with parents. Thus the generic term *hearing impaired,* indicating a hearing loss which may range from mild to profound in a physiological sense, is used throughout this position paper. It has the added advantage of being neutral in emotional content.

Gorelick (1974) supported this notion in examination of responses from 72 preschool programs in Northwest Los Angeles County, where staff members were asked whether they would accept or reject children with handicaps for enrollment in their nursery schools. While 45 (62 percent) would accept a child with "partial deafness," the number of acceptances dropped to 10 (13 percent) for "profound deafness" in a prospective candidate.

In consideration of the general topic of mainstreaming, it must be noted that children with one or more of the following characteristics are *not* candidates for placement in an educational setting with nonhandicapped peers (Northcott, 1972).

> Late identification requiring immediate and intensive special education services
> Severely multihandicapped child
> Extreme social, emotional immaturity
> Irregular hearing aid usage

Assumptions Prior to Placement in Mainstream Program

These would include 1—early detection (birth-24 months); 2—early enrollment in a family oriented special education program with sufficient numbers of families to permit homogeneous groupings of parents and educational alternatives for children; 3—early fitting of hearing aids (binaural, if recommended); 4—full time hearing aid usage; 5—continuing support to parents; 6—a variety of specialists to serve the child and his family; 7—site visitation to the community program in which the hearing impaired child is placed, for purposes of demonstration teaching and consultative services; 8—an auditory/oral method of communication.

Method of Instruction

An early and initial auditory/oral (aural/oral) approach to language learning on the part of a very young hearing impaired child is essential, based in part on the very definition of a deaf child: one in whom the sense of hearing is nonfunctional, with or without a hearing aid, for purposes of ordinary communication.

The Bureau for Hearing Handicapped Children, New York City, provides this functional definition of a deaf child:

"one who has not demonstrated the capacity to develop language through the auditory channel with or without amplification"

The rationale for an auditory/oral method of communication between a young hearing impaired child and his family/teachers includes several considerations.

(1) In the period of natural language development, a child receives his first linguistic information in a natural rhythmic phrasic way and is encouraged by the adults in his environment to match the intonation patterns received through aided hearing. Thus a child with severe or profound hearing loss can induce the rules of his language most naturally, in an oral rhythmic way as do his hearing peers, in connection with experience and conversation in which he is actively involved. (2) The native language or mothertongue of the child (van Uden, 1970) is the English language—its vocabulary, grammatically correct syntax, and semantics—and can be learned spontaneously. It is this distinguished Dutch scholar's premise that every sentence is equally easy for a hearing impaired child to process through his own auditory and vocal mechanism, regardless of syntactic complexity, if it is of appropriate length for his age and stage of development and related to the child's activities at the moment of occurrence.

Under this rubric, the author believes the use of a form of sign language would be relegated to an appropriate place as a second language, linked to American oral language syntax, as determined to be appropriate for selected children of school age. The assumption here is that the child's parents have normal hearing; in the instance of deaf parents, for whom sign language is a native language, every assistance must be given in order to assure their active participation and comprehension of the content of discussion in group and individual guidance sessions. Parent advisers should enlist the active support of neighbors and relatives in providing necessary auditory stimulation on a daily basis (Northcott, 1974).

In light of the findings of Ling and Ling (1974) who examined parent-child verbal interactions among normal hearing 1 and 3 year olds, a word of caution seems appropriate. They found that while parents used full sentences as frequently when speaking to their infants as did mothers of older children, mainly related to ongoing events, imitations and expansions were seldom employed even by mothers of children in their third year. This has obvious implications for the nature of support to parents in their learned behavior of modelling and expanding a hearing impaired toddler's primitive attempts at verbal self-expression.

The Nature of Sign Language

It should be mentioned that there are advocates of the use of sign language, in any one of its various forms, and fingerspelling in addition to and in conjunction with the use of speech, speechreading and audition for very young children. Formerly known as the "simultaneous" or "combined" method, it now bears the label "total communication."

Table 8-1.
Average Decibel Loss, Etiology, and Age of Onset of Hearing Impaired Children*

Pupils	Average Decibel Loss (db PTA)	Etiology	Onset	Grade
Boys				
1	55 **	Unknown	Congenital	1
2	56 **	Jaundice	Congenital	1
3	63 **	Rubella	Congenital	1
4	75 **	Rubella	Congenital	1
5	80 **	Rubella	Congenital	1
6	88 **	Rubella	Congenital	1
7	110 **	Unknown	Congenital	2
Girls				
8	50 **	Drugs	Congenital	1
9	76 **	Premature	Congenital	1
10	76 **	Rubella	Congenital	1
11	85 **	Rubella	Congenital	1
12	85 **	Rubella	Congenital	2
13	98 **	Rubella	Congenital	1
14	110 **	Unknown	Congenital	2
15	110 **	Meningitis	13 months	1

*From Kennedy, P., and Bruininks, R.H.: Social status of hearing impaired children in regular classrooms. Except. Child., *40*:336-312. 1974. Used by permission of the Council for Exceptional Children.
**Pure tone average.

The premise is that in the case of a child with a severe or profound hearing loss, communication of necessity must be highly visual. This is not supported by current research findings and empirical evidence relating to the audiometric assessment of children who have been assimilated in regular classes following early auditory and oral education (McCauley, in press; Kennedy, 1974; Davis, 1964, McConnell, 1974; Pollack, 1971; Griffiths, 1967).

Stokoe (1973), Director of the Linguistics Research Laboratory at Gallaudet College for the Deaf stated:

> "sign language is a language in which what are commonly called gestures do the usual work of words . . . but, most important, it is also a language that has its own morphology, syntax and semantics. Dependence on or derivation from any spoken language has never been proven of the syntax and semology of American sign language" (p. 6, 7).

A few problem areas should be noted, in the use of sign language with very young children whose parents have normal hearing.

1. It is difficult for parents who must attend sign language classes to simultaneously present these signs in full sentences while sustaining the normal rate, rhythm and inflectional patterns of speech from which the child receives his first linguistic information.
2. The question of reinforcement is critical; which behavior will be reinforced by the child's family, the signed word or spoken word, with improvement noted in the desired direction.
3. The use of sign language in conjunction with speech and audition does not result in automatic communication between parents and child since language acquisition follows the same sequence in comprehension and expression: gesture, signal, symbol, symbol referrent.
4. There will not be automatic communication by a child of his feelings and wishes due to the ambiguity of a child's primitive gestures and the need for parents to learn, under formal guidance, the techniques of reinforcement of the child's telegraphic sign language and expansion into full sentences (Northcott, 1975).
5. "Something needs to be added on helping a hearing impaired child communicate with his hearing peers (a parent observed) . . . where does total (communication) fit in here. It's fine for a deaf child to be able to tell his parents that Johnny pushed him down—how's he going to communicate with Johnny? (Comprehensive mental health training, 1972).

In a national survey (questionnaire) of competencies needed by teachers of hearing impaired infants, birth-3 years, and their parents in settings ranging from public and residential schools to speech and hearing centers and hospitals, Northcott (1973) found that sign language, the manual alphabet (fingerspelling) and cued speech as methods of teaching the hearing impaired infant, birth to age three, were rated by both teachers and experts as skills *not* required. They appeared as the three competencies of lowest value on the tables showing rank order of importance according to the ratings of experts, teachers, and subpopulations (B.A. and graduate degrees) within the teacher group.

Fingerspelling and the Young Hearing Impaired Child

Neo-oralism (fingerspelling synchronized with speech) is a method used with infants and preschool children throughout the Soviet Union, although the Director of the Institute of Defectology in 1970 said in the author's presence that a staff member was experimenting with oral-only methods of teaching young children and was "excited by the results." Withrow (1973) addressing to the Soviet approach, pointed out some significant differences between the Russian (Cyrillic alphabet) and English languages (Roman alphabet) and their printed forms.

1. In Russia, irregular spellings were eliminated in the 1920s to provide close congruence between the spoken word and the read word.
2. The Cyrillic alphabet has 33 characters which are consistently used in spelling as opposed to the 298 combinations of the 26 letters of the Roman alphabet which represent the 42 phonemes of English.
3. In the instance of the English language, fingerspelling and speech used simultaneously introduce the notion of "cognitive dissonance" Withrow pointed out, since an average rate of conversational speech is 140 words per minute, whereas fingerspelling rarely exceeds 80 to 90 words per minute. Dr. Withrow used the illustration of the word "phone" with its 3 phonetic values and 5 letters, to highlight the confusion on the part of a preschool child in "developing a true relationship between the finger configuration, the phoneme, the lip movement and the use of residual hearing" (p. 8).

The Rochester method of education (fingerspelling and speech synchronized) is not utilized in the Home Demonstration Program at the Rochester School for the Deaf (where the method originated), the site of a comprehensive parent infant project for children from birth to three years of age. If the parents are hearing individuals, the training approach is auditory. "If the parents are deaf, their method of communication is combined with emphasis on their use of voice. All children use amplification" (Castle, 1974).

An experimental study at Queens College (Meier, 1961) with two groups of parents of deaf babies was designed to explore alternative procedures on language development: one group of parents began fingerspelling for all communication with their young children (18 months to 5-1/2 years). The study was not concluded because the parents in the experimental group discontinued the use of fingerspelling on discovery that their young children responded as well to speech alone, showing by their behavior that they understood what was said to them in connection with their activities.

In conclusion to this examination of alternative methods of communication for language acquisition, it should be noted that the rights of parents in choice of method, are paramount. It is incumbent upon educators to provide sophisticated models using an auditory/oral approach for critical examination by parents of young hearing impaired children.

The choice of method, in effect, addresses to the question of family values and lifestyles. Furthermore, it introduces a predictive factor relating to the educational delivery system for the child upon entrance into the primary grades, choice of friends, and implications for work patterns and economic self realization as an adult.

Regardless of the method selected by parents, the question of congruence between the philosophy and practices of the infant/preschool program and the home is central and critical to progress in the development of communication skills.

Why Mainstreaming?

A Director of Special Education or School Board member may well ask this question relating to the components of educational service provided around the age of three years. It deserves a substantive answer, including these points:

1. It offers the child a model for personal/social/communicative behavior (Northcott, 1970; Luterman, 1973; Kirkman, 1974; McConnell, 1974).
2. It reduces the amount of gesture language initiated by the hearing impaired child.
3. There is positive reinforcement of attempts to talk, which take the form of intrinsic reward but also convey the *power* of speech (another turn in a group game; the chance to pass the cookies, etc.)
4. It cuts down the excessive dependence which may have developed between mother and child (Levine, 1960).
5. It adds a verbal mediating link between the action of play and cognitive development for the hearing impaired child through the presence of highly verbal non-handicapped peers.
6. There is opportunity for increased comprehension and rich interior language stored for later incorporation in self expression through spoken language ("I like it! That's funny! It's mine!)

Dr. Eveline Omwake, past President of the National Association for the Education of Young Children, has stated there is ample evidence that acceptance of a handicapped child during the nursery school year is on the basis of a contribution to group usefulness in play-learning situations.

The Physical Setting/The Funding Sources

Although the placement of a hearing impaired child in a group educational setting with nonhandicapped peers remains a constant objective, the practices and procedures will vary.

At Clarke School and Lexington School for the Deaf and in such diverse settings as the Children's House of Learning, El Dorado, Arkansas (Kirkman, 1974) and Emerson College, in Boston (Luterman, 1974) reverse mainstreaming is offered with neighborhood children being invited to join the group of hearing impaired youngsters.

In the instance of the Special Education Infant/Preschool Public School Program in Minneapolis, Minnesota a cadre of more than 20 nursery schools in the city and suburban districts is utilized for placement of a single hearing impaired child in each (Northcott, 1971). Dr. Fellendorf, Executive Director of the Alexander Graham Bell Association for the Deaf, has indicated that in Sweden the common practice is to reserve one of four chairs at any preschool nursery for a hearing impaired child who is given individual auditory and linguistic instruction on the premises by a team of general preschool educator and teacher of the deaf.

It is an increasingly supported fact that the preschool education of a child is the province of the public school systems in the 50 states (Martin, 1974). The local school district of the child's residence is the local case finder, through the mandatory school census of all children, 0-21 years, and a very likely agency to serve as the coordinator of educational services to preschool age handicapped children, reaching out to other agencies in the community or region in order to provide a full spectrum of services *(State Guidelines, 1974).*

In many states, the same pattern of state aid reimbursement of local school district expenditures for essential personnel, supplies and equipment obtains in programs for prekindergarten handicapped children as in programs for school age children.

The current management-by-objectives approach to any delivery of services to handicapped children mandates that administrators first focus on the necessity of providing services upon the identification of hearing loss in very young children, and then on the method of securing funds to make their commitment a reality. Various titles under the Elementary and Secondary Education Act (Titles I, III, VI, Part B or C) as well as foundation support and expenditure of local tax dollars supplemented by state aids, are available sources of potential financial assistance. Administrators are thus cast in the role of child advocates, in the initiation and expansion of infant/preschool educational services. Be reminded of Pogo who is reported to have said, "We have met the enemy . . . and he is us."

Characteristics of Children Who Are Mainstreamed

UNTESTED WARRANTS AND UNWARRANTED ASSUMPTIONS

There is limited usefulness today in quoting the findings from research studies prior to 1964-1965, when early intervention programs (focusing on parents as the first pupils) were introduced in response to the rubella epidemic in the United States, to support or reject the efficacy of early intervention models which have been developed in the late 1960s. During the past six or seven years the concept of support services to hearing impaired children in regular classes, as a responsibility of the school district of enrollment, became widely implemented. Such studies as those of Kodman (1963) and Young and McConnell (1957) indicate severe language retardation for mild to moderately hearing impaired children attending public school classrooms (Goetzinger, 1962). O'Connor (1961) generalized from a study of 50 pupils who had transferred from the Lexington School between 1945 and 1957, that the percentage of deaf children who are logical candidates for mainstreaming in regular classes is small and that the general age of transfer should be 8 or 9 years.

In contrast, present day studies (Kennedy, 1974; McCauley, 1974; Rister, 1974) indicate that the degree of hearing loss is not equated with ability to function in a mainstream setting. In the Kennedy (1974) study, 11 of the 15 children who were graduates of a parent oriented public school infant/preschool program had a severe or profound hearing loss. They were among 277 children in 13 classrooms in 9 different school districts including Minneapolis.

Children with severe and profound hearing losses were better accepted than those with less severe loss and in 4 instances were among the most popular in the class. Furthermore, they were as perceptive of their own social status as normally hearing children. Rister (1974) reported the degree of hearing loss was no barrier to mainstreaming in a separate study in Texas.

McCauley (1974) studied the interactive behaviors (positive/negative; verbal/nonverbal) of these same children the following year when they were in second and third and (1 child) fourth grade classes. As a group these hearing impaired children did not behave differently from their nonhandicapped classmates, in overall fashion, with respect to these critical variables.

However, certain trends were noted which have implications for inservice and preservice training of general educators. The hearing impaired children tended to interact with a smaller number of hearing children, and there was significantly more verbal interaction with teachers than between teacher and nonhandicapped peers.

McConnell (1974) reported a study involving a small number (6) graduates of the Mama Lere Parent Teaching Home (Infant, birth-3 Years) which indicated the group were above the normal hearing group in total reading percentile and language competence, but not in mathematical competence. It was hypothesized that the concepts of new math were not taught during the preschool years to the hearing impaired group.

Liff (1973) examined the language competency of the early intervention group, using Lee's Developmental Sentence Types (1966) and found it was similar to that of the normal hearing group.

In contrast, Davis (1974) examined 24 hard of hearing children and 24 normal hearing children, 6-8 years of age, who were mainstreamed partially or full time in regular public school classes, on results of the Boehm Test of Basic Concepts which indicates gross representation of verbal concept knowledge and ability to understand and follow directions. Seventy-five percent of the hard of hearing children scored at or below the ten percentile when compared to norms for hearing children their own age or younger. In an item analysis, the poorest performance was on time concepts, quantity, miscellaneous, and space concepts, in that order.

Unfortunately, Davis was permitted to introduce for publication the quantum leap statement which cannot be supported or refuted: "They (note: the 24 hard of hearing children) are probably representative of hearing impaired children in other schools."

Certainly there is need to examine the content of prekindergarten curricula in preschool programs for the hearing impaired, to insure congruence between concepts presented and their usefulness in applied situations in a mainstream program in the primary grades.

In all but the last study described, certain common characteristics of the infant/preschool programs offered in a variety of educational settings (public school or private speech and hearing center) can be noted for each of the mainstreamed "graduates."

All children were

1. Binaural hearing aid users
2. Enrolled in parent oriented, home training infant/preschool programs
3. Placed in mainstream day care/nursery schools for a portion of their weekly educational experience during the infant/preschool years
4. Received individual instruction (language, auditory training) as a supplement (3 above)
5. Taught by the auditory/oral method

"Unloving critics and uncritical lovers" was a phrase chosen by John Gardner, Chairman of Common Cause, as the title of a recent speech. It is applicable to the unwarranted assumptions and generalizations often made by educators of the deaf.

It's good for a hearing impaired child to be mainstreamed at the preprimary level.

The primary mode of communication for prelingually profoundly deaf children must be visual.

He belongs in a school for the deaf.

This kind of simplistic, specious reasoning must be replaced by a team approach to the development of an individualized educational prescription for each hearing impaired (deaf or hard of hearing) child on the basis of daily observation, examination of the results of norm-referenced and criterion-referenced tests, and observations of a child's listening and linguistic behavior by his parents and siblings which are reported to school personnel on a continuing basis.

It would seem useful to examine the verbal and nonverbal interactions of hearing impaired children in mainstream preprimary settings, in consideration of the maintenance of mainstream nursery/day care placement as an integral component of a comprehensive infant/preschool program.

Rankhorn (1974) examined the spontaneous verbal interactions of an experimental and control group of young children: the former group being mainstreamed with children having normal hearing (who were from neighborhood) in a classroom at Lexington School for the Deaf. It was found that the mainstreamed hearing impaired group was more verbal and more oral and auditory than the control group, in number and syntactic complexity of sentences. However, nonvocalized interactions over verbal were still in a ratio of 2-1. For the control group, the ratio was 10-1, with a strong affinity for the less desirable form among those in the self contained classroom which had no hearing children as models for verbal behavior.

The question of relativity would seem to be relevant to the choice of educational setting for group learning experience. It brings to mind the question reportedly asked of James Thurber, "What do you think of marriage?" and his unpredicted response, "Compared to what?"

Dale (1973) examined a group of children in unit classes of normal hearing children age 5-15 years, in contrast to two large day schools for deaf children. One hearing impaired child spoke 3 times in 15 minutes in a group language lesson in contrast to 27 times in a 5-minute period on a one-to-one tutorial basis.

A student of Dr. Mark Ross at the Willie Ross School in Massachusetts examined the environment of children who were mainstreamed in a regular nursery school and found 3 to 4 times as great a number of verbal interactions with hearing children in free play periods as in structured situations. In these instances, in a controlled time sample, hearing impaired children had 51 verbal to 1 nonverbal interactions with hearing children. In contrast, in a situation where hearing impaired children of the same age were grouped together, a count indicated 30 verbal/30 nonverbal interactions. In other words, the chances were 50/50 that the hearing impaired child would talk or gesture to another hearing impaired child.

Castle (1974) reported that hearing impaired children enrolled in private nursery schools made a satisfactory adjustment except for the area of social interaction, the natural setting in which verbal communication would occur. "For the most part, these children played alone, chose their own activities and seemed disinterested in teacher initiated activities" (p.191). However, it should be noted that although reports were sent from the Home Demonstration Program teacher to the private nursery school, no personal contact was made by that individual. One of the questions listed by the authors of the article, asked frequently by early childhood education specialists was "Should they encourage the child to talk?"

In contrast (Northcott, 1973) site visitation to each nursery school in which a hearing impaired child was enrolled, was a routine activity of the parent adviser/teacher in the Minneapolis Public School Infant/Preschool Program from which "graduates" Kennedy (1974) and McCauley (1974) drew their sample of mainstreamed children in the primary grades.

Critical Variables to be Considered

The placement of a hearing impaired child in a regular nursery school or day care center around the age of 36 months does not assure assimilation which Watson (1973) defined as "rendering alike under environmental conditions." An open-ended list of variables to be examined, would include

1. The nature of audiological management (Hanners, 1973).
    A. Signal/noise ratio. Intelligibility of speech depends upon the acoustic environment of the nursery/day care center and the nature of the amplification system utilized in the classroom/mainstream environment.
    B. Sound treatment of the room after identification of its reflection/reverberation characteristics.
    C. Binaural/monaural amplification. Gladwin (1972) examined 120 children age 3—grade 6.
        51 monaural hearing aid users
            31% without an operable aid on any given day
        69 binaural hearing aid users
            10% without either aid, any given day

The concept of the "reserve tank" is applicable here.
- D. A systematic program of listening skill development including the focus on auditory attention, auditory discrimination, and development of short and longer term auditory memory in young children (Pollack, 1970).
  - a. Auditory training incorporated into every facet of daily living. Not a formal training period daily
  - b. Daily routine hearing aid check (Hanners, 1973).
  - c. Activities leading to matching inflectional contour (teacher, child; parent/child); shared music/vocal play
  - d. Moving a child from well inflected jargon to sentences useful in daily activities outside a school situation.
2. The monitoring process: mainstream nursery school/day care center
   - A. Site visitation is critical, on a scheduled basis (6 weeks apart preferably) by a specialist on deafness.
   - B. Workshops, spring and fall of year to permit participatory learning experiences by general early childhood education specialists. Video tapes, role playing, small group discussions, lectures are useful.
3. The hearing impaired child himself; how he organizes his skills
   - A. The question of the child's conceptual tempo (reflective/impulsive)
   - B. How does it mesh with that of the teacher's?
   - C. Who is charged with the responsibility for initial placement/suggested transfer of the child?
4. Play patterns and abilities of hearing impaired children in integrated nursery schools
   - A. Darbyshire (1974) found these characteristics common among 6 children mainstreamed in a nursery at Queens University, Kingston, Ontario, as illustration of preventive action which should be taken, commencing with enrollment of a child and family in a program for the hearing impaired
     - a. Less tolerance for frustration than among normal hearing peers
     - b. Greater dependence on adults for approval
     - c. Dominance level. . . passive and non assertive
     - d. Parents "after 2 years of diagnosis, still in trauma and bewilderment"
5. Curricular model selection: Programmed approach (Bereiter, 1966); Cognitive or open framework (Weikart, 1971); Child Centered (Mayer, 1971)
   - A. Prescott (1974) in an examination of 112 children, 2-5 years, in administration of a day care environmental inventory, found that children placed in a home plus nursery school were highest in cognitive awareness (cognitive restraints. e.g. "This wheel won't fit there, it has to go here.")

6. "A charming nonegocentric character" as van Uden describes a child who expects adults to be useful and responsive to his overtures in play and conversation.

Implications for the Nature and Content of Teaching the Hearing Impaired Preschooler

The following characteristics of activities designed for young children in self-contained classes or in a tutorial situation (one-to-one) are deterrents to the acquisition of the rules of English syntax in a natural, normal way and to development of the ability to speak in well-inflected sentences despite imprecise articulation.

1. A controlled vocabulary, formally taught
2. Unrealistic and prolonged language drills
3. Simple declarative sentences devoid of transformations
4. Emphasis on articulation rather than personal self-expression of ideas
5. Irregular hearing aid usage
6. Minimal linguistic information processed routinely through the child's own auditory and vocal mechanism, with adult prompting
7. Lack of a parent teaching program to facilitate parent competence and confidence in modelling and expanding the child's kernel sentences
8. Lack of comprehensive medical/diagnostic/audiological reports on which to base decisions leading to individualized educational programming.

Participatory Management by Parents

The overwhelming majority of parents have had no previous experience with deafness prior to the birth of a hearing impaired child. The need for a continuing program of guidance and support which is casual, shared, and related to individual child characteristics, is central to the prognosis of effective hearing aid usage by a young child and motivation to learn. The parent program relating to a variety of facets of early child development should include attention to 1—developmental characteristics of young children; 2—behavior management; 3—activities to stimulate language and cognitive development; 4—ways to incorporate the sense of hearing into every facet of the child's waking hours; 5—competence in modelling and expanding the child's earliest attempts at verbal self-expression; 6—practice of the principle of alternation . . . . waiting for the child's verbal attempt, provision of a verbal response or action to indicate comprehension, and encouragement of further attempts at verbal communication by the child in response.

When a nursery school teacher observes that a particular child is "afraid to mess around," parents need encouragement to relax their self-appointed role as pseudo teacher in favor of initiating participatory parent/child activities that encourage listening/learning/cognitive/linguistic development.

One nonthreatening way for parents to slip into the role of active change agents for improved child behavior, which encourages a youngster to hazard a guess, is to invite a mother and father to observe in a mainstream nursery or other preschool group educational setting. The realistic impressions gathered from such periodic and prolonged visitation (an entire morning) can form a basis for shared observations between special education teachers and parents as to the prognosis for continued benefit to a child whose group educational experience is with normal hearing classmates. In turn, the parents can become advocates for change and expansion of present educational services for the hearing impaired in their local school district or region.

Staff Training: Early Childhood Education Specialists

Gorelick (1974) found that teachers knowledgeable about one particular disability were afraid to transfer their new knowledge in the daily handling of a handicapped child with another disability, and recommended that teachers be permitted to express their fears *before* placement of a handicapped child in a regular preschool program.

In the Minneapolis Public Schools (Northcott, 1973) site visitation to a nursery school which has accepted a hearing impaired child, is a routine activity in the professional work week of a teacher of the deaf in the family oriented infant/preschool program for the hearing impaired who also serves as a parent advisor to a selected number of families enrolled, generally a month to six weeks apart. Demonstration teaching and consultative services are an integral component of the support program in the design of an individualized and comprehensive plan for each child, in addition to fall and spring workshops for the staff of all the nursery school/day care centers involved in mainstreaming.

In contrast, Castle (1974) described the dichotomy which exists between special and general educators, in the Home Demonstration Program and the community nursery school, in service and shared observation relating to the hearing impaired child. The question of liaison between special and general educators engaged in direct service to the child and his parents is one which must be resolved if assimilation is to be a realistic goal.

Competencies Not Certification

Certification labels . . . teacher of the deaf, speech pathologist, audiologist . . . are mighty feeble reeds to learn on when considering competencies rather than formal coursework undergirding preparation to provide direct services to preprimary hearing impaired (deaf and hard of hearing) children in a mainstreamed educational setting.

The key descriptors of infant programs for the hearing impaired as delineated in professional journals today are 1—parent education; 2—an auditory and oral method of initial intervention; 3—an experiential inductive approach to learning; 4—early auditory training to encourage listening skill development; 5—group educational experience with hearing children whenever possible.

The mandate for the future is trans-disciplinary support to children and their parents and trans-departmental preparation of specialists in early and special education for the child with speech, hearing and language disorders. A continuing education program must include participatory learning experiences with hearing impaired children at the preservice level, in the mainstream nursery/day care program, as well as acquired skills and knowledge in the core areas of linguistics, learning theory, and cognition. Demonstrated competency will require a combined emphasis on the ways in which young children learn through play (Weikart, 1971) as well as the techniques of implementing a sequential program of listening experiences for the young child to insure his development of auditory attention, discrimination and memory of speech patterns for applied daily usage in communication with others.

Orientation to an Auditory/Oral Philosophy

The question: "What message is conveyed to a nursery school teacher?" is a critical one. The answer lies in the design of an inservice training program initiated by the specialist(s) on deafness responsible for the hearing impaired child's total program, of which nursery school is only one component. Gorelick (1974) reported, "The children in our program quickly imitated the teacher and would turn the hard of hearing child's face toward them when they wanted to speak to him." One can guess that such children are being programmed to speechread rather than to gain their information primarily by listening, with or without the supplement of visual cues as recommended in this chapter (Pollack, 1970).

In another instance, Gorelick (1974) stated, "One mother reported that her four year old son, hearing that their old sick dog couldn't bark any more, suggested that he could teach the dog some sign language. A volunteer who had been tutoring the deaf child had taught the other children in the class some signing." The purpose of placement in a group of nonhandicapped peers must be clearly stated at the time of agreed upon enrollment of the hearing impaired child.

SUMMARY

In conclusion, even though all systems are "go" for a young child, in terms of 1—early identification, 2—early fitting of hearing aids, 3—early family-oriented intervention, 4—mainstream nursery school experience, 5—supportive parents, 6—a multidisciplinary team to serve the child, and family, 7—intensive individual teaching as a supplement to group education, two basic populations can be identified by the time a child reaches the general age of 4 (Level II: a school-based, child-centered program in contrast to Level I: home-centered, parent-oriented):

1. Those children who are realistic candidates for continued mainstreaming in nursery school prior to entrance in a regular kindergarten or first-grade class in their neighborhood school, on a partial or full time basis.
2. Those children requiring a highly specialized, intensive service program of self-containment, taught by a teacher of the deaf.

In many public schools around the United States today, a kindergarten readiness class for the hearing impaired, as an adjunct to the mainstream nursery school/day care morning program, utilizes the regular preprimary curriculum of the local school district for added insurance of potential assimilation during the kindergarten/first grade years.

If there has been a genuine partnership of parents and school team members during the infant/preschool years, the process of working for clarity and then agreement on the appropriate placement among the concerned adults in the child's immediate home and school environment is much easier for all involved.

It should be noted that there are several natural periods during a hearing impaired child's school years when consideration of placement in a regular classroom on a part time (resource room) or full time basis, can be considered. They are 1—kindergarten/first grade; 2—third/fourth grade (when the ability of a child to read inferentially for meaning; use the dictionary; apply knowledge of phonics in word attack skills; present entry level skills within the normal range of behaviors in the classroom in speech, language, academic, personal and social areas augurs well for assimilation); 3—junior high school years.

Those children who are placed in regular kindergarten/first grade classes are generally those who are functionally hard of hearing (regardless of degree of hearing loss as measured by an audiogram). Their ability to gain information through questioning, their ability to respond to open-ended questions like, "What happened next? What does that remind you of? What's funny?" reveals demonstrated application of knowledge of the rules of English language which have been "caught", not formally taught. They are capable of independent judgment, accept criticism and expect to be involved in the action of the moment within any group situation.

An analysis of the 52 children (with the primary disability of deafness) enrolled in the Whittier Infant/Preschool Program, a family oriented regional program for hearing impaired children, 0-4, in the Minneapolis Public Schools* reveals the wide variety of educational settings in which these children were functioning in the fall of 1974. By shared judgment of the

Table 8-2.
Infant Preschool Program: Hearing Impaired Children.
0-4, Minneapolis Public Schools, Educational Placements, Fall 1974

	Children First Enrolled in 1968-1969 ($N = 65$)		All Children Enrolled 1968-1974 ($N = 167$)	
	N	%	N	%
Total enrolled	65	—	167	—
Number multiply handicapped*	11	—	25	—
Number misdiagnosed (i.e., not hearing impaired)	2	—	4	—
Number for whom deafness is primary disability	52	100	138	100
Whittier Infant-Preschool	0	0	19	14
Integrated program	23	44	40	29
Full day integration in home school	(19)	(37)	(35)	(25)
Full day integration of Lyndale or Hamilton	(4)	(8)	(5)	(4)
Partial integration	3	6	13	9
Lyndale or Hamilton	(3)	(6)	(11)	(8)
Anoka	(0)	(0)	(2)	(1)
Self-contained program				
Aural-oral	6	12	28	20
Lyndale or Hamilton	(6)	(12)	(28)	(20)
Total communication	15	29	24	17
Lyndale or Hamilton	(11)	(21)	(13)	(9)
St. Paul	(2)	(4)	(5)	(4)
Wright County	(0)	(0)	(3)	(2)
Minnesota School for the Deaf	(2)	(4)	(3)	(2)
Moved or no information**	5	10	14	10
TOTAL	52	100	138	100

*Two are EMR children now functioning as regular members of EMR classes: one has been diagnosed as a learning disabled child and is partially integrated at Lyndale school.

**Three were known to be integrated before they moved.

parents and school personnel, the method of communication for instructional purposes was either a continuation of the auditory/oral method used in the infant/preschool years, or total communication (fingerspelling, signs, and speech used simultaneously). Thus, with the introduction of a form of sign language for certain children, this method (total communication) became the second language, linked with English syntax and continuing the rhythmic phrasic way of encouraging verbal self-expression.

During the preprimary years, it is imperative to remember that early intervention mandates availability of all possible educational alternatives to accommodate the wide range of presenting behaviors of hearing impaired children who are of formal school age. One, but only one, of these alternatives is integrated placement with hearing peers. It is not appropriate for all children.

At the same time a hearing impaired child's cognitive and linguistic and listening skills are being developed, it is hoped that certain parents are being brought to the threshold of their own understanding to reach the point where they can say with conviction based on appreciative knowledge of their own child's abilities, "Mainstreaming is great . . . but not for my child . . . not *yet,* at least."

BIBLIOGRAPHY

Basic education rights for the handicapped. 1973 Annual Report: The National Advisory Committee on Handicapped Children. Department of H.E.W. Washington, D.C. June 30, 1973

Bereiter C, Engelman S: Teaching Disadvantaged Children in the Preschool. Englewood Cliffs, New Jersey, Prentice-Hall, 1966

Castle D, Warchol B: Rochester's demonstration home program: A comprehensive parent-infant project. Peabody J. Education 51: 186-191, 1974

Cicourel AV, Boese RJ: Sign language acquisition and the teaching of deaf children, Part I. Amer Ann Deaf 117: 27-33, 1972

Comprehensive mental health training in a hearing program: Final Evaluation Report. Title III, Sect. 306. Lake County, Gurnee, Illinois. August, 1972

Dale DMC: Individual integration experiment. Progress Report, to the Chief Education Officer, Haringey, London, August, 1973

Davis J: Performance of young hearing impaired children on a test of basic concepts. J.S.H. Res. 17(3): 342-350, 1974

Gladwin HJ: Initial results from a preprimary program of binaural amplification. Evaluation Report, 1972-1973 UNISTAPS MOdel Demonstration Project, Hearing Impaired Children, 0-6, and their Parents. Minn. State Department of Education, St. Paul, 1973

Goetzinger CP: Effects of small perceptive losses on language and speech discrimination. Volta Rev 64: 408-414, 1962

Gorelick MC: What's in a label. California State University, Northridge. Study sup-

ported in part, Dept. HEW, SRS, Rehabilitation Services Administration, Grant #55-P-45144/9-03, 1974
Griffiths C: Conquering childhood deafness. New York, Exposition Press, 1967
Hanners BA: The role of audiological management in the development of language by severely hearing impaired children. Presented at the annual meeting of the Academy of Rehabilitation Audiology, Detroit, Michigan, October 12, 1973
Kennedy P, Bruininks RH: Social status of hearing impaired children in regular classrooms. Except Child 1974
Kirkman RE, Setliff RC: The children's house of learning: an experiment in early education for hearing impaired children. Peabody J Ed 51 (3): 203-210, 1974
Kodman F: Educational status of hard of hearing children in the classroom. J Speech Hear Dis 28: 408-414, 1963
Lee L: Developmental sentence types: a method for comparing normal and deviant syntactic development. J Speech Hear Dis 31: 311-330, 1966
Levine ES: The Psychology of Deafness. Columbia University Press, New York, 1960
Liff S: Early intervention and language development in hearing impaired children. Unpublished master's thesis. Vanderbilt University, 1973
Ling D, Ling AH: Communication development in the first three years of life. JSHR 17 (1): 146-159, 1974
Luterman, DMA: comparison of language skills of hearing impaired children in a visual/oral method and auditory/oral method. Emerson College, Boston, Mass. 1974

Martin EW: Public policy and early childhood education. Presented at the Education Commission of the States' National Symposium, "Implementing Child Development Programs." Boston, Mass., August 1, 1974
Mayer RS: A comparative analysis of preschool curriculum models, in Anderson RA, and Shane HG (eds): As the Twig is Bent. Boston, Houghton Mifflin, 1971
McCauley RW, Bruininks RH, Kennedy P: The observed behavior of hearing impaired children in regular classrooms. Presented at the Council for Exceptional Children. 52nd Annual International Convention, New York, April, 1974
McConnell F: The parent teaching home: an early intervention program for hearing impaired children. Peabody J Ed 51(3): 162-171, 1974
Northcott WH: Candidate for integration: A hearing impaired child in a regular nursery school. Young Children 25:367-380, 1970
Northcott WH: Competencies needed by teachers of hearing impaired children, 0-3, and their parents. Volta Rev 75(9): 432-544, 1973
Northcott WH: Curriculum guide: hearing impaired child, 0-3, and his parents. AG Bell Association for the Deaf, Washington, DC (revised edition, in press)
Northcott WH: Integration of deaf children in ordinary school programs. Except Child 38(1): 29-32, 1971
Northcott WH, Nelson JV Fowler SA : UNISTAPS: A family oriented infant/preschool program for hearing impaired children and their parents Peabody J Ed 51(3): 192-197, 1974
Northcott, WH: Implementing programs for young hearing impaired children. Except Child 40(3) 1973, 455-463
Northcott WH: Normalization of the preschool child with hearing impairment. in

ME Glasscock (ed): Otolaryngologic Clinics of North America, 8(2), February, 1975
Prescott E: Pacific Oaks College. Pasadena, California. The Day Care Environmental Inventory. Reported at Biennal Meeting of the Society for Research in Child Development, Philadelphia, Spring, 1974. Office of Child Development, U. S. Department, H.E.W.
Rankhorn B: Some effects of reverse integration on the language environment of hearing impaired children. Lexington School for the Deaf, New York, May, 1974
Rister A: Presented at American Speech and Hearing Convention, Las Vegas, November, 1974
State Guidelines: Preschool Educational Guidelines for Handicapped Children in Minnesota. State Department of Education, St. Paul, 1974.
Stokoe WC: CAL conference on sign language. The Linguistic Reporter 12: 6-7, 1970
van Uden AA: A world of language for deaf children, Part I. Basic Principles. Rotterdam University Press, 1970
Watson TJ: Integration of hearing impaired children in nursery schools in England, in W.H. Northcott (ed): The hearing impaired child in a regular classroom; preschool, elementary, secondary years. Alexander Graham Bell Ass'n. for the Deaf, Washington, D.C., 1973
Weikart DP, Rogers L, Adcock C, McClelland D: The cognitively oriented curriculum: a framework for teachers. Washington, D.C. National Association for the Education of Young Children, 1971
Williams, DML, Darbyshire JO, Campbell SM: Play patterns and abilities in hearing impaired children: integrated nursery. Queens University, Kingston, Canada, 1974
Wilson GB, Ross M, Calvert DR: An experimental study of the semantics of deafness. Volta Review 76(7): 408-414, 1974
Withrow FB: Education of deaf children in Russia. The Deaf American 26: 7-8, 1973
Young D, McConnell F: Retardation of vocabulary development in hard of hearing children. Except Child, 23: 368-370, 1957

*Laboratory program, the UNISTAPS Project, Minnesota State Dept of Education. Handicapped Children's Early Education Program. (P.L. 91-230, Title VI, Part C, Sect 623) Dr. Winifred Northcott, Project Director.

Donald I. McGee

9
Mainstreaming Problems and Procedures: Ages 6-12

The increasing interest in the mainstreaming of hearing impaired children is in part a natural outgrowth of the progress which has been made in the therapeutic and educational management of hearing impaired infants and preschoolers in the past two decades.

Mainstreaming of hearing impaired children is not new. Model programs have offered mainstream education for many years. The relative scarcity of mainstream programs has been due to a lack of adequate services for hearing impaired children below the age of 4 or 5 which resulted in inadequate preparation for participation in general education settings. As the consistent use of early amplification has increased, and as the number and quality of preschools has grown, so too has grown the number of hearing impaired children who are able to learn in a variety of educational settings, rather than only in self-contained classrooms.

Professionals have had the opportunity to follow the progress of greater numbers of young children who have had the benefit of very early training. This experience has led us to make some observations which will alter the future planning of programs for hearing impaired children.

1. Children who are provided with early amplification, early auditory and language training, and whose parents receive early counseling, have a higher incidence of successful mainstreaming into general education.
2. Deafness, as defined by pure frequency audiogram, is not prognostic of the development or nondevelopment of useful residual hearing in many children below the age of 4.
3. Most young children who have had very early amplification and auditory

training develop many more auditory skills, and at a much faster rate, than children who receive similar training between the ages of 6 and 12 but who have not had early training.
4. There is an increasing number of young children who are profoundly deaf by audiogram but who develop their residual hearing sufficiently to learn to decode spoken language with remarkable accuracy.

The success which early education has had in promoting a more natural learning of language is evidenced by the larger numbers of hearing impaired children who are ready for mainstream education by the age of 5 or 6. Meaningful interaction with hearing peers is built into the modern preschool, either through reverse mainstreaming or dual tracking. The children, as a result, become prepared earlier to increase their sphere of interaction with the general school population in various types of appropriate mainstreaming throughout their educational careers.

PURPOSE OF MAINSTREAMING

The purpose of mainstreaming is the promotion of natural contact and meaningful communication among hearing impaired and normally hearing children in *age appropriate peer groups.* A secondary purpose is to heighten the expectation levels of achievement for and by hearing impaired students

Mainstreaming implies a strong support program staffed by teachers of the hearing impaired, as well as the existence of a sound general education program. Mainstreaming of hearing impaired children is not a unitary educational approach per se, but subsumes a variety of alternative settings in which individual children can succeed on their various paths toward self-actualization and educational achievement.

Complete mainstreaming is not appropriate for every hearing impaired child. Mainstream experiences which frustrate a child because of inability to participate meaningfully should not be forced upon him or her in the false hope that some incidental benefits will accrue.

While the concept of mainstreaming is often associated with public school programs, it is successfully done in a variety of educational settings. Dr. Connor's description, in chapter 16 of this volume, of the mainstreaming and community involvement at the Lexington School eloquently attests to the viability of mainstreaming in a residential facility.

The remainder of this chapter will deal with mainstreaming as it occurs in public schools and will focus on elementary education. In theory, the public school offers the complement of resources needed to facilitate effective mainstreaming for hearing impaired children. In practice, these resources become fully available only as the result of formal commitments by the school system to develop the best possible program which its resources will allow.

Mainstreaming does not happen anywhere until a person or persons make a commitment to do it and then take the responsibility to enlist the aid of all those who can help to make it work well.

DEGREES OF MAINSTREAMING

The types of educational settings which exemplify mainstreaming are listed in order of the degree to which interaction with normally hearing students is present. One cannot generalize about which type is better than another since this determination must be made in terms of each child as an individual.

Type I: Complete mainstreaming of the student in his or her neighborhood school without supportive help from a specialist.

Type II: Full mainstreaming of the student in his neighborhood school with supportive instruction from a teacher of the hearing impaired or other kind of specialist.

Type III: Partial mainstreaming of the student who is based in a special resource room and attends some general education classes.

Type IV: Team teaching arrangements in which general education teachers and teachers of the hearing impaired cooperatively teach both hearing and hearing impaired students in a general education setting.

Type V: Reverse mainstreaming in which normally hearing students become part of a class of hearing impaired students. This type is most prevalent at the preschool level.

Type VI: Self-contained classes from which students go to general education classes for instruction in one or more academic subjects.

Type VII: Self-contained classes from which students go to general education classes to participate in one or more nonacademic activities.

Type VIII: Completely self-contained classes in which children have occasional contact with normally hearing peers.

The best type of mainstreaming is that which most closely matches the capabilities and needs of a particular student. For groups of students it is necessary to have a variety of alternative plans.

PROBLEMS OF MAINSTREAMING

The primary goal in effecting any type of mainstreaming is that the hearing impaired child feel comfortable in the setting, derive satisfaction and experience success, and that he or she profit from the learning and social activities. The student who passes all general education subjects with high grades but who feels isolated and has no friends in class is not successfully mainstreamed.

The teacher's most difficult problem in bringing the elementary age child into the mainstream is that of monitoring the extent to which the student is profiting from the general education class. In addition, there are other tasks which face the teacher of a self-contained class who wishes to mainstream a particular student for one or two general subjects.

1. Developing a willingness in the general education teacher to include a hearing impaired child in the class.
2. Determining exactly which parts of the general curriculum the student is prepared to pursue.
3. Conferencing with parents and administrators to explain the plan and enlist their aid.
4. Scheduling the times, for mainstreaming and readjusting the schedule of the self-contained classroom in order to work with the student when he or she is available.
5. Establishing some type of efficient feedback system so that the teacher can monitor the student's progress and adjustment.
6. Taking responsibility for educating the general teacher about the management of a hearing impaired student.
7. Solving the many little problems which typically arise.

These tasks become multiplied by the number of students the teacher wishes to mainstream.

More important than the management problems which mainstreaming can create for the teacher are the possible traumatic effects on the child who has not had the advantage of mainstreaming at the start of his or her educational career. Some type of transitional setting is needed which minimizes the negative effects of mainstreaming on the child. In Fairfax County, Virginia we have added a Type IV mainstream plan which appears to answer our need for better transitional experiences for hearing impaired children.

THE FAIRFAX COUNTY PROGRAM

Our program for hearing impaired students in Fairfax employs the first seven types of mainstream options. Approximately two-thirds of our hearing impaired student population, some 200 children, are enrolled in general education classes in their neighborhood schools and receive supportive help from traveling teachers of the hearing impaired. These students, who have moderate, severe and profound hearing losses, may receive up to 1 1/2 hours of instruction per day from the traveling teacher. A few students receive no special help, although their progress is monitored in case they encounter problems along the way.

The program which I am going to describe does not directly involve this group of mainstreamed students. Their characteristics will not be described here but I do wish to make the point that it is the hearing impaired students in this group, multiplied by thousands like them across the country, which do not appear in our professional literature and which are rarely included in our national statistics on deafness. These students do not become the subjects of research studies nor is demographic data on them usually collected. As a result, our clearer understanding of the total, national hearing impaired population is restricted.

The remaining third of our population is divided among our parent-infant program, preschool program, and elementary and intermediate program. In addition, we have a few hearing impaired children who are in other kinds of special education classes: emotionally disturbed, autistic, physically handicapped, moderately and mildly retarded, visually impaired, and language delayed.

We have various types of mainstreaming plans. Our newest plan is Type IV which we are using in the oral communication elementary program at Camelot School.

FROM SELF-CONTAINED TO SELF-ASSURED

Camelot is a medium-size school which was designed and built with instructional pods. A cluster of classrooms around a large open space constitutes a pod, with the addition of an acitivity room, storage closet and office space. The elementary classroom program for hearing impaired children began there a few years ago as a group of self-contained classes located in one pod. The cluster of classes allowed easy access to special materials and promoted sharing and communication among the teachers of the hearing impaired children. The disadvantage of the arrangement was that it effectively isolated hearing impaired children from the rest of the school except for limited mainstream activities.

As time passed, more and more individual children were partially mainstreamed in general education classes for selected subject areas. A type VI program was in effect. Many students, however, were in a Type VII situation, with contacts limited to special events in the general classroom or occasional art, music and physical education activities.

As the general school staff gradually became accustomed to the uniqueness of hearing impaired students, greater sharing and exchange of ideas began to occur between the special and general teachers. It became increasingly apparent to both groups that they had a lot to offer each other. At last a proposal was made that the degree of mainstreaming for hearing impaired students be significantly increased.

When school opened the following September, the organizational pattern was changed from what it had been. The special pod for hearing impaired childred was disbanded. Each special teacher became a member of a grade-level team of general teachers which created a first grade pod, a second grade pod, and so forth.

Within each pod the instructional program was semi-departmentalized and ability groups were identified across the whole range of students, both hearing and hearing impaired. At the same time an intensive assessment of the the hearing impaired children was made.

The results were summarized and a profile was made on each child. This detailed information encouraged and supported greater differentiation among the students according to achievement and decreased the importance placed on hearing loss.

The changes which began to occur as a result of the reorganization continue to intrigue us. One of the first observations made by the staff was that hearing impaired children began to interact with the general staff in ways they never had before. The children began to seek help from the nearest staff member when they had a question or encountered a problem, where in the past they had always gone back to their special teacher for help, even if she were at the opposite end of the building. Teachers also noticed that the children behaved differently than before and that they actually looked different. These were the first superficial changes that were observed but we considered that they were significant in terms of our goals.

The visitor at Camelot is able to observe a variety of changing groups of students. The hearing impaired student is identifiable only by his or her amplification unit. The teacher of the hearing impaired is no longer identifiable by the microphone around her neck since the general education teacher is just as likely to be wearing one too. One may see a language lesson being taught to an equal number of hearing and hearing impaired students; a normally hearing student working alone at a Project LIFE machine; a large-group activity in which hearing impaired children are scattered around the room, no longer needing the security of exclusive contact with other hearing impaired friends; a music teacher conducting an Orff activity with a combined group which is predominantly hearing impaired; a rehearsal for a P.T.A. program in the gymnasium where the acoustics are so bad that the most intelligible speaking part is by a profoundly hearing impaired boy who is being more careful of his articulation than his hearing counterparts.

We do not yet know if the reorganization will produce statistically significant changes in achievement levels of individuals over time. We believe that it will. We do know that the many positive changes we have seen are leading us to develop and expand the options which this type of mainstreaming offers to children. Some of the important advantages of Type IV mainstreaming which we see are these.

1. It permits full time mainstreaming for those students who are ready for it and it is equally suitable for gradually introducing mainstreaming to those students who can participate only minimally.
2. It prevents a child from feeling singled-out or odd because he or she is the only hearing impaired person in a sea of hearing strangers. This feeling is often engendered in Type VI mainstreaming.
3. It provides necessary transition experiences for those children who will someday attend their neighborhood school in general education classes.
4. It provides age appropriate hearing models for children whose school and social experiences have often been atypical and restricted.
5. It enriches and stimulates both students and staff.

HOW IT WORKS

The planning and scheduling required in Type IV mainstreaming necessitates that the teacher's out-of-class time be conserved and protected. The complexities of scheduling the daily instructional program at Camelot requires that teachers be given help beyond that which is usually available to the public school teacher of the hearing impaired.

Curriculum

A full-time diagnostic teacher is assigned to help teachers in the identification of special learning problems and to help them in planning remedial programs. The diagnostic teacher also acts as a curriculum coordinator and helps to interpret the curriculum to teachers. She implemented the plan for in-depth assessment of all the hearing impaired students and created feedback mechanisms which showed the teachers how each of their children stood on an extensive battery of tests and measurements. She also wrote on each child's profile the implications of his or her test performance in terms of possible next steps in the curriculum which the teacher might try. A factor which complicated this task was our ongoing effort to harmonize three separate curricula (a behavioral curriculum for hearing impaired children, a special language curriculum based on sentence patterns, and the Fairfax general education curriculum) into a unitary constellation of instructional objectives.

Without the support of the diagnostic/curriculum resource person, the teachers would not have had the time to organize and perform the many assessment and curriculum tasks which had to be accomplished.

Supervision

In most large public school systems, the concept of classroom supervision fell into disuse long ago. Even in systems which still use the title, the supervisor is typically involved with administration rather than supervision. Schools for the deaf have long depended on their supervisors for quality control in the classroom, but this tradition is now rare in public school.

We assigned a full time position to provide systematic help to teachers in the classroom. The teacher may request a variety of services from the supervisor including demonstration teaching, help in planning, and aid in solving individual problems of instruction. The supervisor also provides regular help in introducing new features into the classroom so that they spread evenly to all teachers throughout the program. She is also available to the general teacher and to the grade-level teams to assist in planning. We do not believe that it is possible to have an effective Type IV program without such a person.

Our school principal is also an important key to the success of the program. Her interest in reorganizing an entire school in order to increase mainstreaming attests to the unity of purpose which is observed in the entire staff. A principal's administrative burden is greatly increased by the presence of special education children in a building. Our program is fortunate that the Camelot principal not only provides an administrative structure within which the program can operate but that she also gives direct assistance to teachers in the classroom and monitors the progress of individual children.

Staff Development

We arrange workshops and staff training sessions on a variety of topics but we feel that the limited time which teachers have is not enough to include all the areas which need to be covered. We believe that the teacher interaction in the classroom with the supervisor and curriculum coordinator as well as with other resource persons, is the most important kind of staff development. Another essential element is our educational audiologist who also responds to teacher requests for aid, as well as routinely monitors the performance of amplification equipment. The audiologist is an experienced teacher of the hearing impaired and is a certified audiologist. This is an excellent combination of skills for our needs because it enables her to work with teachers in the problems of amplification; expand and enchance the auditory training curriculum and train teachers in its implementation; counsel with parents regarding hearing aids and auditory training; condition hard-to-test children in order to obtain more valid audiograms; perform educational evaluations of new applicants to the program; and assist teachers with the problems of individual children.

Our speech therapist too works in the classroom directly with children and teachers. In addition to providing needed therapy, she acts as a staff development agent who increases the skills of the teacher through demonstration and assistance.

PROBLEMS AND PROMISES

We believe our most important long range task is that of continuing to develop more educational and therapeutic alternatives for our population of hearing impaired children. We believe that some type of mainstreaming needs to be a part of each alternative.

The description here of a Type IV mainstream setting is of one kind of integration plan which resolves the problem of over- or underestimating a student's ability to derive benefit from participation in general education as a full-status member of the homogeneous school population. We are opposed to the imposition of mainstreaming on a hearing impaired child whose self-assurance will be undermined by having to cope with more input than he or she is ready to handle. We do believe that most such children can be gradually introduced to mainstream education, however.

We do not believe that the most successful product of our program is the student who is able to go on to complete mainstream education with or without special help. Our most successful student is the one who has made the most progress in terms of where he or she started from.

There are problems which work against the viability of a Type IV program.

1. Teachers and administrators must be completely convinced of the necessity for such a program and that it will significantly advance the best interests of the hearing impaired student.
2. A great deal of extra time in planning and management is required of all staff members.
3. Several teacher support systems are required to facilitate the work which the staff does with children.
4. The program costs as much as a traditional program and the factor of cost reduction cannot be used as a selling point to administrators.

We have confidence that as more students go through the program the objective evidence of increased success of students will lend support to it. In addition to the positive data which we anticipate, our experience has shown that people who see the program in action lose any concerns they may have had regarding the obstacles to be overcome.

The promises which this kind of programming holds out is a sufficiently large carrot to urge us on to an expanded realization of mainstream benefits for children.

1. Since self-actualization occurs primarily through interaction with others, an expanded milieu offers most hearing impaired children a much better chance for improving their perceptions of self than does a restricted environment in which there are few people available to interact with consistently.
2. Through expansion of the child's operational environment, the expectancy level for his or her communication and academic skills will increase. This will occur for the parent, the teacher, and most importantly for the child.
3. When carefully managed, the hearing impaired child's membership in an expanded school community will aid him or her in dealing with and resolving the fears which result from being a representative of a minority group, whether they be conscious or unconscious.
4. A significant benefit of mainstreaming to the teacher of the hearing impaired is that it promotes daily contact with normally hearing children, providing an opportunity to work with a greater variety of children.

MAKING IT HAPPEN

Success is relative. It is not a matter of waiting until you can get the whole pie; it is a process of getting a piece at a time according to a long range plan in which the primary goal is to assemble a whole pie.

Whatever success we have experienced so far in our program comes directly from the dedication of teachers who work very hard to produce positive changes in children. Their work is enabled by a strong commitment from a board of education, a superintendent, and a director of special education who truly believe in what the teachers are trying to achieve.

This shared commitment which we all feel did not spring up spontaneously like a wildflower in the woods. It is the result of dedicated and committed parents of hearing impaired children who, in our county, work as an organized team to effect needed changes, who do not waste their own time with internal conflicts of philosophy, who believe that good educational alternatives can be created for all hearing impaired children, and who see better than most people do, the true potential of their hearing impaired children for equal membership in society.

BIBLIOGRAPHY

Bitter GB, Mears EG. Facilitating the integration of hearing impaired children into regular public school classes. The Volta Review 75: 13-22, 1973

Connor LE: Integration. The Volta Review 74: 207-209, 1972

Leckie DJ: Creating a receptive climate in the mainstream program. The Volta Review 75: 23-27, 1973

McGee DI: The benefits of educating deaf children with hearing children. TEACHING Exceptional Children 2: 133-137, 1970

Nober LW: An in-service program for integrating hearing impaired children. The Volta Review 77: 173-175, 1975

Northcott, WH (ed.): The hearing impaired child in a regular classroom: Preschool, elementary, and secondary years. Washington, D.C.: The Alexander Graham Bell Association for the Deaf, 1973

Northcott WH: Tutoring a hearing impaired student in the elementary grades. The Volta Review 74: 432-435, 1972

Scheeline A: Integrating deaf children into public schools. The Volta Review 73: 370-373, 1971

Charles H. Cosper, Jr.

10

The Mainstreaming of the Junior High and Senior High Student

The great majority of facts and references in this chapter relate to Mr. Andrew Gantenbein's program in Berrien Springs, Michigan. Other situations will refer to the Jane Brooks School for the Deaf in Chickasha, Oklahoma, where I served as a Teacher-Counselor and the Athletic Director for eight years prior to 1967.

In these capacities, I served students from grades 4 through 12 academically, consulting with regular classroom teachers and parents. Examples I mention are taken from among my own students and others I personally observed elsewhere, as Educational Consultant for the Alexander Graham Bell Association for the Deaf, and from my own experience as a profoundly hearing impaired person.

Through the years, I have had students who fell into *three school functioning types* with certain characteristics:

(I.) Those who showed the prerequisite academic functioning skills as observed by qualified teachers of the hearing impaired and by the administration from the starting age of 11 months and/or at age one to the time of kindergarten selection at ages 5 to 7. The academic functioning skills are

1. The ability to follow directions given by teachers,
2. The ability to carry out assigned homework,
3. The ability to participate in class assignments, as a group or alone.
4. The ability to ask for help when one does not understand,
5. The ability to make one's self understood.

These students are required to take the A.B.C. Inventory Test, and the

Metropolitan Readiness Test. A doubtful or borderline student may be placed on trial for an observation period of 2 to 9 weeks by the teacher-counselor of the hearing impaired and the regular classroom teacher.

This group which numbers 50 percent of the hearing impaired population usually moves through the grades with varying degrees of tutoring by the teacher-counselor, from daily supportive reinforcement to the supportive help as the academic needs call for it. But all students are seen daily as part of the ongoing counseling, speech, and auditory training. This group usually moves through the junior high and high school with the basic routine adjustments all school children have to go through. An individual student may be lowered or advanced within the grades in groupings such as: low track, regular track, advanced track. He or she may be even lowered or raised a grade level if recommended by the hearing faculty, hearing counselor, and principal and the teacher-counselor of the hearing impaired, his supervisor, and members of the supportive services.

(II.) This second group of students did not meet the requirements for the transition into the kindergarten or first grade because of failure to meet the necessary criteria for success. These students are placed in the self-contained classes, K, 1st, and 2nd grade for preparation for the eventual transition to the regular third grade. From 3rd to 5th grade level, the class goes to the regular math and science class with their teacher who team-teaches with the regular teacher. These students take the Michigan Assessment Test and the Iowa Test of Basic Skills. At the end of the 5th grade or 6th grade as the individual's case may be. This group usually receives more tutoring time in the Junior and Senior High.

(III.) Of this third group, 10 percent have, by the end of the 5th or 6th grade demonstrated the inability to function in the full-time regular classroom setting. These students are placed in the resource rooms in the junior and senior High and in regular classes for one or more academic subjects in addition to home economics, shop, gym, art, and band. Their program is a four to six year program modeled after the educable-retarded program to prepare them for the world of work.

The evaluation of readiness of students for junior or senior high is based on past educational progress in handling the academic loads, emotional and social situations such as

1. Academic grades, written and verbal reports from the regular classroom teachers, regular counselor and principal, and staff members of the program for the hearing impaired.
2. The graphs of the results of achievement testing-Stanford Achievement Test, Metropolitan Reading Test, etc.
3. Another recommended technique for evaluation is a 6-week period of summer school with the same textbooks and material covered as they would receive in the fall. This helps the teachers decide whether the

pupils could handle the fall placement. It also has another very important advantage: In the fall, the students would be repeating the material covered during the summer placing them more at ease in their new setting and giving them more time to adjust to the class situation and to develop speechreading awareness.

Chronological Age Comparisons

1. Those who are mainstreamed at an early age can be of the same chronological age or one year behind the hearing children.
2. Those who are mainstreamed in the second stage may be the same age or one to two years behind the hearing children.
3. Those who came into a mainstream program from elsewhere or at a late age and continue to make good academic progress may graduate from high school anywhere from age 17 to 21. Example:
   A Korean girl came into the Berrien Springs program at age 12 and was placed in the 4th grade. She made good grades and was on the honor roll through high school, achieving the National Honor Society.

How "old" this child was upon graduating has no significance as long as there was educational progress and the teachers, parents, and the student looked at the positive side of the accomplishments. People of all ages are commended for graduating from college, and so it should be in high school.

As to *the degree of hearing loss,* and contrary to popular belief that the majority of mainstreamed hearing impaired children are only hard of hearing, the majority have severe to profound losses.

The age of onset of impairment of the majority places it at birth. The number of prelingually hearing impaired children has been increasing for some time and early identification affords the best opportunity for early intervention and maximal habilitation.

Emotional adjustment can be just as natural for a hearing impaired child as it is for the child who can hear. Most of the hearing impaired students at the Jane Brooks School and at Berrien Springs have healthy self concepts. They have academic ability, sports prowess, and rapport with other people in the community just like any hearing child. The majority of the parents were handling their children's problems in a normal parent fashion—taking time to "hear" their children and explaining situations whether they stemmed from normal teenage development or had to be related in the light of the hearing impairment.

Usually, some of the problems that affected the academic or social adjustment of the hearing impaired child would be emotional problems coming from the home environment such as: alcoholism, over protection, the lack of a father figure, an absentee parent, or a step-parent, to name a few.

One particular boy, in Michigan, had a good family relationship, but neither parent could read or write above a third grade level. In spite of this drawback, the boy made good academic progress.

In both of the programs, the hearing impaired students did not exhibit deep or long term nonacceptance of their dysfunction. With the exception of a few, they are learning to live with it. Occasionally, some youngsters would have "the hearing loss blues." These came about when one might have not done well in band or didn't get to participate in it; by losing a try-out for cheerleader or pompon girl; losing a try-out for sports, wanting a particular date, or obtaining a certain job.

The power of good oral programs lies in their content and qualified personnel and their ability to teach communicative and social skills in such a manner that the results fall somewhat into the following divisions, from my own observations of students:

Expressive Communicative Skills

Speech: 10% are hard to understand
         60% have understandable speech
         30% are easy to understand
Writing: 15% have limited expressive skill through written form
         70% have near average writing skills
         15% have above average writing skills

Receptive Communication Skills

20% have excellent auditory and speechreading skills
60% have satisfactory or very good auditory and speechreading skills
20% have difficulty in understanding and need repetition or rephrasing of the question or statement on a frequent basis.

Normalization of Communication Skills

Eighty percent are using receptive and expressive skills to the satisfaction of the regular school faculty, parents, and people in the community. Comments like the following are frequent: "I forget that this child has a hearing impairment.", "I seldom have to repeat or rephrase.", "When they come into my shop, I have no trouble understanding what they want or chatting with them."

Twenty percent of the comments frequently heard are: "I have to pay close attention.", "I usually have to ask them to slow down or to repeat.", "Sometimes it is necessary to ask them to write it down".

Modification and Reinforcement of Communication Media

Classroom teachers comment that they write more on the board and use the overhead projector whenever possible. When showing films or filmstrips, they let the student read the description and/or study guide which usually accompanies the material. They prepare an extra copy of the lecture whether it be a carbon copy or a thermofax for the hearing impaired student. They suggest supplemental reading material which they feel will help the student understand the topic to be discussed. As a result of using more visual aids for the hearing impaired students they have noticed an improvement in the other students in class interest and grades. Teacher-counselors furnish the carbon paper notetaker books and a hearing student is selected as a notetaker in courses which are taught predominantly through lectures.

Educational Placements

At the time of entrance into junior high, all hearing impaired students are basically placed in the regular track. At the end of each six week period, the students are evaluated by the regular class teachers, but with a final say by the teacher-counselor of the hearing impaired. The student may be moved, depending upon the evaluation, up into the advanced level or down into the lower track.

Only with borderline students is it advisable to begin them in the lower track and if they experience strong success measured in B's and A's with a C or two to move them up into the regular track.

In the high school, my placement areas for hearing impaired students in order of preference are: college prep; business; industrial arts; general courses; career co-op; work study program.

We also use the option of "two tracking" for a student in any two of the tracks which are available except for the career co-op, which is average or above in skill requirements. There are low, regular, and advanced sections of the others.

After high school, four years of college are available for those who are capable and want higher education. We strongly recommend the two more years of extended training available at a two year community college, vocational-technical school, business college, trade school, or vocational rehabilitation center. Some graduates choose to directly enter the world of work on their own, with parents' or friends' help, or with help from the school and/or vocational rehabilitation.

There is vocational placement available before leaving school through a co-op program, work study program, as a member of the occupationally bound program, and through preplanning with vocational rehabilitation personnel.

Educational Adjustment

From the 6th grade up, students must adjust from having only 1 or 2 teachers (if they team-teach) to the departmentalized system of a teacher (or two) for each subject area. This brings a number of factors into consideration for the student. The ease with which each teacher is heard and speechread is different. Each teacher has his personal style of presenting subject matter and topics of discussion that hearing pupils take in stride but that may present difficulties for the hearing impaired teenager, e.g.:

The teacher
- . . . strictly lectures; closely follows the textbook; uses the blackboard; uses the overhead projector and other audiovisual materials; uses tape recorders frequently; records; and videotapes.
- . . . expects a lot of written reports; oral reports; favors the use of group discussions or panel type situation.
- . . . has groupwork in sections of 3 to 6 with a group chairman, with the delegation of a part of a report to be researched by each member, then, the group puts the whole together and reports to the class.

Each teacher has different methods of checking pupil knowledge of the subject matter, of quizzing, and giving exams. Some of these relate directly to the material covered and some are set up to see if the student can apply the material to hypothetical situations.

For hearing impaired teenagers, as well as children of other age groups, enrollment in a regular classroom is like stepping into a foreign land with different customs and mores. A disciplinarian may demand that students have materials to work with on hand and neatly kept, expecting silence, expecting students to participate in class by asking questions. A more liberal teacher may expect students to work as a group or independently, moving around the room to different sections, or allowed to check out to the library.

The hearing classmates present a wide range of social strata, cultural viewpoints, attitudes and behavioral patterns. Groupings within the junior and senior high involve a cross section of troublemakers, bullies, withdrawn individuals, the stable, the considerate, snobs, know-it-alls, and "upper crust" as well as the loners, those with emotional problems, and juvenile delinquents who are borderline cases.

Problems Faced by Administrators

In order to better serve all students, including the mainstreamed hearing impaired youngster, the ideal class load for the regular classroom would be about 20 pupils. The number of handicapped students within the total regular class load can also present problems. Besides the educable mentally retarded, the hearing impaired, the culturally disadvantaged, there are the "problem" students; the hyperactive, the emotionally unstable, the "discipline problem", the epileptic, orthopedically handicapped, and the low achiever.

School policies should state:

> every child has the right to a regular classroom and clearly spell out to the regular classroom teacher that she is bound by school policy and master contract to serve all children;

> students will be placed in a room by random selection and that any unequalized load of handicapped children will be redistributed;

> teachers do not have the right to refuse to serve a child;

> ignoring a child or failure to serve him can and will result in a nonrenewal of the teacher's contract.

The traditional concept of a classroom with only blackboards is inadequate when hearing impaired children are mainstreamed. The classroom needs to be "sound conditioned" through the use of carpeting, drapes, acoustical tile, noise-free lighting which is nonglare, and located away from the furnace room, band room, and other high noise level areas. The sound conditioning of a room also aids the hearing children by reducing the noise level, lessening eyestrain, and reducing the fatigue caused by trying to concentrate on work amid distractions.

While certain teaching aids might be taken for granted in a hearing classroom, others are an indispensable "must" when hearing impaired children are present. *Needed are:* overhead and opaque projectors, programmed learning hardware and software like the LIFE materials for teaching language, an amplification system either an FM system or an individual hearing aid (If the individual hearing aids are used, the school needs to have a supply of hearing aid batteries, cords, and receiver buttons.), and the use of captioned films.

Tasks and/or Problems Faced by the Teacher-Counselor

1. They are responsible for the final decision on grade and level placement.
2. They need a well-equipped resource room which has a low noise level and is relatively free of distractions.

3. The teacher-counselor is responsible for scheduling the students with the regular class teachers, speech pathologist, and any support personnel
4. They see to the seating arrangement, notetaking services, etc. and handle difficulties as they arise.
5. The teacher-counselor encourages the hearing impaired student to participate in school activities such as plays, school clubs, band, cheerleading, school newspaper, and sports.

In football, several of the hearing impaired boys wear their hearing aids under their helmets. The body aid is fastened to the webbing inside the dome in the helmet and a soft earmold is used.

In the case of behind-the-ear hearing aids, pieces of styrofoam are cut to recess it. A foam rubber pad is also cut to the shape of the styrofoam and glued on the side which touches the face. The whole thing is fixed into the helmet's earpiece. Larry Brown of the Washington Redskins has a custom-made helmet to accommodate his hearing aid. A profoundly deaf boy from the UpJohn oral program in Kalamazoo, Michigan is on the varsity team at the University of Wisconsin. Another, from the Berrien Springs program, is a freshman at Western Michigan University and on the team.

As to social activities, the stumbling blocks of dating for a hearing impaired teenager can be dealt with by the teacher-counselor as in the following examples.

I have had girls come to me and complain that they were wallflowers because they were staying at home on weekends while the hearing girls were out having fun. In some instances, I knew of some hearing girls who did not have a date either that weekend. I lead our conversations to the reasons why those hearing girls might not have had a date for that evening. We go into a discussion of ways to get out and sometimes it leads to the hearing impaired girl asking a hearing boy to go out with her the next weekend to a social function in order to mingle with people. It may take two or three weekends for the boys to take notice and before some of them ask the girls for a date.

Boys who have their own car or borrow their dad's car for dates should have a switch rigged up by a mechanic so that the door courtesy lights can be turned on to provide a soft glow on the girl's face for speechreading. The road map light in some cars does the trick, or in some cases, just leaving the glove compartment open is enough if it has a light. THE DOME LIGHT IS TOO BRIGHT FOR DATING!

Problems Faced by the Regular Classroom Teacher

Generally, the problems faced by the regular classroom teacher are: class load, lack of appropriate teaching aids, discipline, lack of knowledge about hearing impairment, and communication problems.

Problems Hearing Students Face When Associating with the Hearing Impaired Students

At first, the hearing students may not be sure that the deaf students understand them or reciprocally the hearing impaired student may not be sure that he is understood.

At Berrien Springs, the high school counselor came to me one day with the information that one of our hearing impaired girls went to him complaining that her hearing classmates did not seem to understand her in the hall. He was puzzled as this girl had very understandable speech. Suddenly, he came up with the idea of going out in the hall to talk with her. The background noise was so loud she couldn't be heard so he told her repeatedly to raise her voice until she reached the level at which he could hear her plainly. She thought she sounded too loud. He needed to reaffirm to her that she needed to raise her voice in the hall to be heard. Then, he went around to several of her hearing friends and explained the situation and asked them to tell her when she needed to speak louder. After awhile, she became accustomed to raising her voice in noisy situations.

One girl had a bombastic voice that drew undesirable attention. She got along terrifically with people who knew her—both hearing and hearing impaired. But strange students' first reactions were "She's funny." or "What's wrong with her?". The only people it hurt though were her friends. She didn't hear most of the teasing. Her hearing friends, though, called the others down.

Hearing students may forget to keep their impaired classmates informed of events past, present, or future or a change of schedule announced over the P.A. systems. They are not certain the hearing impaired students want to be included in a particular activity.

Hearing impaired girls have to be a little more forward in some social situations with hearing boys such as the girl who likes to dance. She may think the boy is interested in dancing and will ask her, but unless she tells him that she can dance, he may assume because she is deaf, she may not care about dancing.

At times, in their eagerness to understand what is happening, hearing impaired students may ask too many questions while their hearing friend is trying to listen to a third party. Often, the hearing impaired student will walk in on a conversation and begin talking quite unaware that he is interrupting.

Teachers of the hearing impaired can help ease the mainstreaming of their students by volunteering to be club sponsors or assistant coaches as did a teacher in Berrien Springs. Another one, in the LaCrosse, Wisconsin program became the advisor for the Central High Student Council. Thus, hearing student leaders had a chance to ask her about some of the things they observed the hearing impaired students doing. It also greatly facilitated the social assimilation of the hearing impaired students when one of the most popular student council leaders began dating one of the hearing impaired girls he had met in the resource room of the student council advisor.

Communicative Improvement

The hearing impaired student will sharpen his awareness and improve his communicative skills by—

Aural Rehabilitation: Continued work on rhythm, stress, pitch, and the recognition of word patterns.

Speech Development: Working on smooth-flowing speech, articulation errors and correct sentence word usage.

Written English: Working on correct writing style and form, and by developing creative writing skills.

Reading Skill: The development of reading skills: words, phrases, and sentences will transfer to expressive usage in speech and writing.

After all, let's face it, our society is a hearing world. It is in this framework that the deaf must seek ways to surmount those obstacles presented by their disability and learn how to communicate with hearing people. The worst enemies of any hearing impaired person are those whom I call the "thoughtless", the "defeatists" who say, "You can't do it, your speech will not be understood and they won't accept you for yourself."

Through repetitious negativism a child may be brought to the point where he is psychologically defeated and really believes he can't speak or achieve his desired goals. Thus, the child is given a SECOND HANDICAP which he doesn't need, an inferiority complex. The thoughtless, defeatists are indeed the hearing impaired child's worst enemies.

Gloria M. Matter

11

In the Current—With Only One Oar

Sooner or later the child with a hearing impairment will find himself in the mainstream of life. How successful he will be there will depend upon the experiences and skills his teachers and parents will have helped him obtain. Recognizing the inherent value of learning in a mainstream setting for a life in the mainstream, we have attempted to make the Shorewood program for students with impaired hearing a segment of the total general education program established for all students.

The students in the program which uses the auditory/oral approach sustain moderate to profound hearing losses. The graph shows the losses of those students who have completed high school during the last 14 years (Fig. 11-1).

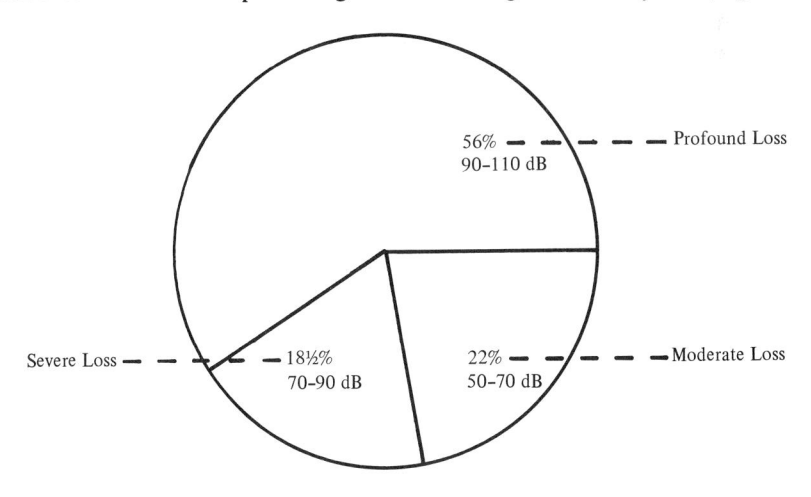

Fig. 11-1. Hearing loss of the 27 students who completed the high school program (500-2000 Hz, unaided).

Such mainstreaming provides the deaf child with a more normal social and learning environment, for it is from his hearing peers that the deaf child experiences the "do's" and "don't's" which educate him socially. Much information of interest today is gained from associations with hearing classmates. Where do most adolescents today learn about and talk about professional football league standings, new automobile designs, or current fashions? Some of this may be acquired from perceptive teachers and parents, but for the most part this is the kind of information that all teenagers learn from each other.

Learning with hearing peers, then, can release the hearing impaired child from the lack of experiences and low expectations a more sheltered child would have. There is a tendency for teachers of the deaf to slow the pace of academic learning or to lower expectations. There is little opportunity for this when a deaf student is mainstreamed in a regular classroom. Then the regular classroom teacher sets the pace and the teacher of the deaf only provides the supportive services.

The student with impaired hearing who attends a regular high school has the opportunity to pursue a greater variety of courses to meet his own needs and interests. Few high schools for deaf students offer courses in chemistry, physics, advanced math, foreign languages, urbanology, black history, or economics. These courses are available in most public high schools.

In Shorewood, the process of preparing deaf students for these expanded opportunities begins at the four year old kindergarten level; the amount of time spent with hearing peers varies, being dependent upon the individual child's readiness to succeed in a particular area. Such individualization means a hearing impaired child could enter the intermediate school with the same experiences as those with normal hearing or with experiences limited to only occasional experiences in a regular classroom.

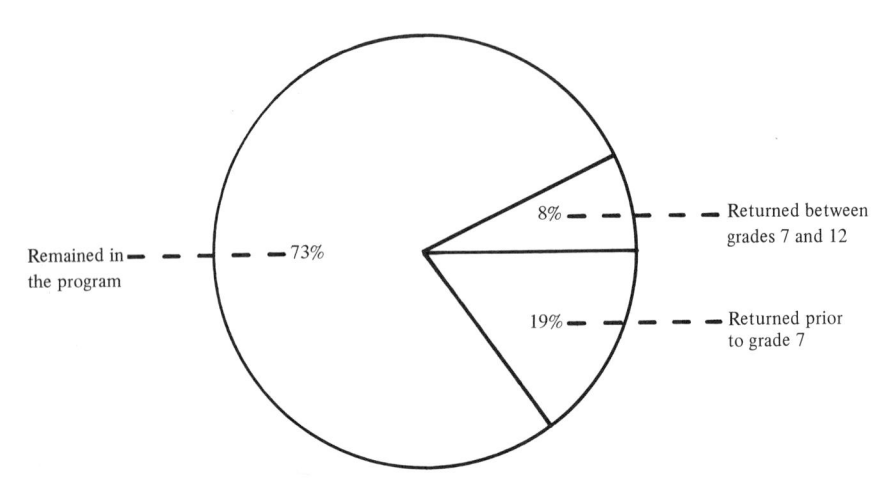

Fig. 11-2. Students returned to their own school district 1960-1974.

Since Shorewood services children from other school districts, who are bussed to Shorewood daily, one goal is to return them to their own districts as soon as possible. During the past ten years, 19 percent of the children in our program have transferred to public schools within their own school districts prior to the 7th grade; another 8 percent returned to their home school between the 7th and 12th grades (Fig. 11-2).

Between 1960 and 1974, we have had 27 hearing impaired students in our high school. Two have returned to the school in their home district to continue without supportive help; five have transferred to other public schools for various reasons; four have received certificates of achievement which are given to students who have not met the requirements for a diploma; and sixteen of the twenty-seven have been awarded regular high school diplomas (Fig. 11-3).

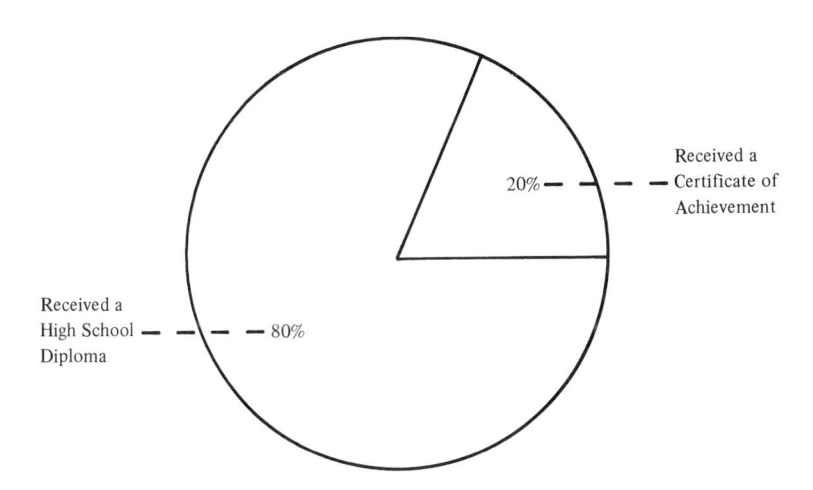

Fig. 11-3 Percentage of students awarded diplomas and certificates of achievement.

Of these sixteen graduates, five went from high school into a vocational training program and then into the labor market and are now either employees or full time homemakers. One entered the National Technical Institute for the Deaf but ten of these sixteen have gone on to attend institutions of higher learning (Fig. 11-4). About 70 percent of Shorewood High School graduates enter college after graduation; 60 percent of the students in our program for hearing impaired students have done so. Four of these ten have already obtained degrees, one from Gallaudet College after transferring there from five semesters' work at the University of Wisconsin—Milwaukee, one from the Rochester Institute of Technology after transferring there from three semesters at the University of Wisconsin—Milwaukee, one from Lake Forest College in Illinois and one from the University of Wisconsin—Milwaukee.

Three of these are now in graduate school, two working towards a master's degree and one is a doctoral candidate; the fourth is employed.

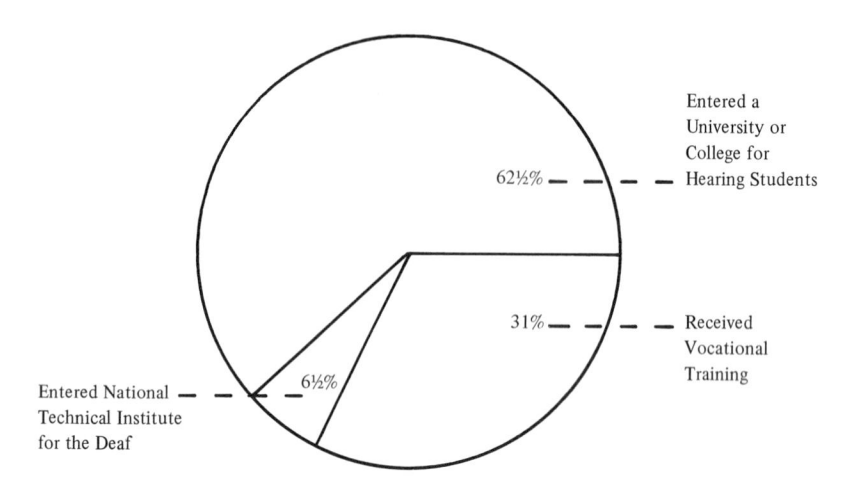

Fig. 11-4. Post-secondary placement of students who received a high school diploma (total number of students—16).

The remaining six are still pursuing their undergraduate work, two in the field of geology at the University of Wisconsin—Milwaukee, one at Concordia College in Milwaukee, one at Waukesha County Technical Institute, one at the University of Wisconsin—Oshkosh, and one at the Milwaukee School of Engineering (Fig. 11-5).

THE ACADEMIC FACILITIES OF SHOREWOOD

The secondary schools into which these hearing impaired students have been mainstreamed in Shorewood consist of the intermediate school, which serves 7th and 8th graders and a high school of approximately 800 students. The curriculum of the intermediate school has been designed around the concept that the needs of an individual child can best be met through the team teaching approach. This flexibility of curriculum makes it possible to mainstream a student for a day, a week, a month, or a semester.

Some students are unable to be mainstreamed into academic subjects such as language arts, math or social studies, often because of special learning problems. These students study these academic subjects at multiple levels with the teacher of the hearing impaired and are mainstreamed only in art, crafts, home economics and physical education. But because of the team approach concept, the teacher of the hearing impaired keeps in regular contact with the

B.S. Degree
U.W.-Milwaukee
Now in Graduate School U.W. - M.

B.S. Degree
Gallaudet College
Now in Graduate
School — — —

Doctoral — —
Candidate
New York
University

— — — — Associate Degree
Rochester Institute
of Technology
Now employed

— — — Now attending a
college or
university for
hearing students

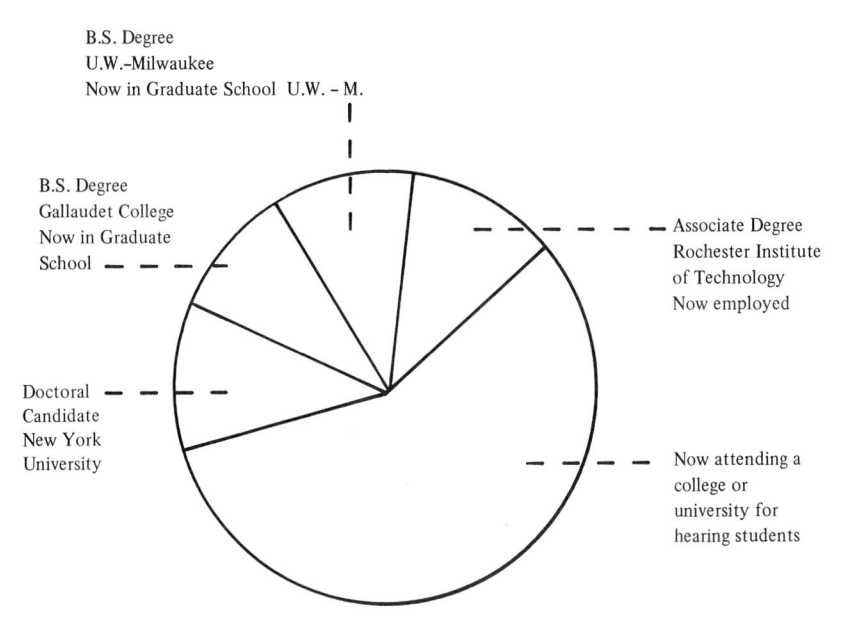

Fig. 11-5. Follow-up on students who entered a college or university for hearing students (total number of students—10).

classroom teachers and is aware of the units being taught or planned for the future. Such contact can provide opportunities for initiation of some students into regular programs, supplementary instruction for those already mainstreamed, and preteaching of some units.

Several years ago Peter entered our program. He had sustained a severe hearing loss and had received his elementary education in special classes for children with learning disabilities. He had no experiences in a regular academic class. However, the teacher of the deaf at the Intermediate School felt Peter might benefit from being part of the regular 7th grade math class. Knowing the math curriculum and understanding Peter's need to succeed, she worked with him on an individual basis on a unit in fractions. Later when the regular 7th grade class was to begin the fractions unit, she placed him in the regular class for a two-week trial.

He successfully completed that unit and finished the year in the 7th grade math class. Moreover, he continued through the 8th grade math course and took a two year algebra sequence in high school, maintaining "A's" and "B's." He is now working in a 3rd year algebra program in a regular high school math class. Not only did this success motivate him academically but his attitude, his behavior, and his self-image have also improved and he is enjoying admiration from his peers that he's never experienced before. His integration is not total, however, for he continues to receive instruction in other academic areas from the special education teacher.

The work of the teacher of the hearing impaired, however, goes beyond giving supplementary instruction to those being mainstreamed. This teacher also assists the regular classroom teacher in planning the most effective method to teach hearing impaired students in a regular classroom. Assistance can include taking notes in the regular classroom during lectures, films, and large group instruction sessions after which she is able to help the student review or understand the material during tutoring periods. Often a tape recorder is sent into the regular classroom so the teacher of the hearing impaired can later transcribe the tapes into written form. In this way, the student has a printed copy of the information and the teacher of the hearing impaired is kept informed of what is pertinent.

Such assistance begins in the intermediate school but continues through high school. Students who have been fully mainstreamed in the intermediate school continue their study in the regular high school program which consists of four academic classes and one period of physical education. They are assigned to the resource room during their two study hall periods.

Those students who are unable to be fully mainstreamed into a regular high school program can earn a certificate of achievement instead of a regular diploma. In high school these young people receive reading and language instruction from the reading specialist and the teacher of the hearing impaired. For these students, we have designed a course in everyday living which includes credit buying, insurance, taxes, social security, bank accounts, and other areas related to consumer economics. They are also being taught how to fill out job applications and how to read want ads. Sometimes they will divide their time between the intermediate school and the high school. They could be in the high school for industrial arts, home economics, and physical education and then return to the intermediate school for academic work in language arts, social studies, and math. This kind of split program is contingent upon the needs of students and the facilities and personnel of the two schools.

Industrial arts, home economics, and art are usually considered non-academic subjects and areas more easily adapted to the students with impaired hearing. Although our students can often be successful in the *practical* aspects of these classes, an unbelievable amount of work is necessary to help them learn the vocabulary and complete the written or oral reports. Some assignments require reading or language skills beyond the capabilities of some of our students but with the cooperation of the classroom teacher, we have been able to find alternatives.

Diane illustrates the way our program works for this type of mainstreaming. She has a severe to profound loss and a suspected learning disability and was enrolled in a regular clothing class. The students in that class were expected to know something about design, color, fiber content, and fabric construction. Each was expected to give an oral report; Diane's topic was "The

Basic Weaves." Each of the three basic weaves—plain, satin, and twill—needed to be defined for the class, the advantages and disadvantages of each given, and examples of fabrics so constructed shown.

With help, Diane was able to gather the basic information. She wove an example of each of these weaves with strips of colored paper and mounted them on large sheets of poster board along with their written definitions. She listed the advantages and disadvantages and labeled the fabric samples. The oral presentation was to be short and simple. Several hearing impaired students became her rehearsal audience. They gave her suggestions such as, "You must look at the audience." and "You can't look at just one person. You must look at people on all sides of the room." These comments were certainly an indication that her critics had learned a great deal the year before in their speech classes with regular students! Subsequently, Diane's report to the regular class was well received and her charts a welcome addition to the bulletin board in the clothing room.

Preteaching, as mentioned earlier, can ease mainstreaming later for the hearing impaired student who has inadequate reading and language skills. We spent an entire school year teaching several of these students the language, vocabulary, and concepts necessary for Driver Education. The following year, these students satisfactorily completed the course with their hearing peers and passed both the course and the state test.

Success for the students in a hearing impaired program is the result of many persons' efforts. The reward for the deaf student and his special teacher is quite tangible; the rewards for the classroom teacher and his hearing peers, though more intangible, are also quite real. In an art class taken by Katie, several weeks had been devoted to art history. The students were expected to know the names of thirty painters, the period of history to which they belonged, and the school of painting. Because the darkened room had made lipreading all but impossible, the art teacher had spent several of her planning periods with Katie going over the slides that she had used. When Katie passed the final exam with a superior grade, the art teacher came to tell me not only how pleased she was with Katie's performance but how personally satisfied she felt knowing that this had been accomplished through her efforts.

Initially the teacher of those with impaired hearing may check with the classroom teachers and the student daily, but eventually the student is expected to request tutorial help. If the student is to row through life independently, he must assume more and more responsibility for completing assignments and understanding the material as he progresses. At this stage, only when a periodic check or a specific request from a classroom teacher indicates a student may have hit a sandbar does the teacher of the hearing impaired step in to set him afloat again.

PARTICIPATION IN CO-CURRICULARS

Academic success, however, should not be the only objective in mainstreaming a hearing impaired student. The student must become involved in the total school program. A high school has a great variety of co-curricular activities ranging from athletics to literary clubs. Some students are anxious to become members of these organizations, but for others the teacher of the hearing impaired must create an interest or need.

Shorewood High has an outstanding drama department and all costumes are made by members of the Drama Club. For hearing impaired students with some ability to sew, this club seemed ideal. The suggestion that they join it, however, was met with a negative reaction by two girls who had been partially mainstreamed. They were finally persuaded to help only because we convinced them the costumes for a particular play would never be completed on time without their help. At first, we spent one school period working in the costume room but within several days, they were voluntarily spending their lunch hours and after school hours sewing. They made friends and became active members of the Drama Club during their remaining years in high school, contributing not only to the costume crew but also the stage crew and make-up crew.

One of them portrayed the wardrobe woman in a scene in "Bye Bye Birdie" and was selected to go as a member of the costume crew to Indiana University when the Shorewood Drama Club was invited to present this production at the National Thespian convention during the summer. Both became members of the National Thespian Society and one was elected to the Drama Club Dragons, the club's highest award which is anually received by three or four of the club's two hundred members.

Unlike Drama Club, some co-curriculars are competitive and require trying out. During the past three years, five hearing impaired girls have tried out for the Pompon Squad, part of our cheerleading group, and three of them have become members.

We have been able to mainstream our students into seventeen of our co-curriculars with one or more students being active in each of the following.

Varsity Football	Dance Club
Swimming Team	Drama Club
Track Team	Pompon Squad
Cross Country Team	Home Economics Club
Wrestling	Chess Club
Baseball Club	Math Club
Golf	Debate Club
Girls' Tennis Team	Ripples (school newspaper)
	Copperdome (school annual)

As a result of their efforts in these co-curriculars, they have accumulated fourteen athletic letters, honorable mention from the Drama Club, and the election of one to the Dragons of the Drama Club.

In recognition of their academic success and co-curricular involvement, the hearing impaired students at Shorewood have been elected to the following honor societies.

National Honor Society, SHS
Quill and Scroll, SHS
Phi Beta Kappa, Lake Forest College

They have also received the following awards.

A letter of commendation, National Merit Scholarship
A Bausch and Lomb Science Award
An American Legion Award
A Scholarship from the Alexander Graham Bell Association

EMPLOYMENT OPPORTUNITIES

Since most high school students have some part-time working experience, we encourage this also. Some of our students have worked as baby sitters, paper boys, stock boys, bus boys, kitchen helpers, office helpers, parking lot attendants, and yard boys. Many of these paid jobs have been secured with the help of parents, relatives and neighbors.

However, we have also created some volunteer jobs to give them additional experiences and develop a sense of contribution and accomplishment. One year, we had a student work in one of the school offices an hour a day, stapling papers, running the mimeograph, stuffing envelopes and doing other routine jobs. This experience was helpful in learning responsibility, getting along with others, following directions, and completing a job. This student received a certificate of achievement from the high school, then further training as a key punch operator and finally employment at Allis Chalmers Corporation.

THE PROGRAM AS A TEAM EFFORT

As I stated earlier, the program for students with impaired hearing at Shorewood is a segment of the total education program, made possible through the cooperation and support of all school personnel, the parents and the students.

The administrators have given the teachers of the deaf free rein in the selection of courses and classroom teachers, but they expect the hearing impaired students to adhere to all school rules. The administrators and the special teachers let these students accept the consequences if they do not.

The guidance counselors provide the same services for the hearing impaired students as they do for the rest of the student body. This includes individual counseling of personal concerns, interest, abilities, life-time objectives, college and occupational orientation.

The teachers of the deaf at the elementary level—there are three of them—have provided the students with the basic skills in language, speech, auditory training, and lipreading and have worked with them on the academic skills in reading, math, social studies and science.

The intermediate school provides additional sequential learning experiences and expanded opportunities in regular classes.

The classroom teachers now routinely accept the hearing impaired students into their classes and are often surprised to learn that deaf students are not educated in regular classrooms in other places. Many faculty members have served as academic tutors to the deaf students in their classes and have given up their planning periods or after-school hours to do so. They have sometimes changed their method of presentation for the class. They have permitted their lectures to be tape recorded and typed. They have provided alternate assignments for the lesser able students and have kept the teacher of the deaf informed of their course expectations. Their actions and attitudes express confidence in the deaf student's ability to learn and to participate fully. Such confidence is essential for success in a mainstream program.

The teacher of the hearing impaired is the keystone to the success or failure of such a program. He or she must develop a personal working relationship with the staff. The faculty is more willing to contribute to the needs of the deaf student if they feel their efforts have been helpful. The teacher of the deaf may need to show a willingness to work on faculty committees or make an effort to mix with other faculty members or hearing students in free hours. It is necessary for this teacher to speak positively about the achievements of the deaf students in the lounge or lunchroom. In this way, the capabilities, not the disabilities, are emphasized. The teacher of the hearing impaired must encourage the special students to express appreciation to the regular teacher for the extra help provided. Positive statements made by deaf students about a classroom teacher need to be repeated.

Since the hearing impaired student must meet success socially as well as academically, the resource teacher should provide the deaf student with more than academic tutoring. The student should feel free to bring all his questions and problems to the resource room, but the teacher of the hearing impaired students must also try to anticipate what the students need to know. If they are going to the Junior Prom which begins at 8:30 p.m., they must be told that no one arrives before 9:15 p.m. Other troublesome questions raised have been: "Do girls buy boutonnieres for their dates?" "Is it customary to go out to eat before or after the event?" These traditions change from year to year and from activity to activity so we need to find reliable sources of such information. Acceptance by their peers is so very important at this time in their lives that not knowing what's "in" could spoil an evening.

I have been the advisor of the Pep Club and now have a homeroom of hearing students. I sometimes enlist the help of some of these in answering some of these questions and helping get my students involved in extra-curricular activities. A high school annual in the resource room is a good reference book for information about clubs, classmates and their names, and staff members. Leafing through it can also lead to discussions and involvement.

Participation in outside activities often is preceded by a great deal of salesmanship on the part of the resource teacher. If our students are reluctant to join an organization which we feel would interest them, we sometimes get a hearing student to invite them or we find out from the faculty advisor what the group is doing. If the club is having a bake sale to raise money, it will need advertising posters. We try to convince our students that making a poster is something they could do. In the beginning, we may have to provide the idea but in a short time they catch on. They often are willing to participate if they can be made to feel needed and wanted and able to contribute, but the student who is not fully mainstreamed academically will often require a great deal of salesmanship.

The independence which is our goal is encouraged by the teacher of students with impaired hearing. Particularly at the high school level, problems should be solved with the student and not with his parents whenever possible. We have to help him make a decision by showing him possible consequences: "If you do this, what do you think might happen?" "If you don't do that, but you do this, what do you think might happen?" Then we need to step back and allow him to decide and accept the ultimate responsibility for that decision. One of my freshman boys failed to complete three written assignments for his English class one week. When he was asked by me why he hadn't turned them in, he said he was busy with his biology. He then complained that he had received three "F's" and asked me to explain to his English teacher how hard he was working in biology. He wasn't at all pleased when I told him that those "F's" were the result of his decision and if he didn't like "F's," he had better decide to complete his Engligh assignments.

It is very easy to allow the hearing impaired student to use his hearing loss as an excuse for not doing something. We must be aware of the difference between the problems deaf students meet as a result of their handicap and the problems all teenagers confront in the process of growing up. If our deaf students have tried out for the pompon squad and were not selected, it is not because they are deaf but because there were others whose performance of the routines was better. Occasional failure is part of life. If we don't allow students to develop a personal resiliency in coping with failure and accepting success as they grow up, they will never be able to row in the current of life.

Some of our students will cruise in the mainstream of education and later in the mainstream of life with relative ease. For others, it will be like rowing against the current with only one oar. These students may encounter more sandbars, maneuver more slowly, but by providing them with successful experiences which help develop confidence and a positive self-image, they will be able to sustain themselves in coping with the demands of reality.

Helen R. Golf

12

What Do You Do If The Mainstreamed Hearing Impaired Child Fails? or Mainstreaming: Sink or Swim

Many people have used the term mainstreaming to describe a wide variety of programs. Too often, as the subtitle may imply, it is a situation in which hearing impaired children are expected to function in a regular classroom situation completely independent of supportive personnel. It is unrealistic to expect that very many, if any, of these children will be successfully and optimally educated without some sort of supportive help. I would like to define mainstreaming in the following ways.

1. Regular classroom placement with indirect or direct supportive services from an itinerant hearing specialist.
2. Regular classroom placement with resource room support.
3. Regular classroom placement with supplementary support from an academic tutor.

With the indirect services, the specialist probably would not actually be working with the child, but would be providing information for the regular classroom teacher in terms of modifications in the programs, materials and procedures. This indirect service might also include some short term speech and language assistance which the teacher and the parents would be expected to carry over. There may be a few children who can be successful with only this indirect service. In contrast, in direct services, the itinerant teacher would provide some sort of continuous, on-going service directed to pupils. This might be regular sessions each day, but more probably sessions several times during the week. In some cases, it might be a period of daily intensive service for a limited period of time. This type of service needs to be as flexible as possible to best meet the individual needs of the child at any particular time. Of course we all have to have schedules, but hopefully they won't be so inflexible that individual needs cannot be met at the time they most need to be met. The itinerant specialist is also the liason person who in many cases provides most of the necessary information to the regular teachers about the needs of the hearing impaired child.

A second option for mainstreaming would be regular classroom placement with resource room support. Students following this option should be able to function effectively in a regular classroom for at least half the day and then receive resource teacher support for the other half or part of the day. This time may be spent in the resource room, or the resource teacher may be working in the regular classroom. Ideally, the person serving as a resource teacher would have had experience with normal hearing children plus experience with the hearing impaired. This kind of experience would enable the teacher to be more realistic about skills which are necessary for the child to function effectively in a regular classroom and also to better meet the special needs. Unfortunately, people with these qualifications are difficult to find and many times we must make concessions and compromises.

Resource help can be either individual or group work. When there are normal hearing children who need the same kind of help as the hearing impaired, then, by all means, the resource person should work with both groups of children instead of isolating the handicapped children in a separate room or in a smaller group in the regular classroom. Although the resource person's primary responsibility is to the hearing impaired, he should be available to work with any children in that particular situation. In many ways, it is better to work with the children within the regular room rather than removing them from the classroom.

There are several advantages to this type of arrangement. The resource person's willingness to work with both hearing and hearing impaired children in a team approach establishes better relationships. The fact that the resource teacher is working with both normal and hearing impaired children reduces the likelihood that a child will be labeled as either "special" or a "failure" by himself or by others. Although these children are intensively involved with at least two teachers, they don't seem to lose the feeling that they belong in one class, and yet they are receiving the special help and assistance they need. The amount of time spent with resource teacher support should remain flexible. The amount of help needed will vary a great deal from child to child, and may also change from time to time. Sometimes the needs of these children can best be met with the resource teacher in the regular classroom, and at other times, removing the child or the group to the resource room may be advisable.

The resource teacher should be very careful not to say to the regular teachers, "I am the expert. I will take these children out of the classroom, work with them, fix them up and then bring them back to you." Children often perform at very different levels when they are in small groups out of the classroom as opposed to competing in a regular classroom situation. Working with children in the regular classroom may also give the regular teacher more insight into the needs of these children. A great deal of learning can take place if people are willing to compromise, share ideas, accept the strengths of others, and be as open as possible.

The academic tutor would probably function in very similar ways to the itinerant specialist. This tutor may or may not be a specialist in the area of the hearing impaired. Any work done by this person should certainly be coordinated with the regular teacher. Although a child may be receiving supportive help, certain parents might want to provide additional help, particularly in the area of speech, and might use a tutor for this purpose. A tutor should also be considered if the option for mainstreaming is a private school. This certainly is an option for some children, particularly when regular public school classes are crowded. Many parents would opt for private schools with smaller classes where children can receive more individual attention. Even with smaller classes, in most cases, the hearing impaired child is going to need extra supportive help.

The options just described are the only ones which I consider to be mainstreaming. Now we need to focus on the second part of the original title—failure. Failure can be defined in a number of ways. There are many parameters that may contribute to failure and it certainly can be more than academic failure. Some things that might be considered failure are equally present in the lives of many normal hearing children, as well as those having a hearing impairment.

Failing children have not developed self-respect or a good self-concept. They may not have mastered the reading, verbal or computational skills that the schools are trying to teach. They may have been socially promoted through the grades whether they know anything or not. Many children have not learned to play the testing, memorizing, non-thinking kinds of games that are carried on in many classrooms where the payoff is the right answer. Some children are constantly trying to figure out what answer the teacher wants and if they don't find that answer, they are not making it. Another example of failure in many cases is the child who is not getting A's and B's and thus is in the failing majority. Many children are afraid; they are afraid of failing or of displeasing their parents, many of whom have unrealistic expectations.

Many teachers' expectations are extremely low. We really are not challenging many of the children in our classes. Those to whom we aim our teaching are very often even below the median of the group. Those children who are slow learners, behavior problems, and those who exhibit various kinds of other problems very often receive the majority of the teacher's attention. The average and above average children frequently just sit in class and end up being turned off toward school and learning. They are bored because so many things that they are called upon to think about are really very trivial and dull; they make very limited demands upon children's intellectual potential.

Children often seem to be very confused. There are tons of words being poured out over them every day. Some teachers seem to equate talking with teaching. Frequently teachers tend to do all the talking and their students are never given the opportunity to express themselves. There is also a tremendous difference between teaching and learning. Most children have developed only a tiny part of their huge capacity for learning, understanding, and creating.

Many people are anxious to discuss children who fail. Let's flip the coin over. A child who is failing is either in an inappropriate program or someone has programmed him incorrectly. We as educators and administrators must be able to develop educational programs and place children in educational settings where they are going to succeed; where the opportunity for success is optimal. The development of educational programs that ensure success for children is dependent upon having a continuum of services which will meet the needs of all the kinds of children we see every day.

The starting point for a continuum of services is, of course, identification at as early an age as possible. Intensive audiological assessment takes place in the early years. Using this particular model, periodic reassessment at about age five and above should be done at least yearly, with additional testing available whenever it seems advisable. The parent-teaching program, basically for children from birth to three years of age, is the first type of educational program. If you are dealing with children who come from a regional area rather than an urban one, the parent-teaching program may need to extend beyond the age of three, as there may not be any other options for placement of children who are between the ages of three and five. This parent-teaching program should be heavily oriented toward parent involvement rather than being tutorial or child-oriented.

From ages three to six, there are several options for most children. One option would be a nursery and/or kindergarten program for hearing impaired children. This program might consist of only hearing impaired children, or there might be a combination of children of comparable age, some with hearing impairments and some normal hearing children. Another possible option would be to mainstream the hearing impaired in normal nursery schools and kindergartens for part of the day and then supplement these experiences with classes for hearing impaired children during another part of the day. These classes should be designed to meet the special needs of pre-school hearing impaired children, particularly in the areas of language and speech. Regular preschool and kindergarten classes cannot provide enough reinforcement.

At age six there are more options available. The one listed first is labeled a "transition class" and is proposed for children between the ages of six and eight. There are many children in this age range who are quite close to being

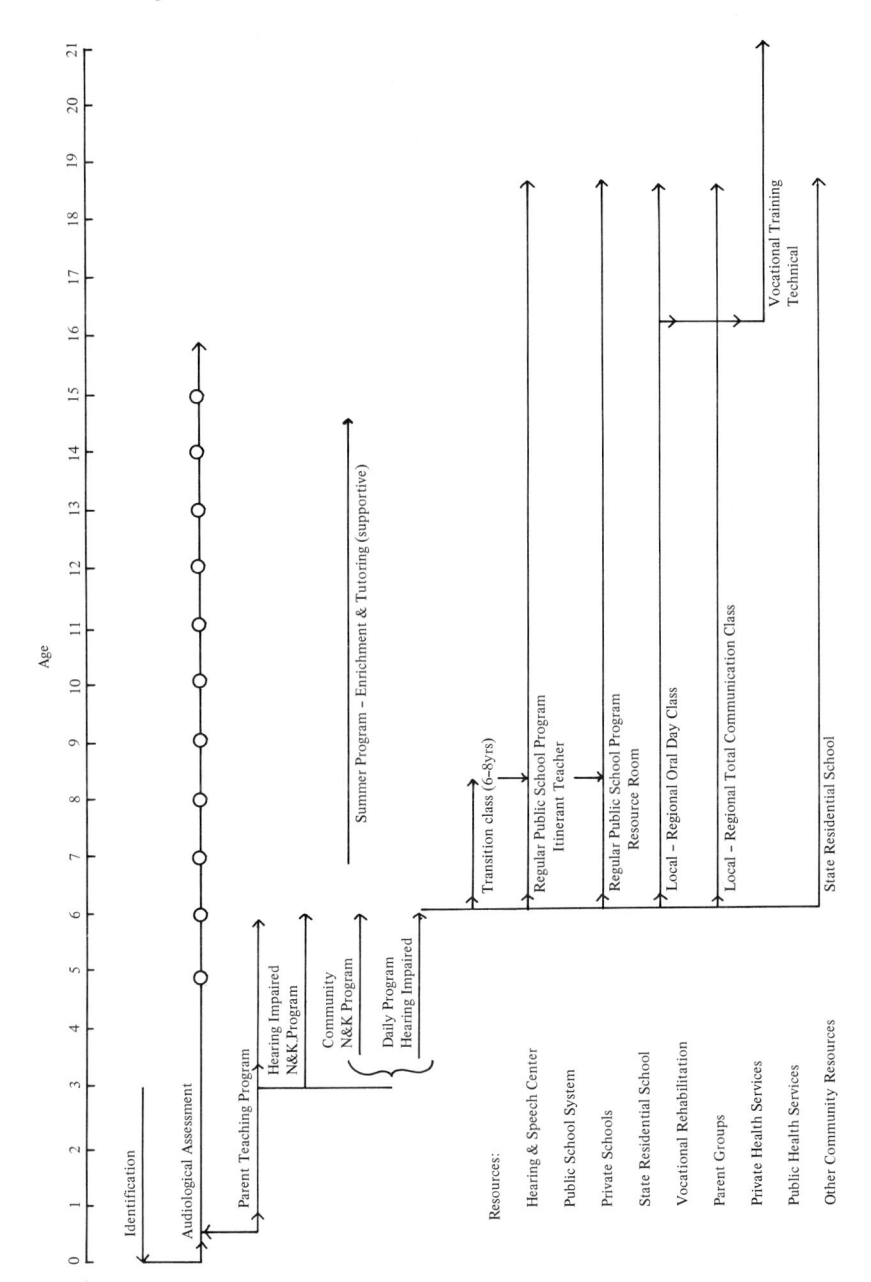

Fig. 12-1. Continuum of services for the hearing impaired.

ready for resource room mainstreaming. The class would be similar to a self-contained class and would be situated in a regular public school where the children could be mainstreamed for all nonacademic activities. There might possibly be some children in this class who could mainstream for at least one academic subject. I would advocate using regular public school materials and presenting them in a manner similar to the one used in the regular classrooms. This type of class should not academically retard these children as so often happens in too many self-contained classrooms. Working with a smaller group of children than would be found in a regular classroom, children learning basic academic skills would have more opportunity for individual attention from a teacher knowledgeable about the special needs of hearing impaired children. A good deal of emphasis would also be placed on language development.

The next two options are those discussed in the definition of mainstreaming—regular classroom placement with supportive services from either an itinerant teacher or a resource room teacher. Establishing resource rooms at various levels provides more flexibility in meeting individual needs than itinerant services, and also more immediate help and support for regular classroom teachers.

Two other options are the local-regional oral and total communication day classes. In many areas it is very appropriate to provide services on a regional basis. There are certain smaller school districts where there is no appropriate placement. The only supportive services for hearing impaired children in many of these localities is an itinerant teacher who may or may not be knowledgeable about the needs of these children. For certain children who live in these rural areas, itinerant support is not going to be enough for them to be successful. The only other local option which may be available is a special education class which is generally similar to a traditional "little red schoolhouse." A more realistic placement for children who are not ready for mainstreaming would be to take advantage of the existing services within a larger urban area by bringing them in for services. This eliminates placing them in a sink or swim mainstream situation where sinking is almost inevitable. The local-regional oral or total communication day classes are located in a regular public school where the students are with normal hearing children for everything nonacademic and where some of the children, particularly those from the oral classes, may be able to mainstream for certain academic subjects.

As students from the two options above, and possibly some from other options in the continuum, reach the ages of fifteen or sixteen, some type of vocational/technical education should be available. It is advantageous and more realistic to use existing facilities within the school district rather than to try and provide separate and distinct services for hearing impaired children. Manual interpreters will need to be provided for some students, depending upon their communicative skills. Some students may need the help of a resource teacher in the classroom with them.

For the majority of children, our goal is to educate them whenever possible in the local public schools. The last option suggested is the state residential school. For some children, particularly those who live in very rural areas, there is no question that the state residential school can provide a much broader continuum of services than the local school district could possibly provide.

We should try to incorporate as many of the various community resources as possible. The more we can capitalize upon existing services rather than duplicating them, the more effective our programs can be. When there are enough options, recommendations can be made based on where the child will function best, and where the best opportunities are to meet long range goals. Our aim is that eventually the hearing impaired students will be educated, productive, and contributing members of society, rather than being among the thousands of students who leave school or even graduate with such a meager education that they are destined to very menial employment for the rest of their lives.

One of the problems facing us even with a continuum of services is that parents inherently have the idea in the back of their minds that success equals mainstreaming. We are obligated to prepare parents very early that there may be a variety of options that will be appropriate for their child's needs, and that it is not possible for all hearing impaired children to be mainstreamed at the first grade level. We should maintain as much flexibility as possible in our ability to move children from one option to another. Placement of children in programs other than those presently defined as mainstreaming should not be equated with failure, either by parents or teachers. Very often, teacher attitudes are poorer and their expectancies are lower the further away they are from the mainstream options. With so much emphasis and enthusiasm being placed on mainstreaming and mainstreaming being equated with success, anyone who does not reach that goal is too often considered a second class citizen. We cannot afford to lower our standards or expectancies for any group. We have a tremendous obligation and responsibility to all these children to meet their individual needs realistically and effectively, and not to be influenced or guided by the mechanics which a system may dictate.

We as educators and administrators must establish realistic criteria for placing children in mainstream programs. We are often pressured by teachers and parents to mainstream children too soon or at a grade level where the child is unable to cope. Some of the essential questions which we must ask are: (1) Does the child have the receptive and expressive communication skills, concepts, and at certain levels the academic skills, so that reasonable success can be anticipated in the regular classroom? (2) Is the child going to be able to learn new material when it is presented in the regular classroom or only when he is in a one-to-one or small group situation with a special teacher? (3) Is the child sufficiently mature socially, emotionally, and physically to function effectively in a regular classroom? An out-going personality is certainly advantageous to the child. (4) Is there sufficient supportive help available and is the regular class enrollment small enough so the regular teacher will have some time to help the hearing impaired pupil solve his problems? A hearing impaired child realistically adds between three and five pupils to a regular class. We must also consider teacher competency, personality, and the teacher's willingness to accept a hearing impaired child. We certainly are not going to ensure success for a child who is being forced upon a teacher. (5) Are the parents and other members of the family willing to help and support the child who is mainstreamed? Are they able to help him develop solutions to problems he may have in adjusting to the regular class environment? All of the above factors must be considered carefully and recommendations and decisions must be made on an individual basis.

After carefully selecting the children to be put into the mainstream, we also have an obligation to provide effective monitoring and evaluation of these children. This should be done periodically and I would suggest a team evaluation at least once a year, ideally twice a year. There should also be careful, ongoing evaluation by the regular classroom teacher, the itinerant or resource teacher and a coordinator or supervisor so that children who are having problems will be identified and modifications made before failure occurs. When careful monitoring is taking place, essential intervention at critical times is possible.

Some of the major myths of mainstreaming need to be presented and dispelled.

Promises Promises

Early identification, early amplification and early training will enable hearing impaired children to enter first grade with their hearing peers. The future of many hearing impaired children is dependent to a large extent on the medical, audiological, and educational intervention services they receive prior to the age of six. Early identification, early amplification and early training gives many hearing impaired children the opportunity to learn speech and language by listening in the early years, just as normal hearing children do. Some hearing impaired children will be ready to enter first grade with their normal hearing peers. But too many promises to parents only add more feelings of failure and guilt if their children are not yet ready for mainstreaming.

Learning Language By Osmosis

The hearing impaired child needs only a regular preschool or kindergarten program in order to learn language. Early exposure to normal children seems to have a very positive effect on social adjustments. In regular preschools and kindergartens, hearing impaired children have the opportunity of listening to normal speech and language of their peers. In an environment where everyone talks, the hearing impaired child will be more motivated to speak himself. He will also be exposed to functional language connected with child-centered activities and this will aid in concept development. Normal preschools and kindergartens certainly supplement more specific training, but parents and educators should not delude themselves that this will take the place of more specific speech and language training.

Success Breeds Success

Success in integrated preschool and/or kindergarten automatically predicts success in the elementary school mainstream. What is termed "success" in preschool or kindergarten may not be sufficient for successful mainstreaming. Many of the preschools and kindergartens are mainly interested in the socialization of children. A child with very limited speech and language may be fairly successful in many preschool and kindergarten settings because so many of the activities require little or no language. They may have been termed successful, but many of these children lack the necessary communication skills or may not be socially or emotionally ready to be mainstreamed.

My Kid Is Now Normal

Normalization is one of the outcomes of mainstreaming. Parents of young hearing impaired children are frequently the ones who are the most insistent that the child be mainstreamed. They seem to feel that somehow the fact that he is mainstreamed will make him "normal" or, at least, there will be some appearances of normality. In some cases these are the children who most need more special training. Time lost from education during early years can never be regained and we will never be successful in patching people up. You can only patch so long and then the whole bottom drops out. Psychologically, some children are being placed in situations breeding frustration and continuing failure and may suffer very traumatic effects. For children who are not ready for mainstreaming, we may in fact be isolating and de-normalizing them.

We Can Breathe Easier Now

Parents can breathe a "sigh of relief" once a child has been mainstreamed. The parents' responsibility to their child certainly does not end just because he is mainstreamed. In fact, it is very possible that more responsibility is added at this point. Parents' roles as language teachers and academic tutors never seem to end. Although a young child may adapt satisfactorily in the lower primary grades, as the levels of communication and educational expectations become more advanced, it is possible that a child may require additional help or alternative educational placement.

Teacher Knows Best

A teacher of the hearing impaired can make the best evaluation as to mainstream placement. The best evaluation a child can receive results from a multidisciplinary approach. Each person provides the detailed information for which he is specifically trained while simultaneously evaluating the child as a whole child. The psychologist, social worker, audiologist, itinerant or resource teacher, supervisor or coordinator, regular classroom teachers and others can provide, as a team, a much more detailed and comprehensive evaluation that any one person could provide independently. A teacher of the hearing impaired is not always the expert and no one person can be all things to all people.

The Audiogram Tells All

The audiogram indicates the kind of placement the hearing impaired child needs. Most of us would agree that emphasis should be placed on *how* the child functions rather than on *what* the audiogram may indicate. Audiograms certainly can provide useful information and certainly should be considered, but speech, language, basic concepts, reading ability and achievement in other content areas, and social and emotional maturity may be better indicators of appropriate placement for the hearing impaired child.

Mainstreaming should *not* be a sink or swim proposition. Nor should it be an either/or approach.

SECTION III

Administrative Aspects of Mainstreaming

Leo E. Connor

13

Administrative Concerns for Mainstreaming

Throughout the past five-to-ten year period, the Special Education and General Education communities have been moving closer on a collision course. Many Special Educators have "gotten a message" that began with a whisper and is rising to a shout. It says "mainstreaming!" On the other hand, most General Educators thought that "those handicapped kids" were taken care of in special schools and special classes and somewhere in institutions or on home instruction. So General Administrators may be genuinely bewildered by this shout of mainstreaming. They may agree with what they hear about the theory of the idea, but the practical implications—Stop! "You proponents are really talking about a revolutionary concept in education (i.e., putting deaf kids in regular classes) and although I, as a general administrator, may not know much about mainstreaming, maybe you as a Special Educator don't know much about it either."

The thesis of my chapter is that Special Educators and, in particular, the educators of the deaf, as well as general educators, must do more planning, conduct more discussions, evaluate better and be clearer in their objectives and programmatic techniques for mainstreaming, than they have been up to the present.

CAUTIONARY NOTES

A heady combination of forces has merged in recent years to create the dream of mainstreaming deaf children. But too many proponents seem to forget that there are obstacles to such a concept. Haven't you talked to educators who cite the need for quality programs for normal children and the detrimental effects of mainstreaming? So, while special educators talk about appropriate services, zero reject concept, litigation and the rights of the handicapped, there is also an opposing chorus that talks of the triage problems and scarcity of resources or accountability and lack of definitive data. Under such complex and contradictory pressures, an administrator of a general *or* a special education enterprise may well become confused and retreat into inaction, delays or opposition to the initiation of a mainstream service.

The history of the education of deaf children could be instructive at this point and should be made known to general education administrators. Although simplified in the following description, the changes in the education of deaf children add up to gradual but seemingly inevitable shifts in our educational system. From 1817 to 1920, the majority of deaf children were educated in residential schools. From the early 1900s to 1970, an increasing number of deaf children were educated in special classes of regular schools, while the residential schools percent of day pupils also rose steadily. Starting in the 1960s, and increasingly in the 1970s, a variety of new organizational patterns began to emerge, including resource rooms where a special teacher kept the homeroom for deaf children and sent them out to regular classes. Other organizational possibilities included itinerant teachers of the deaf, who worked with regular class teachers who had deaf students, or consultant educators of the deaf, who gave workshops on techniques, methods and programs to regular school administrators, supervisors and teachers to help with the increasing number of deaf children who were entering regular classrooms.

From the field of Special Education currently have come such concepts as "the least restrictive environment" and the "deinstitutionalization" concept which deals with "the prevention of problems in community programs and the return to each community of all handicapped children." But how does an administrator (general or special) reconcile these ideal statements with the practical ones of the triage which is defined as the choice of the least damaging alternative among negative possibilities? Please remember that the triage concept emerged on the battlefield of World War II where surgeons with limited personnel had to decide on whom to operate among the dozens or hundreds of casualties from a particular battle. Stated in civilian terms, the question might be, should a severely retarded baby be permitted to die or should extraordinary means be employed to retain his life? In educational fiscal terms, the application would be, if a decreased amount of money is available, whose program is to suffer?

At the administrative level of operations, the questions raised regarding school fiscal resources and accountability are real ones. These questions cannot be swept aside in a show of ideal rhetoric concerning the needs of deaf children. If a general school administrator has conflicting claims between spending $15,000 for an extra teacher and equipment to mainstream 5 to 10 deaf children, or for an extra teacher who can provide 30 disadvantaged children with a better educational program—then the choice is a real one. And deaf children might lose in such a case. Advocates for deaf children must be prepared to explain, to convince, and to succeed in whatever local fashion makes for progress toward a more effective educational program.

ADMINISTRATIVE CONCERNS RELATED TO MAINSTREAMING

It seems clear that most of the questions raised by the topic of mainstreaming deaf children will be basically ones that come down to a favorable or unfavorable decision by a special school administrator. Whether the state laws require mainstreaming, or the local district newspaper advocates this new trend, such educational programs sooner or later revert to the administrator's decision, the resources that carry it out, and then the teacher's willingness to implement that decision in an effective manner.

What are the components of an administrator's decision? Probably the earliest components are an administrator's level of knowledge and insights which turn into his or her priorities.

What have educators of the deaf been doing to increase the level of knowledge and insights that administrators have concerning the potentialities of deaf children? Far too often we have concentrated so much on our own techniques and objectives that we have failed to communicate with the regular school administrator or the Special Education Administrator in charge of all handicapped children's programs in a city, a county or a local district. Too often some of us think of persuasion as the act of sending a parent of a deaf child to the educational establishment. We are convinced that parents have but to ask and the portals will open. Or we think that an influential politician or a local newspaper or a deaf adult statement will persuade all of the community concerning the righteousness of our cause.

When will we educators of the deaf stop talking about the "rights of children" as if everyone agreed on their practical definition, and instead offer specific plans and resources concerning the proposed rearrangement of programs and practices so necessary to effect mainstreaming objectives? On a practical level, are we willing to limit our requests to a slow, experimental beginning; can we include realistic and effective evaluation procedures in any proposed plan; do we show the general administrator where extra State and Federal resources are to be located; have we available a certified teacher ready and willing to carry out a program? These are examples of the preplanning that must be established before Special Educators can move from the theoretical discussion of "needs" and "rights" of handicapped children to the practical agreement that next September a resource teacher of the deaf will be employed in our local community.

Perhaps the preparation period is the least understood of all in the decision-making of an administrator. No experienced administrator can or will give immediate assent to a new idea for an educational change or innovation until he has been thoroughly briefed or exposed over time to the concept. There will always be the exceptional community where the administrator or a board member or an important local official has a close relative who is deaf so that much of the readiness and groundwork for favorable decisions have been accomplished.

But the usual case is more apt to be the local community and school leadership which has a stereotype already firmly in mind. It can be that deaf children have always gone from this local community to the state residential school. Or it may be that deaf children have had such a low profile that their mention is automatically equated with extra costs, segregation, and some esoteric techniques. It could be that a recent failure of educational efforts for the blind or the crippled have confused the administrator in regard to the present requests for the deaf.

In almost all cases, the introduction of the concept of mainstreaming will be affected by the important factor of time and timing. Time, in the administrative lingo, means that planning and meetings and question answering will consume long weeks and probably many months. A parent's or an educator of the deaf's expectations cannot be based on unrealistic time schedules such as, "Well, I wrote a letter or had my meeting with the superintendent 4 weeks ago!" Instead, no action is to be expected if that is all you did.

A multifaceted attack on the establishment of a school district should be planned from the beginning by the proponents of any new program. The attack must be direct and devious; simple and varied; understandable and complex; easy to achieve, yet permanent in commitment; offering advantages and profit as well as work and headaches; respectful yet threatening; within the organizational pattern yet involving many segments of the community! In short, a request for a new departure or change in established programs should be recognized as a battle involving many factors, including reputations, other power groups, community perceptions and mores, as well as overly committed resources, and the legitimate needs of large groups of children.

Even an administrator's agreement in principle with your objectives may not be sufficient. You may have to find allies from other educational areas who see your program as an advantage to themselves. You may have to balance your overwhelming desire for direct pressure and immediate results against the administrator's desire to take the credit or allow him an "out" so he can escape reprisals from other pressure groups. Are you ready to compromise on the extent or schedule of your proposal? Have you anything to trade or will you work for someone else's pet project in exchange for a fragile alliance?

Innovators of ideas sometimes forget the further steps of planning which deal with possible failure of the services after initiation and the subsequent years of a program. An administrator can never forget these important elements. He or she should be provided with contingency plans for most forseeable elements. For example, what happens if the regular teachers resist, or the deaf children hate their new classes or the parents of the deaf child get the regular staff too upset, or if first-year results are only half of what was expected? What happens when the deaf child and his parents find out there is no audiologist or electronic technician available to fix hearing aids in the regular school? What happens when the local principal finds out that this wonderful specialist you've sold them, the teacher of the deaf, has never taught normally hearing children, cannot answer the faculty's questions about genetic counseling, and probably knows as much about an electromagnetic free-field broadcasting unit as the principal does?

Most articles and books concerning mainstreaming seem to start with the "Three L's" of recent special education history. These are legislation, litigation, and leverage. Legislation, of course, deals with local or state mandates for new organizational patterns. Litigation concerns the Pennsylvania case, or the District of Columbia Mills case, or some other precedent establishing the legal force that requires governmental groups to do something for handicapped children. And leverage usually revolves around local pressure groups and reaching the policy making level for the influencing of administrative decisions.

But from the administrative viewpoint, the action level of mainstreaming is more bothersome and has not been written up in the journals. How and who will train regular classroom teachers to work with deaf children? Are parents of deaf children interested in getting their child admitted to this new proposed program or will they in the future be continuing aggravators? Are state officials offering cooperation now to a local district with the expectation of failures to emerge and later utilization in their own resistance to mainstreaming? How can anyone tell if a deaf child is ready to face the tremendous pressures of a new educational program while it is going through a shakedown period? Have the universities been preparing teachers of the deaf teach in the usual special class programs, or do such teachers really know what is necessary to succeed in a regular school? Will these mainstreamed deaf children be the one added burden on the regular school staff that will tip the balance negatively against the other successful experiments going on for other than handicapped children?

What many administrators are discovering about mainstreaming is that it is not a simple matter of "either mainstreaming *or* special schools and classes" but that the concept includes both of these and more. It seems clear that special schools and special classes are going to be required in the future for many deaf children. But mainstreaming demands an additional set of alternatives, such as resource rooms, itinerant teachers, hearing handicapped consultants to the regular class teachers, supervisors and administrators, and perhaps other organizational arrangements.

Thus, I return full circle to the administrative question I started with: Are educators of the deaf ready with sufficient knowledge, experience, and techniques to make this complex, interrelated series of new and old organizational arrangements really work? Where has it been tried and what were the results? If a particular local district is being asked to experiment and be the "first one," then how can the teachers, staff, parents, and community be prepared and assured that a detailed plan is available that can respond to limitations yet still produce sufficient results that will be better than whatever was accomplished in the past.

Many administrators will ask further honest questions, such as: since deaf children are a severely handicapped group of low incidence, how can a diversity of organizational requirements be arranged with such a small number of children? Can educational and professional judgements predominate over the hopes and desires of parents who usually want to hear that their deaf children should be educated in "the least restrictive environment?" Does this "least restrictive environment" mean the deaf child has to fail before he/she is moved downward in the organizational hierarchy? Do we have criteria, agreed upon characteristics or results, and do we really know which deaf child belongs in the mainstreaming effort?

ADMINISTRATIVE GUIDELINES FOR MAINSTREAMING

Administrators, whether special or regular educators, are always looking for guidelines regarding the complexities which beset their professional activities. This section of the chapter seeks to offer such generalizations regarding administrative actions that may have direct application to the questions raised about mainstreaming.

First, it seems clear there are a number of possible organizational arrangements that could be initiated and/or retained to deal with deaf children. If a county or city superintendent or director of special education has been sending all deaf children off to a state residential school, then mainstreaming offers new possibilities. But administrative reassurance should be offered that in any one city or district only limited patterns can be initiated. Advocates of mainstreaming and administrators alike would be wise to concentrate on one or two aspects of the spectrum in order to provide a quality program that can be effectively implemented. A resource room, and/or a self-contained special class for the deaf in a community, would be a major step forward into mainstreaming if nothing except a residential school had been available in the past. Administrators, therefore, are advised to limit their choices and for a several-year period to supervise and evaluate such a new program before facing the next set of organizational variables.

Second, in any adventure into a new program, administrators are advised to rely principally upon proven teaching and supervising personnel. This means that fully prepared, certified and experienced teachers of the deaf must be available, as well as knowledgeable supervisory or consultant staff, to oversee the direct service components. Although exceptions to this guideline are possible, it is my stipulation concerning any new program that it has the best chance of success when unproven personnel are not asked to find themselves as well as to prove the program. Thus, a reasonable extension of this administrative guideline is to work on all aspects of the overall plan but refuse to put it into effect until the right kind of personnel become available in your community.

Third, the real goals of this new program are not to prove whether mainstreaming will work, or whether your district or city is adopting the latest trend in Special Education, but rather, are 5 or 10 or 20 deaf children in this new arrangement receiving a better educational service than was available previously? Thus, the administrator's focus must be on educational results for the children rather than whether the new program makes parents feel better, or whether it complies with a state directive, or relieves the pressure from a local group.

An aspect of this guideline is also the reasonable request from the administrator that the results for deaf children be provable ahead of the initiation of a new program. That means that if better social and academic results are its objectives, then such results should be not only theoretically possible but that data from other localities and programs be indicative that this new concept has actually worked. The burden of proof should be on the shoulders of those who want something different.

Fourth, an administrator should be able to make a distinction between the new program itself and the deaf children who are involved in such an experiment. This guideline means that if one or several deaf children try out the resource room or the itinerant program and do not like it and perhaps return to what the older arrangements were that the mainstreaming effort itself may not be at fault. Thus, a new program requires a fair trial of sufficient length which may continue over several years and involve varied personnel before a final verdict is rendered concerning its success or failure.

Fifth, it seems important for an administrator to know that there are different types of deaf children. Deaf children are moderately and severely deaf; they have excellent communication skills or they have none; deaf children can be bright, retarded, extroverted, emotionally disturbed, motivated, or passive; they have interested and supportive parents, or they can come from a distressed home background; they can have special language or learning problems, or they can be perceptive, fast-learning individuals. In other words, every administrator must know what are the characteristics of the deaf children he/she is being asked to mainstream. Depending upon the known level of skills and the personality patterns of a group of deaf children, the chances for such children to enter upon and succeed in a regular class or resource room or an itinerant program can be predicted.

Most past research studies have indicated that what we now call mainstreaming and what some people have called integration can be successfully achieved by deaf children who have most of the following characteristics: (1) understandable speech; (2) reading levels equal to the grade they will enter; (3) secure and hopefully outgoing personalities; (4) supportive parents; (5) average or better IQ; (6) early and consistent auditory training.

CONCLUSIONS FOR ADMINISTRATORS

Tentative answers to other specific questions of administrators are offered from the recent literature. Normal children may reject those handicapped children who 1—are bused in from other neighborhoods (Goodman et al, 1971); 2—are perceived as less competent than normal peers (Gottlieb and Davis, 1973); 3—act in antisocial or unpredictable ways (Goodman et al, 1971; Iano, et al, 1974); 4—look different physically and/or have coordination problems (Gottlieb and Davis, 1973); 5—are not accepted by the regular classroom teacher (Gottlieb and Budoff, 1973).

Administrators should know that the field of Special Education is not united on the value of mainstreaming. Where Dunn (1968), Lilly (1970), and Deno (1970) led in the conceptualization of the trend, later modifications have been offered by Adamson and Van Etten (1972), Sabitino (1972), Reger (1973), Snapp (1972), and Ohrtman (1972). Budoff in 1972 summed up the current perception of mainstreaming by saying, "integration of severely handicapped children into the regular classes requires a school with a broad range of options, preferably one that is philosophically and structurally organized to deal with heterogeneity among children."

Perhaps the following list of my own personal conclusions can be of generalized aid to other administrators.

1. Exceptional (e.g., high achieving) deaf children are able to maintain themselves in regular classes and, depending upon individualized evaluation, planning and support, should be mainstreamed.
2. Mainstreaming of deaf children requires supportive services and specialized educators of the deaf who can aid deaf children in maintaining a success pattern in regular classes.
3. Limitations of deaf children (e.g., emotional problems, hyperactivity,

deficits in communication skills, or multiple handicaps of any kind) will preclude such deaf children from being mainstreamed.
4. Formulating an individualized educational plan for each deaf child that includes his current and future academic, social and vocational needs will offer a realistic profile to assist administrative decisions concerning deaf children.

As a final statement of administrative aspects of mainstreaming, may I offer these reflections. Mainstreaming of more and more deaf children is here to stay. It is a viable opportunity for deaf children that can be of greater or lesser effectiveness depending upon the extent to which a community will commit itself to the effort. If the local general and special administrators in charge of such programs are willing to plan, to work, and to closely supervise, the mainstreaming of deaf children can become an integral part of the educational services for that community. The battleground for the establishment of such a program should be in the minds, hearts and discussions of adults who are parents, teachers, supervisors and administrators. The deaf children who are the subject of such debate should not have their lives uprooted and their learning environments changed until a reasonable chance for success can be guaranteed.

BIBLIOGRAPHY

Adamson G, Van Etten G: Zero reject model revisited: A workable alternative. Except Child 38: 735-738, 1972

Budoff M; Providing special education without special classes. J School Psychol 10: 2, 1972

Deno E: Special education as developmental capital. Except Child 37: 229-237, 1970

Dunn L: Special education for the mildly retarded—Is much of it justifiable. Except Child 35: 5-22, 1968

Gottlieb J, Budoff M: Social acceptability of retarded children in nongraded schools differing in architecture. Amer J Mental Deficiency 78: 15-19, 1973

Gottlieb J, Budoff M: Attitudes toward School by Segregated and Integrated Retarded Children: A Study and Experimental Validation. Cambridge, Mass.: Research Institute for Educational Problems, 1972

Goodman, H., Gottlieb, J. and Harrison, R.H. Social Acceptance of EMR'S Integrated into a Nongraded Elementary School. Cambridge, Mass.: Research Institute for Educational Problems, 1971

Iano RP: Shall we disband special classes. J Special Ed 6: 167-177, 1972

Lilly S: Training based model for special education. Except Child 37: 745-749, 1971

Ohrtman WF: One more instant solution coming up! J Special Ed 6: 377-381, 1973

Reger R: Resource rooms: Change agents or guardians of the status quo. J Special Ed 6: 355-359, 1972
Sabatino DA: Resource rooms: The renaissance in special education. J Special Ed 6: 335-347, 1972
Snapp M: Resource classrooms or resource personnel? J Special Ed 6: 383-387, 1972

Lee F. Auble

14

Mainstreaming in Southwestern Michigan

My purpose is to tell you something of our efforts in Berrien Springs, Michigan which have led to success in mainstreaming. I must admit that this was not a concern when we first began our program for hearing impaired children. Our concern was for the individual child. However, we inevitably became involved in mainstreaming because of that concern.

What I have for you is something of a testimony as to what I've seen. It's been my privilege to live with the Berrien Springs program—actually to live in the center of it, as it's grown from nothing, to a program which serves the needs of 125 hearing impaired children in a 600 square mile area with a total population of 60,000—in a time span of a dozen years. I can tell you about this, not because I've done it, but because I've seen it happen, and I've had the rewarding experience of having arranged the framework on which it grew.

I remember my first introduction to the education of hearing impaired children—a mother came to me to talk about the possibility of allowing her daughter—age 4 with a profound hearing loss—to attend our kindergarten the next year, just to see if she could make a go of it for the year—preparatory to enrolling in a state boarding school some 200 miles away the following year. We talked about it, the mother, the school principal, the potential kindergarten teacher, and I. The teacher, who was—after all—the one really concerned felt that it was worth a try.

Experience that year indicated that we couldn't cut it—we needed help if we were going to provide education for a deaf child—but we did become convinced that with trained help it could be done. That same year Michigan established legislation which provided state financial encouragement and a plan whereby local programs in special education could be established. You know that the old adage that birds of a feather flock together is no idle expression. Half a dozen children with hearing problems were identified and we were challenged to establish a program. We found a teacher, trained in the field, who was willing to try, and whom we thought had potential. Her main qualifications were a dynamic personality and a strong voice. She believed in speechreading, and amplification, but most strongly in her own voice. You could hear her efforts at communication with her charges all over that 15 classroom building even when she had the door closed and she often left it open. But the 7 children with whom she started our program have succeeded. The girl whose mother started our whole interest graduated from our high school as a mainstream member of the student body and has gone on to college work. One of the boys who was a member of our original group finished high school last spring with a strong academic record and was an outstanding athlete in three sports. He is now attending college and playing football. Both of these young people attended typical classes beginning with the junior high school. Of course there were problems, difficulties, obstacles—but they were overcome successsfully.

Now back to the building of a program—we soon found that in any random group of handicapped children there is such a variety of problems, such a spread of ability, that one teacher can't possibly cope with the situation. We needed help and we needed a greater number of children to justify the help.

This didn't come all at once, but it came gradually. The number of children was the easiest. Make an honest effort to help someone and you'll find several others who would also like help. Getting additional staff members was more difficult—but it happened. Our first teacher—the one with the strong vocal chords—found that her nerves just couldn't take it. We found Andy Gantenbein teaching a similar program in a nearby town in a basement room, and convinced him that if we were to pool our efforts we could do better. I don't know that he really needed convincing—it was more a matter of giving him an opportunity. That's what I have for you as a message. Give capable people the opportunity.

The opportunity consists of setting up a policy and an administrative structure which will allow, encourage, and promote hearing impaired individuals to live and learn as regular, normal members of society, and to begin that experience as early as possible.

As I think back to what Andy's program was when I first visited him, I remember it as being labeled Special Education, meaning something different than the normal school program. The students were set apart and had little in common with the rest of the school. We have come to regard this as something we want to avoid. The only thing special we want is special effort. This implies special provisions and special arrangements, but not unless absolutely necessary. Many of us tend to be overprotective and under confident of handicapped children. Nothing could be further from their need. Life is real for them and we must keep it that way. To allow special concessions unnecessarily prevents a good deal of potential development.

Certainly, we could make things easy for a hearing impaired child by an "understanding" attitude—by lowering standards and expectations. But this philosophy does no one any good. Hearing impaired children must make an *extra* effort—and they can. Perhaps we're able to be successful in this, or rather *they* are, because schools (and society) don't expect the extra effort, and those who start back of even can keep up, with effort, because those without the handicap don't realize their potential either. There's a message in that observation. My point here, though, is that the school's policy should not only make the extra effort possible, for handicapped pupils, but it should expect it. A pupil who has a handicap can't expect to solve a given problem in the same time span, and with no more effort, than that exerted by those who don't have the handicap. All of us recognize that we have to try harder to do certain things than some other individuals do. Of course, a hearing aid is bothersome—but with the right attitude it's no different than red hair, or freckles, or any other individual characteristic as far as looks go. It does take maintenance and acceptance if it is to reach maximum effectiveness. Similarly, a pupil who misses part of a teacher's explanation will fall behind if he doesn't get special tutoring every day to guard against this—so it must be policy to keep hearing aids in top condition, and tutoring and counseling help must be provided daily.

As we developed our program and the number of children grew, we found some who really needed only a little encouragement and daily maintenance in order to make a go of it in a typical classroom. This led us to wonder how many others could do so. We began to try, on an individual basis, placing children in normal classes in specific subject areas, such as math or science at the level of their accomplishment, without too much attention to their age. We sent along with them a teacher trained in working with them, on a sort of team teaching basis with the regular classroom teacher. This worked so well that we expanded it to placing 2 or 3 selected children in each of several typical classrooms with special consideration for the teacher. We considered these pupils as requiring extra time and decreased the class size in rooms to which they were assigned. We learned through experience how to judge which children could succeed and at what level. We place less emphasis on age than we had expected we should. We found that age variation is not the problem it would seem to be.

I'm not claiming that every hearing impaired child can succeed in a typical classroom if given enough special attention in addition. But I am saying that many of them can—provided that they're given the chance and proper support. As I've indicated, that support includes an administration which will make it possible for the extra effort to be made. It should be policy that typical classroom experience is intended for every pupil, and that he will be excused from it only by admission of the staff that it's impossible for the child to profit from it. Today in many states we're providing for the first time, buildings constructed so that pupils confined to wheel chairs may attend. Is it any more unexpected that classrooms be sound-conditioned so that hearing aids will work properly without creating confusion for a pupil who has a hearing problem? Is it any less proper to provide amplification equipment for those with hearing loss than to provide large type books for the visually handicapped?

Of course, just making the extra effort possible, even requiring it to be made by the pupil, won't get the job done. Those who make up the staff must be dedicated to its accomplishment. Children with handicaps must be welcome in classrooms, must be accepted, and must be treated as regular members of society. Teachers, who are looking for the easy day, and the early arrival of pay day won't do. But many teachers adopt these attitudes because of a lack of challenge. Most people who are in the profession today are there because they're interested in the work—or at least they began that way. If the school attaches an importance to a given task or facet of education or procedure, the staff is likely to respond, given encouragement and time—and what greater encouragement than the thrill of knowing that a person, who can hear very little of what you're saying audibly, is able to keep up with your class and accomplish as much as any of his fellow class members.

We require no teacher to accept handicapped children, but we give special consideration to those who do, and we make it a little uncomfortable socially, I suppose, for those who don't accept the challenge. As far as possible we employ classroom teachers who are trained in the field of education of the hearing impaired and we give consultant help, set up team teaching situations, provide special equipment, etc. to encourage the staff all we can. But they're the ones who make it happen. And we try to give them the credit. The rest of us merely make it possible.

As we've talked with others about our effort and the things which have worked for us, we do observe that we have a few things going for us which all communities don't have and it's only fair to mention them so that they may be considered in setting up new regional programs. We are a small school system in a small town. We get and feel more recognition in our community than the same program would in a large city. We can, using small vehicles rather than typical school busses, transport pupils as far as 25 miles without imposing on them physically. That transportation program, by the way, is one of the biggest problems. The drivers become key people in the effort—as message carriers and observers of what's happening and what needs to happen.

We're centrally located in the area we serve. Our school buildings are built in a campus type arrangement so that pupils, teachers, equipment, busses, etc. can get from one classroom to another within minutes, even by walking. We have enough racial and ethnic integration to avoid any problems in that area.

If you don't have all these advantages your task is more difficult. It may seem even impossible—but don't accept it as such. You—like the typical student in the typical public school—probably aren't realizing your potential either.

Of course nothing—or very little—today, is free. Somebody has to pay the bill and you can't expect to accomplish much of anything extraordinary without finances. We're blessed with a state department of education which is supportive. Many is the time we've had to call the state office to ask consideration for a teacher who seemed to have great promise but who lacked some fine line detail in certification—or to ask for liberal interpretation of a rule of finance that would allow a new idea to be tried—and more often than not we've been pleased with the word received.

Money is one area where the term Special Education is worth playing up. It has an appeal to the taxpayer which is hard to refuse. And it's good sound economics, also. A handicapped person who can become a mainstream, self-supporting member of society is well worth an extra investment. Every facet of financial resources must be explored. The local taxpayer, state and federal funds, local civic groups, fund raising programs, etc. all have their place.

But we always consider the cost, when we want to try something new. We seldom give up because of cost but we consider it. There are ways of doing things—even if they're costly—if you believe they're essential. Sometimes that most expensive thing can be obtained free more easily than you can raise the money to pay for it, if you ask the right person to help you.

So, in summary, there seem to be 3 considerations if mainstreaming is to succeed. You must have a school policy structure and adminstration which will allow and promote it. You must have a staff which believes in it, and will work to see it accomplished, and you must have a financial base on which it operates in order to pay the bills.

Andrew R. Gantenbein

15

Components For Normalization Of Hearing Impaired Children in a Public School Setting

For the past decade, Berrien Springs has dealt with the many questions surrounding children with hearing losses in a public school setting. In order to generalize about where we are, it is felt that some explanation is in order regarding where we came from and where we think that we are going.

The regional concept of our program was effectuated in the school year 1963-1964. Growth in terms of children and staff has slowed down. We hope that growth in terms of services will never stop.

It was my feeling in the beginning that unless we gained an enrollment of at least fifty children, it would be difficult to build any kind of comprehensive program. We had only about fifteen children then. Those fifteen children represented at least four different educational thrusts, as we see it today. Separating those program components was and is still the most important aspect of our school even though we are serving nearly 130 youngsters at this time.

Now, it is not numbers that we seek, but specialized professional personnel who can deliver services. One of the biggest lessons that we learned was that a teacher of hearing impaired children can't do it all. Most states have recognized hearing loss as a reasonable way to return state monies for local-regional programs. Teachers who qualify with state departments of education as specialists with hearing impaired children however can't handle every problem that a child may have. State funding can work against normalization if it tends to lock hearing impaired children together for fundable membership units under certain labels.

PARENT PHILOSOPHY AND CITIZEN APPROVAL

Basic to all education is the general acceptance of an educational philosophy by parents and citizens. This has a very special meaning to us because we are dealing with questions which go beyond the usual generalizations about middle class aspirations. Language development and communication of society at large, dictates that whether we like it or not, children will be faced with the need to read, write, speak and receive the English language. No one would argue that George Bernard Shaw was wrong when he tried to convince the English speaking world that English spellings should be changed to a phonetic system. Yet we are faced with the reality that he and those who agreed with him since haven't been able to change that base, and we must eventually teach all children the English alphabet and spellings. The likelihood of any sizeable component of our society becoming bilingual is even more remote. The chances of any kind of language communicated on the hands being that second language is nonexistent.

People do not need research to tell them this. It is understood that there is no easy way out. Children with hearing losses either learn to communicate orally or miss critical opportunities for a lifetime. Most people want their child to have a shot at every possible opportunity and they expect the school to give their child the skills which will give their child an equitable choice and a chance.

COMPONENTS FOR NORMALIZATION OF HEARING IMPAIRED CHILDREN IN A PUBLIC SCHOOL SETTING

An Auditory-Oral Preschool

By terming the preschool "auditory-oral" we are simply stating some goals—the most important one being that there is a chance to stimulate a young child's residual hearing and take that child through the normal steps of hearing development. When this happens, a child who would not have normal voice quality, speech, and language at age 6, will have all those things and will be able to cope in a normal classroom setting starting in kindergarten. This one new possibility has revolutionized the whole field during the past decade. Our program follows an Acoupedic approach pioneered in this country by Doreen Pollack.

We have reorganized the traditional preschool structure, introduced nursery programs within our school with hearing children on a two to one ratio and generally effectuated a broader base of behavior models for young hearing impaired children. In addition the preschool staff has developed one of the first curriculum guides utilizing an auditory approach.

It has been said over and over that the three most important factors in infant programming today are early identification, early amplification and early training. We will never achieve any of these goals in our society until there are mandatory high risk registries in every state health department in the nation and that this data is made available to programs for hearing impaired children.

A Diagnostic and Treatment Preschool

By establishment of hearing goals, we also automatically recognize children who are not going through these steps developmentally. There are two general reasons why a child would not go through the normal auditory developmental stages. The first is because he began too late and the other is because he has additional problems. In other words, in the latter case, it may not be the peripheral hearing loss that is causing the trouble. People trained to deal with hearing loss have also been trained, in many cases, to see the whole world through damaged ears. Other specialists in education, psychology, and medicine must be involved in the school to help sort these problems. Just because a child with a hearing loss has trouble with the English language doesn't give us the right to say that methods designed to assist children with hearing loss are going to always be the answer. We know that some children with normal hearing have trouble with reading and talking.

A Parent Program

Parents of very young children like to feel the security of being in a program that knows what they are doing. They must have a "gut level" feeling that the program can do the job. They need to feel the enthusiasm, affection, and involvement of the professionals. You can articulate this in "how to" books and pamphlets, but what really counts is that you have secure professionals who know where they are going. There are several levels of parent involvement. Some parents can give more than others. There are leadership roles in Local, State, and National activities which only parents can fulfill.

A school must be secure within itself to deal with parents on all levels. We have found that placing cassette tape recorders in homes, allows use of voice recordings on cassette tapes for daily communication and for daily evaluation of parental work with children in the home.

A Hearing Management Program

Teachers and parents have never demonstrated that they could shoulder the total responsibility of hearing management. The concept that parents should be responsible for all the management of a hearing aid has never worked out well. Built into every program must be funds and systems which allow for school control, of most all the factors, because the school is the only party capable of delivering day by day services.

This is not to say state crippled children departments, otologists, audiologists, hearing aid dealers, parents and teachers still do not have autonomous roles. But most of the money and control had better come out of the program if the school ever hopes to deal successfully with the questions of appropriate consistancy of hearing. In Berrien Springs, we hire the Educational Audiologist who schedules children at the Constance Brown Hearing and Speech Center. He also takes the aids up for electro-acoustical analysis, and counsels parents and staff. The school provides all the batteries, earmolds, cords, and pays for services. He also does the paper work and leg work in dealing with third party agreements.

Many programs feel that by purchasing expensive auditory training equipment for use at school, this will in someway compensate for poor hearing management of individual hearing aids. Unfortunately it not only fails to compensate for sloppy management of individual aids, but fails to duplicate or improve most individual amplification systems. Before any school should go into duplicate amplification systems, it should learn how to monitor one system properly. There are some different hearing theories which suggest expensive complicated instrumentation. Enactment of any of these programs will take unique leadership management.

A Strong Multisensory School Program

Many of the move-ins and slow starters are perfectly capable of learning all forms of the English language through visual-oral methods. These children and others are mainstreamed through partial participation in the elementary levels leading to fuller participation in the regular classroom by junior high age. Areas of expertise must be maintained in speech development, language development, speechreading, auditory training, cognitive learning and reading. Strong supervisors and strong teachers must continually work together to build any kind of comprehensive program.

Even children with normal hearing become "visual-oral" when they go into first grade and learn how to read. It is not uncommon for children with good auditory function to fail in reading. It happens in the Public Schools all the time. This can happen to our hearing impaired children with good hearing function unless there are specific kinds of criteria that are available to teachers of hearing impaired children. Standarized achievement tests give good normative data but will not provide enough information for teachers of hearing impaired to make valid judgements in reading, language, and speech. The reading and language evaluations of Helen Woodward are ones which have been extremely enlightening to us.

A Diagnostic-Developmental Department

There are children who will be seriously brain damaged, emotionally impaired, mentally impaired or whatever. They need more, and in some instances, different help. We have an alternative program in Berrien Springs. It is not total communication. For many of these children, pure old manualism would be a difficult task, much less talking and signing at the same time. We use some of the methods of McGinnis perceptual motor abilities and linguistic techniques of our own. Children are evaluated within this small department and dealt with in somewhat of a clinical fashion. Three or four of these children are considered to be a class load. Teachers have full time aides and departmentalize for more intensive services. The most important aspect of this department is that we expect to continue to work with these children, with or without complete diagnosis. In other words we do not plan to give up.

A Behavioral Management Program

Behavioral problems are not just with children. Professionals and parents are continually modeling poor behavior as well as good behavior. A program needs to have it together within itself before teachers can manage children. Management techniques are readily available to everyone in education. Positive behaviorial attitudes are not related to methods. For some children, teaching hardly begins until there is inner control. These more serious cases must get special programming and services.

Goals

It is my belief that a school must have a living, visible record of expectations for every level and department. Revising the document each year, allows the staff to communicate about critical issues. Excess writing of lesson plans, behavioral objectives and other daily plans for the sake of paper accountability is a sham without a comprehensive plan. Supervisors have to be pretty insecure to demand more paper turned in to them by teachers than they can intelligently evaluate each week. Teachers and parents alike need basic educational end goals tied to a distinct school plan. From this plan, a consistant and continuous program may grow. This program must lead to programs and occupations past the school system. Figure 15-1 is an illustration of our own particular plan.

Administration and Supervision

There are many ways to effectuate interaction among general educators and teachers of hearing impaired children. But there is only one way that will

Fig. 15-1.

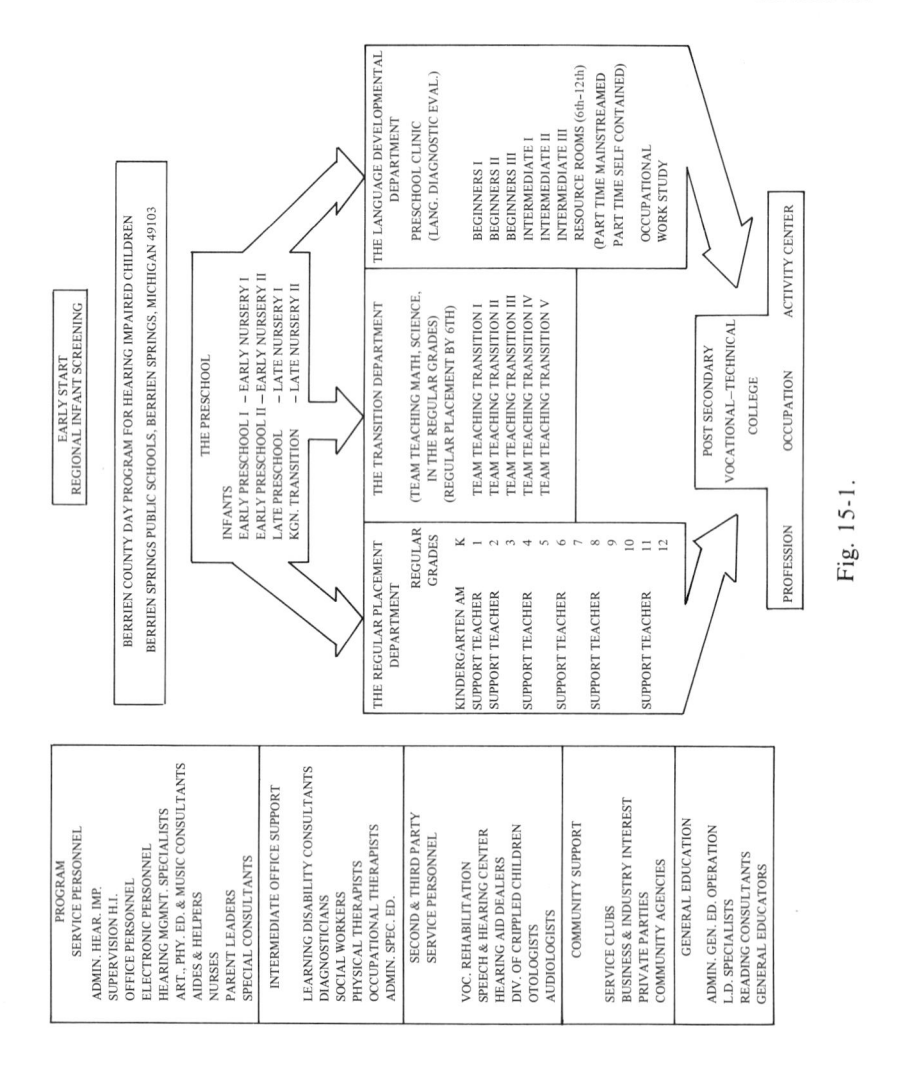

EARLY START
REGIONAL INFANT SCREENING

BERRIEN COUNTY DAY PROGRAM FOR HEARING IMPAIRED CHILDREN
BERRIEN SPRINGS PUBLIC SCHOOLS, BERRIEN SPRINGS, MICHIGAN 49103

THE PRESCHOOL
- INFANTS
- EARLY PRESCHOOL I – EARLY NURSERY I
- EARLY PRESCHOOL II – EARLY NURSERY II
- LATE PRESCHOOL – LATE NURSERY I
- KGN. TRANSITION – LATE NURSERY II

THE TRANSITION DEPARTMENT
(TEAM TEACHING MATH. SCIENCE, IN THE REGULAR GRADES)
(REGULAR PLACEMENT BY 6TH)
- TEAM TEACHING TRANSITION I
- TEAM TEACHING TRANSITION II
- TEAM TEACHING TRANSITION III
- TEAM TEACHING TRANSITION IV
- TEAM TEACHING TRANSITION V

THE LANGUAGE DEVELOPMENTAL DEPARTMENT
PRESCHOOL CLINIC
(LANG. DIAGNOSTIC EVAL.)
- BEGINNERS I
- BEGINNERS II
- BEGINNERS III
- INTERMEDIATE I
- INTERMEDIATE II
- INTERMEDIATE III
- RESOURCE ROOMS (6th-12th)
  (PART TIME MAINSTREAMED
  PART TIME SELF CONTAINED)
- OCCUPATIONAL WORK STUDY

THE REGULAR PLACEMENT DEPARTMENT
REGULAR GRADES
- KINDERGARTEN AM — K
- SUPPORT TEACHER — 1
- SUPPORT TEACHER — 2
- SUPPORT TEACHER — 3
- SUPPORT TEACHER — 4
- SUPPORT TEACHER — 5
- SUPPORT TEACHER — 6
- SUPPORT TEACHER — 7
- SUPPORT TEACHER — 8
- SUPPORT TEACHER — 9
- SUPPORT TEACHER — 10
- SUPPORT TEACHER — 11
- SUPPORT TEACHER — 12

POST SECONDARY
VOCATIONAL–TECHNICAL COLLEGE

PROFESSION   OCCUPATION   ACTIVITY CENTER

PROGRAM SERVICE PERSONNEL
- ADMIN. HEAR. IMP.
- SUPERVISION H.I.
- OFFICE PERSONNEL
- ELECTRONIC PERSONNEL
- HEARING MGMNT. SPECIALISTS
- ART., PHY. ED. & MUSIC CONSULTANTS
- AIDES & HELPERS
- NURSES
- PARENT LEADERS
- SPECIAL CONSULTANTS

INTERMEDIATE OFFICE SUPPORT
- LEARNING DISABILITY CONSULTANTS
- DIAGNOSTICIANS
- SOCIAL WORKERS
- PHYSICAL THERAPISTS
- OCCUPATIONAL THERAPISTS
- ADMIN. SPEC. ED.

SECOND & THIRD PARTY SERVICE PERSONNEL
- VOC. REHABILITATION
- SPEECH & HEARING CENTER
- HEARING AID DEALERS
- DIV. OF CRIPPLED CHILDREN
- OTOLOGISTS
- AUDIOLOGISTS

COMMUNITY SUPPORT
- SERVICE CLUBS
- BUSINESS & INDUSTRY INTEREST
- PRIVATE PARTIES
- COMMUNITY AGENCIES

GENERAL EDUCATION
- ADMIN. GEN. ED. OPERATION
- L.D. SPECIALISTS
- READING CONSULTANTS
- GENERAL EDUCATORS

offer any security to the parents and teachers. This is for the administrators, starting at the top, to want a quality school system for all children.

Local-regional programs must have knowledgeable support at state, regional, and local levels. If there was any one factor which could be picked out as the determinant for growth of Berrien Springs, it is that first class administrators in state, regional and local levels saw the need for a program and worked together to help establish it. It goes without saying that there would have been no program if our local superintendent, Lee Auble, our regional director of special education, Walter Wend, and our state consultant, Mary Blair, had not been able to work together for this purpose.

Within a program, a supervisor who knows programming and has taught hearing impaired children is needed. Teachers cannot exist in a vacuum. Unless there is a continual monitoring of performance and objectives, the higher level administration is powerless to effectuate good teaching. Some school systems tend to invent hopeless situations and then wonder why hearing impaired children never get very far.

Mainstreaming Agreements

Mainstreaming agreements, or lack of them, is one of the great problems of society today. The term "integration" suggests some of these problems. Unless there is a good school system for all children, it is folly to try to solve the problems of hearing impaired children in the typical classroom.

There are numerous ways that a program for hearing impaired children can support and profit from a typical school setting. There are some classes and departments that can get along perfectly well away from public school settings. The preschool for example, may run its own nursery program and not be attached to a public school building. It really doesn't matter. But most generally speaking children should have their classes in the same buildings where they participate in regular classes. Hearing impaired children should not be spread all over town. Teachers, who are dealing with similar problems need to be located in the same building and have intercoms to connect to a central supervisor. A program needs its own office and staff of professional, clerical, and electronic technicians. Teacher aides should be fundable. Many a program has grown, because aides and volunteers filled in until professionals could be hired.

One of the most frequently asked questions today is "Do you have any trouble getting regular classroom teachers to accept hearing impaired children?" My answer is that this really is unimportant. The most important question should be "What goes on in a given classroom of normal children?"—one that you want a hearing impaired child to attend. If, for example, a typical classroom third grade teacher has thirty children, two of which are in need of deep psychological therapy, ten of whom have learning disabilities, five of whom are neglected at home, fifteen of whom are poor readers, five of whom are bright and bored and so on, do you really think that this teacher is doing you a favor by taking a hearing impaired child? Where do you think she should file the paper telling her how to deal with the hearing impaired child in the regular classroom? The answer is, right next to the pamphlet on teaching the child with a learning disability, the rules and regulations dealing with the rights of mentally impaired, the "suggestions" for helping the child with a reading problem, the behavioral management form for intervening with the emotionally disturbed child and the court papers on the neglected child. Let's be frank about it. There are some regular classes where we do not want hearing impaired children. Teachers of hearing impaired children lose control of the academic and behavior situation when the child goes into regular classroom. Everything must be assumed to be OK, just like we assume everything is OK for our normally hearing children in a regular classroom. If these assumptions can't be safely made, then it is the program's responsibility to do better. Mainstreaming involves considerably more than dropping hearing impaired children in a regular classroom.

Team teaching arrangements, which put hearing impaired children in small groups with hearing children on homogeneous cognitive-levels, are most desirable. These arrangements allow for both teachers of regular classrooms and special ones to profit. Schools which keep hearing impaired children locked into self-contained fish bowl settings are setting up a destructive strategy for the hearing impaired child's own self-concept, not to mention the impossibility of "Little Red Schoolhouse" goals for group strategies.

There are many mainstream models which can cost very little and benefit all children. General educators are generally open to plans which broaden their experience and help all children, if this plan does not *add* to their problems. This rule of thumb can open many doors.

There are some models of teaming which may be used.

PLAN 1 Ability Group and Divide by Two: hearing and hearing impaired children go to two rooms, dividing total number in half for each teacher.

Subjects: Math, Science
Grades: 3-6
Advantage: Less children in both groups

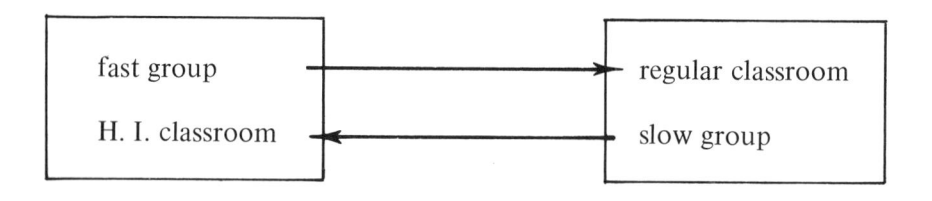

| fast group | → | regular classroom |
| H. I. classroom | ← | slow group |

PLAN 2 Reverse Mainstreaming: the two teachers agree on a smaller number of hearing children who will join H.I. children for a subject.

Subjects: Math, Science
Grades: Any
Advantage: Integration when you can't get it any other way

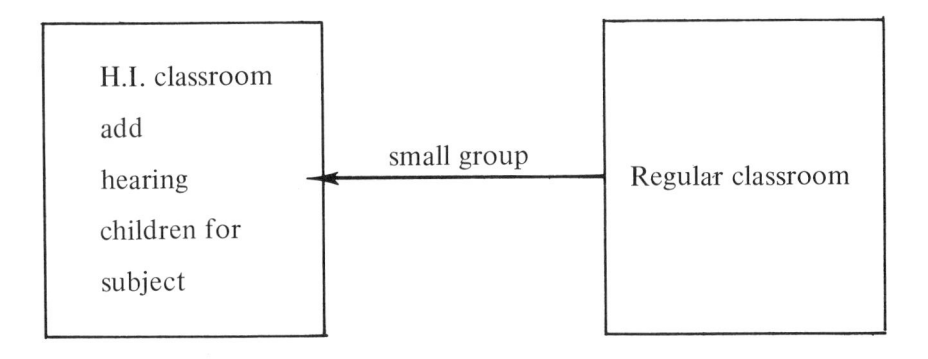

```
┌─────────────────┐                    ┌─────────────────┐
│ H.I. classroom  │                    │                 │
│ add             │   small group      │                 │
│ hearing         │◄───────────────    │ Regular classroom│
│ children for    │                    │                 │
│ subject         │                    │                 │
└─────────────────┘                    └─────────────────┘
```

PLAN 3   In the regular classroom, Ability Grouping: the teacher of hearing impaired children takes class to regular classroom where he or she teaches a small group of hearing and perhaps, hearing impaired children while the regular teacher has larger group of hearing and H. I. children.

          Subjects: Math, Science
          Grades: 3-6
          Advantage: Helps regular teacher by controlling a few different children

```
┌─────────────────┐                    ┌──────────────────────┐
│                 │                    │ Regular Classroom    │
│                 │                    │         ┌──────────┐ │
│ H.I. classroom  │───────────────────►│         │ small    │ │
│                 │                    │         │ group    │ │
│                 │                    │         │ lesson   │ │
│                 │                    │         └──────────┘ │
└─────────────────┘                    └──────────────────────┘
```

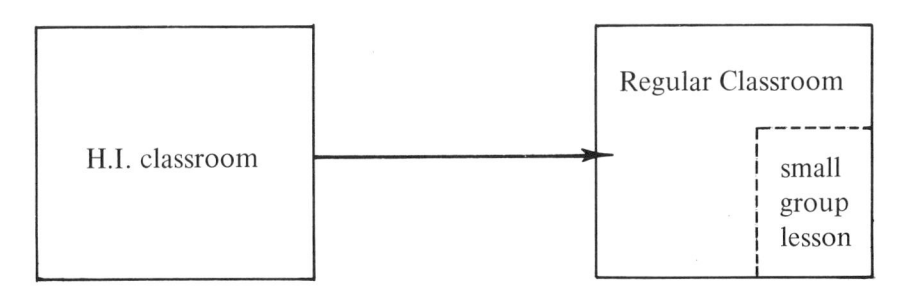

PLAN 4   Full Scale Team Teaching: entire three hour middle of the day block spent in Regular classroom. Teachers take different subjects or units and provide support for each other in materials and media.

Subjects: Math, Science, Specials (art, physical ed., music)
Grades: 3-6
Advantage: Gives H. I. child strong identification with hearing classroom, allows for beginning and ending of day to concentrate on speech, language, and reading in small groups

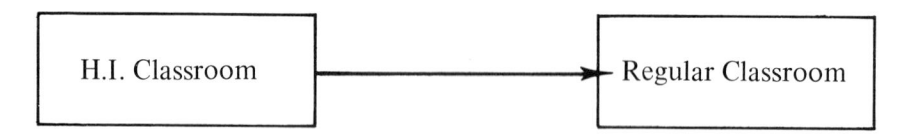

H.I. Classroom ⟶ Regular Classroom

PLAN 5 Modified Team Teaching: teacher picks out only one subject block schedules next to lunch and recess and specials (art, physical ed., music). Teams with regular teacher in her room.

Subjects: Math or Spelling
Grades: 1-3
Advantage: Early participation in grade classroom without need for strong academic skills; good identification with regular classroom and maximum time in self-contained class

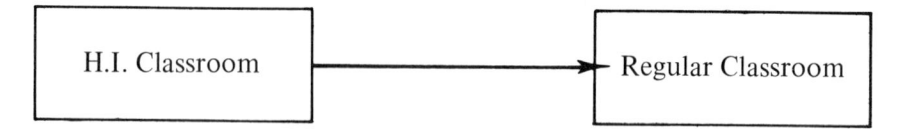

H.I. Classroom ⟶ Regular Classroom

SECTION IV

Exemplary Programs and Materials

Leo E. Connor

16

Deaf and Hearing Children at the Lexington School for the Deaf or— Mainstreaming the Special School

For the 1974-1975 school year of the Lexington School for the Deaf in New York City, there were 360 deaf students enrolled between 3 and 21 years of age, of whom 80 percent were day pupils. There were 43 normally hearing children enrolled full time in the classes with deaf children, and there were 29 deaf infants together with 15 hearing infants under 3 years of age. At the close of the school day, about 150 normally hearing children from the neighborhood utilize the Lexington School for the Deaf as a community center and join the Lexington deaf children of all ages for recreation, clubs, teams, and joint social activities. Each evening the Lexington Teen Center enrolls deaf and hearing teenagers between 14 and 19 years of age in a variety of social, recreational and cultural activities, while the Lexington Community Adult Education Center offers courses to hearing and deaf adults from age 18 and up. The evening education students include current and former Lexington deaf students, together with deaf and hearing parents, neighbors, staff and community persons in an adult learning program. During each school day, the Lexington School has over 75 normally hearing volunteers in its classrooms for a 3- to 6-hour period, along with its full-time 150 employees.

This is a summary of what is going on at the Lexington School, which includes deaf and hearing children. How did it start; why has the Lexington School for the Deaf been "turned on" to hearing children and where are we going? I hope that this chapter can answer some of the major questions frequently asked about our intense effort to mainstream the special school named Lexington.

BACKGROUND

In January 1968 the Lexington School for the Deaf moved from its cramped and inadequate inner city site to a larger, four-building campus outside of Manhattan, but still well within New York City. Our 7-acre campus is located in Queens, one of the five counties of New York City. Queens is three miles from downtown Manhattan and is a bedroom and industrial area of the city. It has slightly over 2 million people, which probably makes it the 6th or 7th largest city in the United States.

Planning for our expanded facilities was a five-year process, with parents, Trustees, governmental officials and staff involved in evaluations, concept, discussion, educational and social trends and fiscal considerations. The final statement in 1969 of Lexington's objectives will give you the flavor of what is called our 1970-1980 blueprint.

The guidelines adopted by the Lexington School to carry out its fundamental purpose are as follows.

1. The deaf child is a child with a communication problem who is to be educated as an integral part of the hearing world.
2. The Lexington School should provide the most progressive, modern educational program possible to continually improve its own endeavors and to provide the model from which deaf children everywhere might benefit.
3. The Lexington School must provide the highest possible level of personnel in this endeavor to improve, to achieve and to lead.
4. The earliest years of life are the optimum period for establishment of effective auditory-visual-speech skills and for maximum growth of the hearing impaired individual.
5. The Lexington School's resources should be utilized in the development of public awareness and a knowledgeable understanding of deaf persons.

Thus, the Lexington School for the Deaf started a ten-year period of endeavor to become a Center of Services for the Hearing Impaired. Its fundamental aim of having deaf and hearing infants, children, youths, and adults live together was not a futuristic one or one to take place after graduation. It was accepted as a commitment for the *now* period of deaf children's life and work. If deaf and hearing people were to be integrated into an easy and mutually helpful relationship, then it had to be accomplished at every stage of life and learning. We overtly rejected the concept that deaf children were to be educated separately, but we did not reject the basic reasons for requiring specialized teachers and services.

The Lexington School had begun, during the 1968-1969 period, to accept normally hearing children into its three- and four-year-old nursery classes. In 1970-1971 we added the five-year-old level to our deaf/hearing class groups, and in 1973-1974 we went up to the six-year old, first grade classes. Then, in 1974-1975, we enrolled normally hearing children in our seven- and eight-year-old deaf groups, thus providing a full day, mixed educational program at the six-, seven-, and eight-year-old levels to our half-day three- to five-year old classes.

In terms of our Community Center and Community Education programs, as well as our Volunteer activities, each of those is a full-fledged, serious endeavor to offer to deaf children and adults as much organized educational and social interactions as possible with hearing people. We believe that it is not sufficient to throw the burden of interaction onto deaf people and to allow them to "sink or swim" in this complex business of growing up in a hearing world where the vast majority of recreational, vocational, neighborhood, and cultural activities were created for and cater to the normally hearing individual.

The Lexington School believes and acts on the assumption that deaf children must learn to live with hearing people. This does not stop at the classroom door but attempts to show each deaf child that his entire school and his recreational environment should be filled with social and communicative interaction with hearing children and adults. It particularly seeks to prove to teenaged and adult deaf people that it has not abandoned them to their own resources. We are willing to offer a counterbalance to the usual deaf adult environment found in most cities or metropolitan areas of the United States as a continuation of our programs with deaf and hearing children. We are willing to face the complex difficulties of working with deaf teenagers, young deaf adults, and older deaf adults in a mixed, integrated, mainstreaming effort.

The Lexington School's Teen Center operates four nights a week, with a one-to-one or two-to-one ratio of hearing and deaf youth between 16 and 25 years of age. It has regular teams and group sports; it offers a snack bar and social area for conversation, table activities and dancing; it plans weekly excursions to cultural, athletic and artistic events; it involves its deaf and hearing young men and women in useful as well as interesting projects all the way from rebuilding a car motor, to poster making for school events, to organizing a party for old people or retarded children.

At one level of our adult educational program, the Lexington School operates a Community School. Starting with one night a week, it has recently spread to more evenings. Deaf and hearing persons from any section of the New York area are welcome to pay a $12.00 fee to take a semester course in any of the offered subjects. Currently, we have courses operating for almost one hundred deaf and hearing people in art, judo, folk-dancing, lipreading, guitar, stitchery, physical fitness, basic English, and crafts. At least 5 deaf and 5 hearing persons must enroll before we run one of these courses. The response has been good enough that we will probably double our enrollment and course offerings next year.

This Lexington Adult Education Program is in addition to the Deaf Adult Education Program which Lexington personnel organized at a New York community college in 1973. There, deaf interpreters are provided in any one of the 60 adult courses if four or more deaf persons enroll at the beginning of a semester. This college program was planned and initiated by the Lexington School, but we deliberately planned for an advisory group of deaf adults and college administrators who operate that program. Our hope is that both the smaller deaf adult program at the Lexington School and the larger adult program at LaGuardia Community College of the City University will be able to offer different objectives and opportunities to deaf and hearing people.

Lexington's Mainstream Program:

1. Over 100 profoundly deaf children transferred fulltime into regular school programs before age 15 since 1969.
2. Fifty percent of all deaf infants go into regular nurseries; twenty-five percent go out to regular classes by age 12.
3. Six nearby elementary and high schools provide us with partial mainstreaming.
4. High school vocational training is offered off campus in regular vocational and technical high schools or training programs.
5. Sixty percent of 12th grade graduates go on to post-secondary education.

OBJECTIVES AND RESULTS

The objectives of educating deaf and hearing children together must extend beyond the obvious ones of benefiting the deaf child. Before discussing the results of this program for the deaf, I'd like to cover two other aspects: the reactions by parents of hearing children and the kind of curricula that Lexington School advocates for deaf and hearing children.

Perhaps the most frequently asked question regarding the Lexington deaf/hearing educational program is, "Why would parents of hearing children send them to your school?" Such a question did not arise during the five years that hearing children attended our nursery classes for three- and four-year olds. It appeared only when hearing children were admitted to our kindergarten classes, and rose to a crescendo when they entered our first and second grades.

The answer lies in the evaluations and conclusions made by parents of the hearing children. They requested that the Lexington School not terminate their children at the end of nursery and then at the end of kindergarten and, a year later, at the end of first grade. Thus, the Lexington School was responding to parental requests, and we do not seek transfers of hearing children from other schools. Hearing children who had experienced a nursery and kindergarten program with deaf children were requested to continue in our school because of what the parents saw as benefits from our classes and as a comparison with what was available in nearby private and public schools.

Parents of hearing children have expressed clearly the value they placed on our education program. They appreciate the small classes (7 deaf and 7-8 hearing children per class), the motivated and effective teachers, the individualization of instruction, the stress on child development, as well as language and speech training and, finally, the type of curriculum and involvement permeating our school.

The curriculum approach utilized throughout the Lexington preschool and elementary departments is a child development, open classroom, project oriented, individualized program. It seeks to involve children wherever they are, to bring families into the learning process, to respond to functional and immediate concerns of children and their environment and it relies heavily upon innovative, knowledgeable faculty and volunteers who have an open approach to assistance, ideas and opportunities, and a stress upon useful language, reading, speech, and academic skills and experiences.

This nontraditional curriculum requires an active involvement of teacher and children in direct experiences which can be used to foster desired skills. The class atmosphere and relationships are personal and enthusiastic. Each child must succeed at his/her level of abilities or else the subsequent dislike for the learning process stops all educational and social progress.

Basically, then, it is the consumer (the deaf and hearing children) and the parents and the teachers who are causing the Lexington School's hearing/deaf program to succeed and to expand. As long as faculty members can plan for and create the classroom climate for deaf and hearing children's learning, then all of our parents will be supporters of this unique educational program. Actually, it is the Lexington School's parents of hearing children who are our best recruiters of new students. They talk to their neighbors and bring them in to visit and to participate so that as of today we have a "waiting list" of hearing children in the three- to five-year-old age range who want to enter our classes for the deaf. To complete the picture, you should know that this is not a free program since parents of hearing children must pay tuition and transportation charges at the same rate as they would in a New York City private school.

Teacher support is offered in a variety of ways. Teacher aides assist in each classroom where deaf and hearing children are enrolled. Consultants from nearby universities offer inservice supervision and course work so that teachers of the deaf feel confident regarding their skills and competancies for hearing children. Summer workshop and course work add to the teacher skills and abilities in any areas of educational development that needs strengthening.

Evaluations are a major aspect of the deaf/hearing program. Since the deaf/hearing program has developed over a six-year span, it has been looked at, resisted, discussed and experimented with incessantly. Parents and faculty have been the most critical and most supportive. For at least a one-year period, hearing children were not accepted into the first grade level (6-year olds) because no Lexington teacher was confident enough to try it out. Finally, when parents of hearing children and Lexington teachers agreed on a strong evaluation program, the experiment went ahead.

Formal evaluations of speech, language, reading, arithmetic, and social relationship are performed on an annual basis. All standardized achievement scores for the deaf children have improved significantly during the past two years, as compared to five- and six-year-old deaf groups of five years ago. While the increases are not large (about three months average), because of the small base, and while our number of children is not large and therefore not considered reliable, the standardized scores tend in the direction of betterment and therefore support our clinical convictions and parental/faculty opinions.

DISCUSSION

The Lexington School's main purpose in educating deaf and hearing children together is to mainstream the special school. We will continue to integrate or mainstream individual deaf children by transfers to regular schools. But we also have an explicit objective to insure that every deaf child must live and learn together with hearing children. This does not mean that all deaf children must leave a special school and attend a regular class. This does not mean that all deaf children must or can get by with itinerant teachers or resource rooms. We have seen too many young deaf children placed in ordinary nurseries and kindergarten classes before they have appropriate speech, language, auditory and speechreading skills. We will not accept the mainstreaming concept that every deaf child should be experimented with by "being placed in the least restrictive setting" until he fails. We do not believe that the lessons learned over the past 100 years in U.S. education about the values and achievements of special classes, special schools, and special teachers should be ignored.

The Lexington School considers itself a realistic but innovative school in that its aim is to be sure that all deaf and hearing people live and learn together. That means again that every deaf child in the Lexington School will be exposed to hearing children on a daily, continuous full time basis and that they must learn and live together for the entirety of their educational careers. We are saying that special schools can remain special but should be a part of the mainstream. We are proving that parents of hearing children will send their children to a special school if it's good enough. We are showing that teachers of the deaf are excellent teachers of normally hearing children and that whether judged by critical observers, standardized tests and/or clinical analysis that deaf and hearing children can be helped educationally in an open and project-oriented curriculum environment that also involves the recreational, social, and cultural aspects of their lives.

Audrey Simmons-Martin

17

The Central Institute For The Deaf Demonstration Home Program

Mandating education of handicapped children to be "a part of rather than apart from" society can open Pandora's Box. Recently, I had the pleasure only an old teacher can enjoy. I ran into a former student and his wife celebrating their 18th wedding anniversary. It was David, who at age eight, asked me where was Dr. Max Goldstein's field? He had read Dr. Max's obituary and it mentioned that Dr. Goldstein was *outstanding* in his field.

David and his wife Barbara represent true mainstreaming to me. As parents of three sons, they participate in their community actively. Tolerating my probing, they answered questions regarding their life style. David is a computer programmer who works on nuclear war heads. He leads the team which plans, supervises and evaluates the underground nuclear explosions in Nevada. Barbara, who is also profoundly deaf, is a housewife whose hobby is fine arts.

Asked about their social set, they replied that their friends were parents of their sons' friends, neighbors in their subdivision, members of their church and business associates. Only of deaf people would anyone ask the next question but I couldn't resist. David and Barbara's prompt response was—yes, they have deaf friends too, but they choose friends because they like them, not because of their hearing status.

David and Barbara both received their elementary education at Central Institute for the Deaf but went on to secondary schools for the hearing in their own communities. Finishing there, they each went to their State Universities where they received their degrees.

Permit me to take this opportunity to relate another anecdote from my experience. Melinda, also profoundly deaf, began in the Parent-Infant

Program at the age of 17 months and mainstreamed at the third grade level. Recently, I received two news articles about her from the Collinsville, Illinois, newspaper. One began, "Five North Junior High School students have been cited for outstanding achievement," and it continued, "Altogether 21 maintained straight A averages during the year." Both of those numbers included Melinda.

The second article started with—"Out of 149 bowlers, Melinda, ıry and Jim represented Camelot Bowl in State competition bowl play-offs in DeKalb, Illinois. Melinda, with a 124 average bowled in the junior division competing with over 120 at the state level."

Now let me tell you about Matt who was referred to us at age six years, 10 months. He was said to have learning problems. From a clinical setting he had been placed in public school. Beginning with kindergarten he continued to fail each year. His language was quite immature. This was demonstrated by a recorded language sample. As we worked with him, we came to see that despite the fact that he wore a hearing aid, his residual hearing had not been trained. For Matt, public school integration meant severe segregation. It was four years before he was enabled to hold his own in his neighborhood school and function "as a part of rather than apart from" the mainstream.

Dan was another moderately hearing impaired child failing in the mainstream. At seven years of age, when he was referred to us, he was using limited jargon, that is, connected syllables spoken with sentence-like patterning, but with few intelligible words interspersed ("boy," "girl," "man," "happy," "playin' "). It was three years before we felt that he could compete with his hearing peers. I am happy to report that he not only competes now but excels. Dan now attends high school in his home town.

It is my fear that *successful* mainstreaming is only a dream if the requests I receive for information and help are any indication of the problems that it can create. The following is but one letter indicating a predicament that is repeatedly reported.

Washington School
October 23, 1974

Dear Sir:

I am a teacher of primary special education. Recently a ten-year-old deaf girl was placed in my class. I am not trained to work with the deaf, however I do know the hand alphabet.

I am wondering if you would have any literature which would help me in teaching this little girl. She is not retarded but is very bright, however this is the first time she has attended public school.

CID Demonstration Home Program

I would appreciate your prompt attention to this matter. I need any literature that might be helpful.

Thank you very much.

Sincerely,

Mrs. A   P

At Central Institute for the Deaf we believe that all children should be mainstreamed as soon as possible but we do not recommend mainstreaming when it will only lead to the cruelest kind of segregation. Cases need to be reviewed frequently in order to ascertain what placement is best. The factors we consider are

Linguistic development
Communication skills
Verbal intelligence
Academic skills
Social and emotional maturity

Linguistic Development

The disparity between the child's chronological age and his linguistic age should not exceed one year. This requires evaluation of sentence structure and vocabulary as well as the appreciation of the nuances of speech.

Communication Skills

We must evaluate the child's ability to follow not only the teacher but peers as well. Consider the difficulties communicating in a classroom with hearing children. Listening with hearing aids imposes problems due to the noise level. Watson reported kindergarten and primary classes to have 69 dB of noise and the constant ambient noise was 55 dB. Classrooms have reverberant walls, floors and windows. Reverberation time is 1 to 3 seconds in most classes.

What happens when the speaker is 9 to 10 feet from the child's microphone? What is the signal-to-noise ratio?

Because listening in a classroom of children is difficult, the hearing impaired child must also lipread. Hence he must be free to view the speech of whoever is speaking. It is difficult to have a single favorable position since children move around to centers scattered about the room. But his classmates have as much to give the hearing impaired child as does his teacher. How often does the teacher ask questions for which the hearing impaired child will miss the answers. If the respondent is behind him, he will miss the answer and will not be able to evaluate his own ideas.

Skill in communication also means producing sophisticated speech that is intelligible. The hearing impaired child's speech must be understood by both teacher and classmates. Speech which is understandable for people used to deaf speech may not be so intelligible to the lay listener.

Verbal Intelligence

Verbal intelligence is a factor affecting mainstreaming because of the pressure exerted on a child if the operating cognitive level of the classroom is above his ability level. The concept and vocabulary load of today's kindergartens reflect the impact of cognitive developers and thus the curriculum load is heavy even in the early years.

Academic Skills

Before a child is accepted into the mainstream, he must be able to handle the curriculum of the receiving school. He needs to be able to acquire academic skills that his classmates are accomplishing. Failure is detrimental to his self-image. He knows full well when he is only promoted on a social or chronological basis.

Unlike the often discussed reading plateau, it has been demonstrated that reading scores of properly placed deaf children increase with training (Lane and Baker, 1974). Since reading is the basis for academic success, failure in this direction certainly leads to frustration.

Social and Emotional Maturity

The immature child finds it difficult to mainstream, whereas the socially adaptable may make good mainstream material. But isn't this also true of hearing children?

It is our opinion at Central Institute for the Deaf, that it is better to be cautious than overly optimistic. It is better to start the child in a program when we know he can succeed and gain confidence, not when he will fail and withdraw in defeat.

While we do not feel that mainstreaming is the route for all hearing impaired children, we certainly strive for that placement as soon as the child is ready. The thrust of our counseling with parents is directed toward their knowing their own child and helping them set realistic goals with him in mind. It is they, after all, who have the responsibility of managing their child. It is they, who must be knowledgeable about the needs of their child in order to carry out their responsibility.

However, parent involvement requires more than just transmission of information. The Parent-Infant Program aims toward increasing parents' understanding of their children *and* developing competence in dealing with them.

The greatest need of a hearing impaired child is a parent who can understand his problem, adjust to it, and do something constructive about it. The process, what parents do, how they do it, how much they do and how persistent they are in doing it is important.

A substantial number of young *hearing* children seem to reach age six very poorly prepared for future learning experiences, including formal education. Such being the case, how can we expect the situation with the hearing *impaired* child to be different?

White and his colleagues have systematically and intensively observed how some families manage to do an unusually *good* job with their young children and have looked to ways in which the experiences of the first six years of life can be used to encourage maximal development of human competence. They concluded that under the variety of early rearing conditions prevalent in modern American homes, divergence with respect to the development of educability and overall competence first becomes manifest sometime during the second year of life and becomes quite substantial, in many cases by three years of age (White and Watts, 1972).

As a matter of fact, he boldly states that the mother's direct and indirect actions with regard to her one- to three-year-old child are the most powerful formative factors in the development of a preschool child. He further suggests that if a mother does a fine job in the preschool years, subsequent educators will find their chances for effectiveness maximized. Much of the basic quality of the entire life of an individual is determined by the mother's action during those first two years.

Superior mothers are designers who make their home a safe place in which the children can play. They provide a rich, but not necessarily expensive variety of toys and household objects and they allow the children to roam all over the living area.

These activities include perceptual training through all sense modalities. How important it is for the hearing impaired child to learn the sounds these objects produce and how vision and hearing supplement each other. Needless to say, this learning cannot take place without early amplification.

On the other hand, White found that the less effective mothers "protect" their hearing children and possessions by ruling a large number of places out of bounds. They restrict the child's instinct to explore. Restrictions of playpens, gates and high chairs over long periods of time suppress a child's curiosity severely and impede cognitive development.

Unfortunately, in our Parent-Infant Program we are not seeing enough children before they reach the age of two. Our reported tabulation for the 62 children seen in our Parent-Infant Program in the 1973-1974 school year showed only 20 children enrolled in the age range of birth to 18 months, whereas 28 were 18 to 36 months and 14 over 36 months of age.

To be an effective parent does not mean hovering over a child for most of the hours in the day. What effective parents seem to do, often without knowing exactly why, is to perform excellently the functions of designer, consultant and authority. They design a physical world, mainly in the home, that is suited to nurturing the curiosity of the one to three-year-old. Furthermore, mother is generally permissive and indulgent. However, she is not a "namby pamby." Her child is not allowed to drift aimlessly but rather knows the limits at all times. Nevertheless, the child is encouraged in the vast majority of his explorations.

When the child confronts an interesting or difficult situation, he often turns to his mother for help and mother responds. Importantly, these interchanges are focused on the *child's* interest of the moment rather than the mother's interest or need. The talk, which is considerable, is at a level the child can handle. She talks about the child's object, his clothes his toys, his concerns, his interest. She *matches* her language to *his* thoughts. She talks in sentences appropriate to his intake level and she uses similar language day in and day out.

Why not adapt activities of the effective parent in child-rearing to the needs of the hearing impaired child rather than develop a frustrated, anxious, insecure parent? Why not have the parent of the hearing impaired infant do the same thing while getting down to the child's eye level and within his acoustic range? That is what we attempt to do in the Parent-Infant Program. We try to lead parents to being superior parents and adapt the patterns used by the superior parent who is effective with her hearing child.

The very young hearing impaired child initiates every bit as many of his own activities as the hearing child. For him these are the vast majority of his activities. Like the hearing child he concentrates on ego-centered *nonsocial* more than *social* interchanges. It is to these activities that parents must match meaningful language. It is the language that is applied to the *child's* thought that takes on meaning.

This concept of parenting is relatively new to the literature and therefore a difficult one for many young people to apply. It is understandably frightening to think that it is they, the parents, who have the greatest impact upon the development of their child. Add to that responsibility the task of coming to grips with hearing impairment and all its implications. The total impact can be overwhelming.

For this reason parents need opportunities to ventilate and interact with others confronting similar problems. For this reason we provide group sessions in addition to the weekly one hour individualized sessions. In the groups we try to apply group dynamics. There, we hope we ease some of the burden.

If the performance of mothers during these early years is extremely important, then educators need to show more concern for this problem. If this behavior is important for parents of the hearing child, we can certainly generalize that it is even more urgent for parents of the hearing impaired.

Pity the parent who is confronted with conflicting philosophies! "Teach him the unisensory way! No, lipreading is the route to go! Oh, by all means use total communication! No, instead use Ameslan! Oh, no, use fingerspelling! No, use Cued Speech!" No wonder parents write as this one did for *The Deaf American* in 1972

> . . ."When will it ever end? Why can't professionals understand that parents of deaf children cannot be constantly torn apart by a methods battle? Why must we and our deaf children be constantly in the middle of the "big experiment"?
>
> . . .Most parents are not linguists, nor do they want to be. Few understand what you are talking about when you say "sign in concepts." They only want to have their deaf child become as much a part of their world as possible with the least possible adjustment demanded on the part of other members of the family.
>
> . . .I have come to the conclusion that no one understands what it is like to be the parent of a deaf child except another parent of a deaf child. Professionals that I thought understood the confusing role of parents are apparently not really tuned in. I am tired of having these people blame parents for all of the ills in education and psychological adjustment of their deaf children.
>
> Many deaf adults find it difficult to understand hearing parents of deaf children because they have never walked in our shoes. Some take their frustration against their non-communicating parents out on the new generation of parents who are doing everything within their power to communicate with their deaf children. I do not understand professionals and deaf adults who are so tuned out that they won't try to understand the needs of parents.
>
> My heart aches for mothers and fathers of deaf children who are being caught up in yet another methods battle. I could cry—and I do."

The dynamics of the family can be altered by the siblings; and also those outside of the core family, such as grandparents and sitters. Our Parent-Infant Program includes as many individuals in the child's environment as can attend. The program offers some practical guidelines, including knowledge of how a child's language and his mind develop, and knowledge of hearing and the implications of a hearing loss. Parents need to be alert to the conditions which will give the child the greatest advantage in receiving the available auditory signals. They also need to know the value of stimulation and language input.

We believe that it is critical that we view each family as unique. We do not believe that frightened and grieving parents should be offered stereotyped solutions or be pressed for awesome decisions. At a time when they have not yet begun to come to terms with the diagnosis, or to understand child-rearing habits, parents should not be urged to make a decision that will affect the permanent life style of their child. Rather, we believe they should be given support and help to know their child as an individual. Some parents begin sooner than others to accept the situation and to mobilize themselves to help the child.

The very uniqueness of families presents difficulties in the Parent-Infant Program. Some parents handle principles regarding their child's management quite well and these make application easily. Other parents seek and need specifics. They are the ones who want a "cookbook" telling steps one, two and three. For these parents, application and consistency are most difficult.

Some parents read and believe everything simply because it is in print. Others don't need to read at all to be good parents. Often parents find that great help comes from other families who have had similar experiences. For some, the generalization of the discussion to their own problems is only achieved by patient direction by the teacher-counselor.

Parents tend to be selective listeners and some don't listen at all. It is not uncommon to hear a parent reply after being told the same thing by teacher-counselor, nursery teacher, classroom teacher and principal:

> No one told me that before.
> I never heard that.
> Why didn't someone tell me?
> Oh, it's good to hear that at last.

That same parent very likely will ask the same questions for several years to come and will make similar replies for all those years. Aggressive attempts must be made to encourage questioning and to work on the basis of honest communication. By all means, however, respect the psychological defenses, including denial, which might be employed by parents.

Two cases will serve to illustrate longitudinally the changes in parenting which enhance the development of hearing impaired children.

CID Demonstration Home Program

The first child is a hard of hearing boy who is now mainstreaming. It is very significant that in spite of his moderate to severe hearing loss, at three years and three months of age, he was not talking. He had a few vocalizations but not intelligible speech. His mother had the makings of an efficient mother but was so overwhelmed by the handicap, the task, and resentment, that she seemed to extinguish any good that might occur. Obviously if this child had continued in the situation as originally engineered by his mother, his gains in linguistic and auditory ability would not have been accelerated.

At first, his mother expressed little if any pleasure in working with Greg. She appeared cross and impatient. She restricted Greg's attempts to explore and create; her attention was to the task and not to Greg.

Within four months, his mother was laughing with Greg and working *with* him. She used the activity *he* initiated to provide expanded language input. Greg responded to the change in mother's behavior toward him, so that both mother and son reinforced each other's positive efforts.

After another seven months, the mother was comfortable in constructing interactive situations herself. There was warmth in her voice and substance in her words. Accordingly, Greg progressed from the silence of the initial session to the meaningful production of sentences after one year. At six years of age, Greg entered the first grade of his local school for hearing children.

The next case is a longitudinal study of a profoundly deaf child whose parents needed help in designing their child's activities. She is presently receiving an appropriate education in a school for the deaf.

Sarah's parents began in the Parent-Infant Program when Sarah was 17 months old. Her mother's initial focus was on getting the *task* accomplished; for example, at block play, mother's language was: "Here's a square, put it in the hole. Here's a rectangle. Put it in the hole. Here's a trapezoid. Put it in the hole." She could not see that Sarah preferred to *shake* the container.

After five months, her mother learned how to adapt her language to the input level that a toddler could handle. She taught concepts through language: "Open the box." "Open the door." "Open the refrigerator."

It was not until several months later that Sarah's mother learned to match her input to *Sarah's* interests and to modify her focus according to *Sarah's* actions. And, she was comfortable doing this. She smiled at Sarah and the child no longer needed to stamp or grab or cry.

Soon after, Sarah demonstrated a growth spurt in communication skills. When her mother tuned in to Sarah's gestures, Sarah readily imitated her mother's language translation. Her vocalizations, which were reinforced, increased in frequency. She watched her mother's face and, at first, understood many words in combination with a situation; later she responded to the words alone.

When she was three years old, Sarah began group and individual work with a teacher of the deaf. Because of her home training in being receptive to communication, she readily acquired an expressive vocabulary and could recognize and produce sentence models of experience-based language.

In summary, I would like to make two points.

1. Before recommending mainstreaming you must critically and realistically evaluate the child's ability in language, communication, verbal intelligence, academic skills and social and emotional maturity.
2. Besides education of the child the best preparation for mainstreaming is early parent education.

BIBLIOGRAPHY

Lane HS, Baker D: Achievement of the deaf: Another look. Volta Rev 76; 489-499, 1974

Rhodes MJ: From a parent's point of view. The Deaf American. p. 20, 1972

White B, Watts J: Major Influences on the Development of a Young Child. Englewood Cliffs, NJ, Prentice-Hall, 1972

Mark Ross

18

Model Educational Cascade for Hearing Impaired Children

One of the main reasons I had left my university teaching position three years ago to assume a directorship of a school for the deaf was to try to accomplish just what the title of this chapter states and that is to develop a workable educational cascade for hearing impaired children. In the years I taught clinical and rehabilitative audiology, served as consultant to a number of programs, and directed or assisted in the operations of speech and hearing clinics, one constant frustration was always apparent: we could never accomplish what we knew could be done, because we never had more than a piece of the action. We could, and did, develop programs that existing schools were not interested in—such as parent-infant programs, but on reaching the magic age of three or so, the children were transferred to someone else's care. We were able to test children's hearing, recommend and inspect their hearing aids, try to help the parents through all their anxieties and uncertainties, but in truth our effectiveness was limited because we could see the children only once or sometimes twice a year. For all we knew—and sometimes to our consternation we did find out—all our efforts could be voided because of something that happened two minutes after the child left the clinic.

Many experiences like this have convinced me that the usual method of delivering educational services to hearing impaired children had to be drastically overhauled to be truly effective. For years, it seems, the different people engaged in providing services for hearing impaired children have battled over the ascendency of their personal view, with the parents and children often bewildered innocent spectators on the sidelines. Often, each of the professions involved, have ignored, rejected, or simply been unaware of, the possible contributions of other professions. Physicians have not been sensitive to the nonmedical implications of a hearing loss; Audiologists and Speech Pathologists were so busy battling with teachers, via incomprehensible reports, that they frequently overlooked the rest of the educational process; and teachers have traditionally tried to be and do everything for the children, from acting as surrogate parents to psycho-social counselor, but meanwhile being unfamiliar with developments in such areas as audiology and psycholinguistics which required the input of other professionals besides themselves. The only thing, it sometimes seemed that these diverse professions could agree on, was in the adversary relationship they had developed with parents, whose natural anxieties regarding their children seemed to be simply exacerbated by the professionals who, while honestly trying to help the children, too often viewed other professionals and parents as impediments.

It's a harsh picture I've just drawn, and in truth, I think unduly harsh on the individuals concerned. Rarely have I ever met a professional working directly or indirectly with hearing impaired children who was not truly dedicated and committed to their work and the children. The very intensity of their complaints about other professionals and parents testify to their emotional investment in their responsibilities. As I examine the situation, it seems that we have all been caught in a systems' trap; we have been trying to exercise our responsibilities within educational models which are themselves prime generators of the conflicts we deplore. Our problems, and the lack of coherent, organized, and superior educational services, are predictable from the systems under which we usually operate. Our failure is preordained.

I felt three years ago that there had to be a better way. Here and there around the country, one could see attempts and elements of programs in which many of the pieces were being fitted together. We are trying, at the Willie Ross School, to fit more of the pieces into place, though we certainly have a ways to go and no certainty of success. We have now, however, in my judgment, the skeleton of a workable plan, one that works for us with the population base we have and the educational structure in the state. One important fact should be kept in mind, however, throughout this chapter, and that is the difference between our intentions and our performance. We all have good intentions, and if we were to be rated on this aspect alone, we'd all score 100 percent. It is what we actually do that is most important. How well, in other words, do our children achieve, and can we attribute possible superior achievement to the educational model we are using? To me our model has very attractive face validity; we shall eventually see, as we examine the data we are continually collecting, if our actual results are in accord with our intentions.

We are a small day school but we offer a number of alternative programs to meet the specific psycho-social and educational needs of children in the Greater Springfield area. At the present time, there are 10 children enrolled in the parent-infant program, 32 children in our itinerant program, and 60

Model Educational Cascade for Hearing Impaired Children

children who are enrolled in one of our full-time programs. All of our children are under 11 years of age, since the school's beginning can be traced to the Rubella epidemic of 1964-1965. One primary educational focus of the school is the fostering of natural speech and language development through an auditory approach, with, however, other options for children who are unable to make their maximum progress with this method. One primary goal of the school is to mainstream as many children as possible, through a carefully developed sequential series of programs, using both tests and observational criteria to evaluate readiness to progress to a next higher level. Again, as will be made clear, we have other options besides full mainstreaming for some of the children. Figure 18-1 presents an overview of the school's structure.

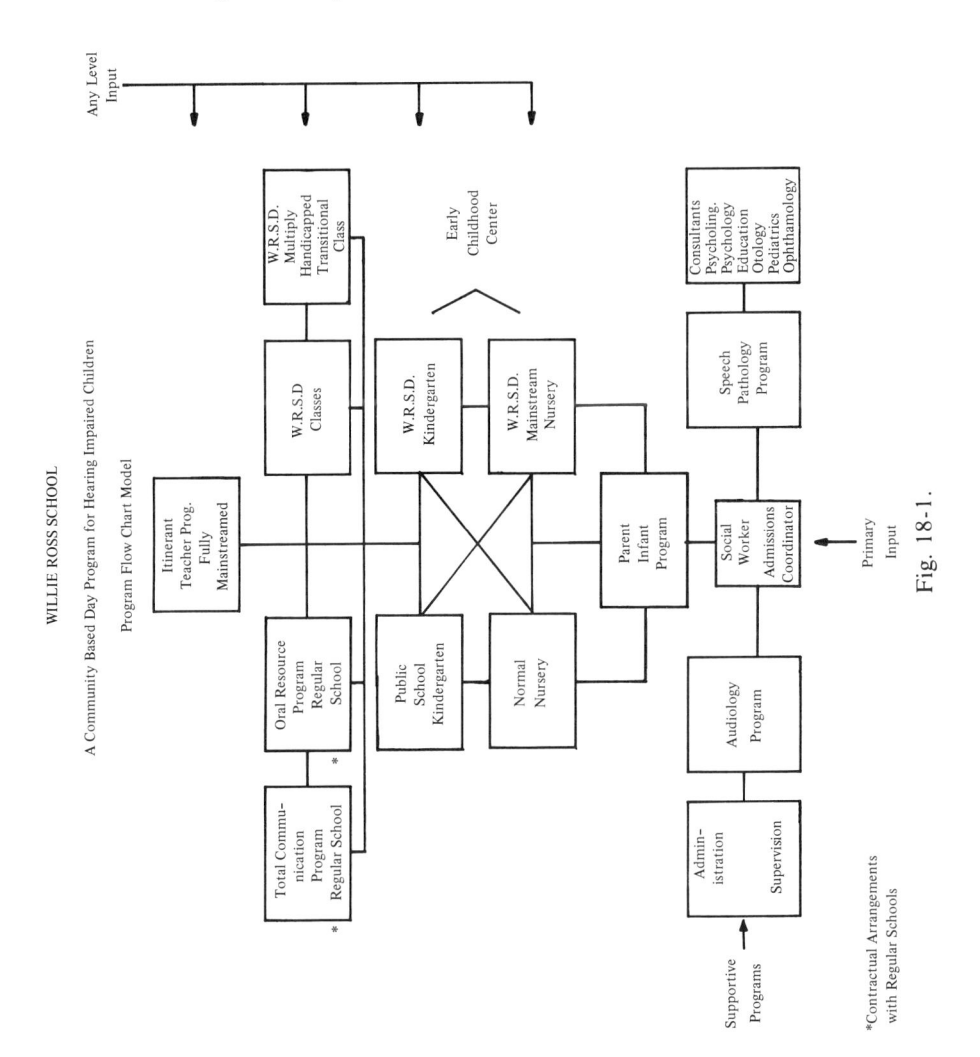

Fig. 18-1.

Let's begin by considering the supportive services. It's my contention that hearing impaired children require even more supportive services than normal hearing children. Unfortunately, they usually get less. I don't think any school or program for hearing impaired children is complete or can be effective without a strong audiology service. Testing hearing is one of the least, though indispensable, functions they serve. They are continually evaluating hearing aids and auditory trainers, through listening and electroacoustic techniques, and modifying their characteristics when necessary. One cannot make the maximum use of residual hearing without trained professionals on the spot working full time for this goal. We take our own ear impressions and make some of our own earmolds. We have a large number of loaner hearing aids which we use frequently. Visits to the classrooms are made on a very frequent basis and teacher or parent referrals are handled expeditiously. In our school, we presently have three full-time audiologists, one of whom only works with the school population. Another coordinates the audiology program and evaluates out-patients, and the third manages the parent-infant program. We are attempting to adhere to the proposed "guidelines for audiology programs in educational settings" developed by the Joint Committee on Audiology and Education of the Deaf, of which I am co-chairman.

Our audiology services include visits by our otology consultant, who comes to examine the children three or four times a year. If this seems like a lot, the results of his examinations indicate the necessity. The first time he evaluated all of our children, over 50 percent of them had suspected conductive problems in addition to their basic sensorineural hearing loss. The usual observations were impacted wax, fluid in the ears, retracted eardrums, enlarged tonsils and adenoids, and the like. In his most recent visits, we find that fewer than 10 percent of the children require otological care, and we attribute this to the regular examinations and treatment received by the children. We supplement the physician's examination with tympanometry and stapedial reflex measures; often, it is the results of these tests which suggest the need for the otological examination.

Another one of our supportive services is the speech pathology program. There are four full-time speech pathologists on our staff, one of whom works full-time in our mainstream nursery program, of which more later. Each child in our full-time program receives individual therapy at least three times per week. Therapy goals are selected with the cooperation of the classroom teacher, who reinforces and supplements the individual therapy objectives. Periodic conferences are held between the classroom teachers and the speech pathologists, in which the child's current status is discussed and new objectives are formulated. Each child is administered, at least once a year, a complete speech and language evaluation, using some standardized tests and one speech test we are currently developing. Parent involvement is solicited with all of the children and, for some children, a home therapy program is devel-

Model Educational Cascade for Hearing Impaired Children

oped. We also have a working relationship with several of the nearby universities, and graduate students in Speech Pathology and Audiology receive practicum experience here, supervised by the Coordinator in Speech Pathology (and by the Audiology Coordinator for Audiology students).

Social services are the responsibility of an MSW social worker, who coordinates all admissions procedures, agency contacts, and arranges or conducts individual and group counseling with parents. Teachers consult and refer social and psychological problems to her. The social worker is also heavily involved in the parent-infant program, working very closely with the other professionals involved with this program. Our experience with the social worker's contribution has been very positive; we have learned that a vacuum existed for needed services which we were not truly aware of.

Other supportive services include a psychological examiner, who tests the children routinely and on referral, an ophthalmological consultant, who screens all the failures in our visual screening program, and, as needed, consultants in psycholinguistics and general education. All supportive services are completely integrated with the education program and are components of the total services we provide each child.

Our educational efforts begin when we first detect the hearing impaired child and not at some arbitrary age. Hopefully, the child is no older than one year of age when he is enrolled in our parent-infant program. Children are placed in this program when it is determined that they have a permanent hearing loss. Usually, a number of visits are required before this determination can be made. After medical clearance, hearing aids are fitted to the child—either binaural body or binaural ear-level aids—and the parents enter into weekly informational and counseling sessions. Home visits are made biweekly with office visits by the parents and the child on alternate weeks. The parents are given demonstrations and instructions in the exploitation of the home environment for maximum speech and language development. The first priority is to assist the family in working through their feelings about having a handicapped child. This is a crucial step on which depends the success of much of our later efforts with the parents and the child. We emphasize the parental role because, for the young child, the parents are his first and most important teachers and his home is his first and most significant school. We are convinced, and our conviction is supported by many national authorities, that the traditionally poor performance of many hearing impaired children rests in large part on the absence or the ineffectiveness of early intervention programs. The first three years of life are the most crucial in terms of speech and language development. Unfortunately, it is only relatively recent that programs for three years olds have become widespread, much less for children less than three years of age.

When a child reaches three years of age, he can be enrolled in our own nursery or a normal nursery, and followed by one of our itinerant teachers.

This decision, as other educational decisions of the school, is made by our own evaluation team, who use both objective test results and subjective impressions to make their recommendations. Generally a child is recommended for normal nursery school when he has demonstrated the capability of learning through an auditory-oral mode and when his communication skills are sufficiently developed to permit some meaningful communication with normal hearing children. Usually, this means the child should be at the two word stage in language development.

Our nursery is organized on a mainstream basis with ten normal hearing children and approximately six hearing impaired children in each nursery class. The class is staffed by a regular nursery school teacher, a teacher's aide, and a speech pathologist knowledgeable in audiology, psycholinguistics, and child development (we have also used teachers of the hearing impaired in this position). Each hearing impaired child receives individual tutoring each day; additionally the parents of the hearing impaired children (usually the mother) visits and consults with the speech pathologist each week. Our goal is to stimulate the growth of speech and language via an enriched and maturationally appropriate language input, tied to ongoing and relevant experiences. We have found, as a bonus, that the behavioral models supplied by the normal hearing children have resulted in a substantial improvement in the socialization of the hearing impaired children.

From the nursery, there are again two possible alternatives for the children. In one, the child is moved to our auditory-oral kindergarten, conducted in our own facility. The children in this kindergarten receive an intensive preparation in first grade academic readiness skills, still emphasizing a natural language development approach. Specific remediation in pre-academic skills is given when needed. For this class, we are sometimes able to have them accommodated a half day in a regular kindergarten (accompanied by one of our aides) and sometimes not, depending on the available space in a nearby public school. The key to the child's readiness for the next mainstream step is the child's ability to communicate orally, although social and cognitive status and performance on standardized tests of speech and language are also considered. His performance on these latter measures should be no more than two years behind his normal hearing age peers; beyond this, he cannot be considered a candidate for a full mainstreaming program, and would instead be transferred to our resource rooms located in public schools.

The second kindergarten alternative uses a total communication approach. Children for whom our evaluation team considers not appropriate for a primary auditory-oral approach are transferred to this class, which is physically located in a nearby school in which we rent rooms. These children are scheduled for individual speech and language therapy by one of our speech pathologists on the same basis as the children in our other classes. A natural language Seeing Essential English (SEE) sign and finger spelling system is utilized. The goal is to develop language competency through this method, which precisely follows English syntax and generally follows English morphology, and then to use this competency for increased educational achievement and oral skills. The children are mainstreamed with the normal hearing children in the school for art, physical education, and other non-academic activities; in the future, we hope to develop some academic mainstreaming as well. They receive the same battery of tests the children in the other kindergarten receive, and thus a direct comparison of achievements is possible. No child is transferred to a total communication program without the parent's approval.

Children leaving the kindergarten program have, at the present time, three educational options available. In one, the children can continue in the total communication program. We hope to eventually sequence this program right through high school, along the lines of what is now being accomplished in two locations in the eastern part of Massachusetts. The parents of the children in the total communication program are asked to attend weekly classes in the SEE method as well as intensive three-day workshops in the summer. The maximum use of residual hearing and the maximum development of oral skills is stressed in this as well as in all other programs in the school.

In the second alternative, the children are enrolled in one of our transitional rooms located in public schools. We now have two rooms in a local public school. Two additional rooms are located in another public school. These rooms are staffed by our teachers and aides, with frequent visits by the staff of our supportive services. Each child is individually programmed in terms of his ability to profit from selected classes and experiences with the normal hearing children. This is accomplished in consultation with the teachers and administrators in the public school. The Willie Ross teachers are responsible for liaison with the regular classroom teachers; their efforts are supplemented by formal orientation programs at least once a year. We view this program as a kind of a half-way house in which we can determine a child's readiness for full "mainstreaming." The logic of this program rests on the lack and deficiencies of objective or subjective criteria to predict successful or unsuccessful "mainstreaming." Rather than depending only on general predictive criteria to make this judgment, it seems more sensible to directly assess our efforts in this regard. So we observe the child in the regular classes, evaluate his performance, psycho-social status, communicative interaction, and personal desires, and, from this information, judge how ready a child is for mainstreaming in his local school.

The third choice from our kindergarten is the mainstream program, to which children can also be transferred from any of our other programs. Our own evidence, and the literature, suggests that elementary school age children are candidates for the mainstream program when (1) they possess sufficient residual hearing capacity to permit audition to serve as a primary input mode for speech and language development, (2) they are not more than two or three years behind their normal hearing peers in standardized tests of speech and language capability, (3) they can produce intelligible oral speech in unstructured situations (4) and when they possess those indefinable but recognizable personality characteristics which bespeak a tough, resilient, gregarious, and inquisitive child who can "make it" in spite, rather than because, of us. The best criteria, however, as indicated above, is the actual observation of the child in a normal classroom setting.

When a child is transferred to a mainstream program (and this decision, as well as all other educational decisions, is made by our own evaluation and placement team), he is assigned to one of our mainstream consultants who can play a number of roles depending on the needs of the children and the public school. She can provide direct tutoring and services to the child, or she can consult with teachers, tutors, speech pathologists, and other resource personnel in the school regarding the child. In practice, we do provide more consulting than direct services. Our rationale is that the child is in a regular class five hours a day and that it is more important to ensure that this period of time is used effectively, rather than directly tutoring the child just an hour or two a week. The mainstream consultant conducts orientation programs for the teachers in the regular schools, evaluates the child's deficiencies and makes recommendations to the local personnel, troubleshoots hearing aids and auditory trainers, and generally acts as a bridge between the local school and the Willie Ross School. The children in the mainstream program are regularly scheduled for complete audiological and hearing aid evaluations twice each year. They also receive a complete speech and language evaluation by our own speech pathology staff, who relates these results and the consequent recommendations to the child's teacher and the local speech pathologist. One of the goals of the mainstream program is to gradually diminish much of our involvement to the degree the local school is able to provide for the needs of a specific child.

An additional alternative provided for in our educational model is a multiply handicapped auditory-oral class (a few other multiply handicapped children are dispersed through our total communication program). These are basically mild to moderately hearing impaired children who have flunked normal school, or children with additional mild emotional, intellectual, or physical problems. We view most of these children as eventual candidates for a regular school, though perhaps not a regular class in such a school. We do not yet have a multiply handicapped program to accomodate children with severe secondary problems accompanying their hearing loss. This is one of our future goals. Such children are now managed in mainly residential environments, frequently in institutions focusing on other than hearing problems, and they, too, deserve an opportunity to learn in a less restrictive environment.

Completing the educational alternatives the school provides is an oral class for profoundly hearing impaired children, whose primary sensory input modality is visual rather than auditory. These are children whose oral progress has been slow, but sufficiently steady to encourage continuation in this mode, or whose parents have made an explicit decision to select an oral program rather than the recommended total communication program. This is a legitimate alternative, appropriate for some hearing impaired children. We have found, however, that with the combination of an intensive early auditory-oral program, which prepares children for mainstreaming, and a viable total communication alternative for those not candidates for an auditory-oral approach, that there are an insufficient number of children available who can be appropriately placed in this program to permit new classes being organized. For the occasional child who does fit this category, we have either referred, or the parents have elected, a residential placement, although we would have preferred to have this alternative available on a day-school basis.

In every class and program, in every clinical and educational contact, the participation of the parents is actively solicited. We make the same observation in our school that has been made in many other programs and schools: the child who is "making it" best is the one whose parents are actively engaged in the educational process, defined to include not just academics, but everything that inputs on a child and has implications for his progress and status. This kind of participation doesn't just happen. It must be a primary goal of every educational program dealing with hearing impaired children. We may not succeed with every parent and every child; we do have an obligation to try with all of them. From the day the diagnosis is first made, from the time when parents cannot fully comprehend the enormity of the handicap or of the tasks required of them, through all the years of the child's schooling, we try to keep our obligation to the parents in mind. Individual counseling and group meetings go on constantly. We're human, we slack off, we let our failures influence us unduly, but, as a program, we're committed to continue our active efforts to engage the parents in our mutual goal, fostering the well-being of the children.

In describing our day program, I did not intend to imply that residential placement is not often a preferred alternative for many hearing impaired children. It is, and often the only kind of placement that makes educational and social sense for a particular child. We make this recommendation when we deem it necessary. It is my preference, however, other factors being equal, to attempt to educate hearing impaired children on a day basis—particularly at the preschool and elementary age level. A day program cannot be successful, the educational alternatives and academic and clinical flexibility cannot be obtained, unless the program can draw on a sufficient population base to permit the organization of the complete educational cascade. As one unfortunate by-product on the current emphasis on mainstreaming, we are finding that local school systems are attempting to organize their own "little red schoolhouse" for hearing impaired children. These programs usually consist of a motley, heterogeneous group gathered together in resource or transitional classes, unsupported by skilled diagnostic or ancillary services, or the odd hearing impaired child floundering and being overwhelmed in a regular class. Mainstreaming is a desirable educational goal and some hearing impaired children can attain it. The physical presence of a hearing impaired child in a public school should not, however, be used to measure the success of this goal. We are concerned with their performance and their feelings, not where they are physically placed. Nor should mainstreaming be sought for its economic rather than its educational implications. We are lately seeing the occurrence of a tremendous advocacy for the tip of the educational cascade—full mainstreaming—not for its presumed benefit for the child, but because some officials are finding it cheaper to educate the child in a regular school rather than provide the special help a child needs in a special, and more expensive program. Of course, this motivation is never explicitly stated, nor is it unmixed without a certain degree of self-deception, professional ignorance, and altruistic intentions. While we must frequently face the harsh constraints of economic reality, and realize that we cannot do all we would like to do, the first priority of a professional educator should be his advocacy role as the authoritative spokesman justifying the best possible program. If the educational administrator assumes as his first priority the business manager's role, then the profession has lost its most powerful content advocate. I'm all for accountants, bookkeepers, and business managers, but when I'm talking to an educational administrator working at the higher bureaucratic level, I hope to assume that beneath all the economic constraints of the situation, the professional educator is still peeking through with values intact.

Providing the educational alternatives in a cascade model is a necessary but not sufficient factor in determining the feasibility of such a program. There has to be an organized and skilled evaluation and placement team, representing the supportive and academic services, which recommend the specific educational plan and placement for every child. We've just formalized this committee, and, as a by-product, are finding improved intraschool communication. All services get a chance to see the child from the other point of view. No educational decisions are final. The essential placement flexibility is easily obtained, within a cascade model, as long as all the components are administered centrally. The more agencies involved, the more complicated simple educational decisions and alternate placements become. Since the child's teacher is a member of the evaluation and placement committee, the success of the recommendations can quickly be assessed and other options explored. A teacher's request, through the administration, can quickly activate the committee so that problems and issues can be continually explored.

In summary, what I have described here is an educational model which appears to be working for us. Although the specifics may change depending upon state and local requirements, the essential ingredient of real, not just nominal, alternatives for different children, can be provided most anywhere. The basic commitment has to be to children and not methods.

Helen Hulick Beebe

19

Deaf Children Can Learn to Hear

Norman Cousins, in the Golden Anniversary issue of Saturday Review, August 1974, editorialized that the opportunity of the Saturday Review "is to argue for the proposition that human beings are equal to their needs, that a problem can be resolved if it can be perceived, that progress is what is left over after the seemingly impossible has been retired, and that the crisis today in human affairs is represented not by the absence of human capacity but by the failure to recognize that the capacity exists."

Relating Cousins' philosophy to the need of educating the hearing impaired we could say the problem has been perceived and that the seemingly impossible has been retired if we are willing to settle for providing the hearing impaired with limited academic education but the crisis has been in limbo for some time, namely, providing the hearing impaired with adequate auditory/oral communication to achieve their full potential as human beings.

It has been my privilege, aided by my invaluable colleague Antoinette Goffredo, to help retire the seemingly impossible task of teaching the deaf to hear.

Pioneering is not easy but it can be very exciting and rewarding. All of you will have been exposed to living proof that profoundly deaf children can learn to hear and to acquire speech and language via acoustic pathways. In 1944 when I had my first opportunity to use what has come to be called the unisensory approach with a profoundly deaf child, I had no proof positive nor had I observed any case which demonstrated that this approach was valid. All I had to go on was the theory learned from my teacher, Emil Froeschels, M.D., namely, that even minimal amounts of residual hearing in a hearing impaired infant if stimulated with auditory training in unisensory fashion could lead to the development of spontaneous speech and eventually to oral communication adequate to allow him to matriculate in a regular school program. The theory had been known for centuries and had been described in this country by Goldstein in 1939. However, until the advent of wearable hearing aids after World War II, implementation had not been practicable.

I was astounded by the results of my first case. Here was a profoundly deaf child (etiology, maternal rubella), audiogram as follows.

I.S.O.	250	500	1000	2000	4000
	R. 75	R. 105	R. 100	R. 120	R. 125
	L. 80	L. 100	L. 100	L. NR	L. NR,

She literally heard nothing without amplification, but learned with amplification to converse, repeat stories, etc. via acoustic pathways alone. The quality of her speech and voice became so close to that of a hearing person that it belied her deafness (Beebe, 1953).

I soon became aware of other workers in the field stressing auditory training, for example, Wedenberg in Sweden, Ewing and Whetnall in England, Huizing in Holland, and later Pollack, and Griffiths, in the United States. Today there is living proof throughout the world that the unisensory approach is viable.

As conceived in our program there are seven requisites to an effective unisensory approach.

1. Early detection of hearing impairment
2. Fitting of appropriate binaural amplification to be worn during all waking hours
3. Intensive auditory training of even *minimal residual hearing,* and forcing the use of (amplified) hearing by eliminating visual clues. Thus the name "unisensory," unisensory as opposed to the multisensory training approach used in traditional programs.
4. Full family involvement
5. The use of the chewing approach to develop and maintain a natural voice quality
6. Therapy on a one to one basis
7. Educational placement with hearing peers

EARLY DETECTION

By early, we mean in the first few months of life if the hearing loss is congenital. Every month of delay makes it more difficult to train the child. Quoting from Whetnall and Fry, (p. 125), "Whether the deafness is perceptive or conductive, the young child will always have in addition a central lesion, which is of a physiological or psychological nature, due to the fact that the patterns of hearing are not present at birth. Deafness interferes with the normal 'spontaneous' development of these patterns by the simple process of depriving the brain of sound." The medical profession to which parents turn when they suspect a hearing deficit must be made more generally aware of the critical responsibility it holds to refer parents without delay to appropriate facilities.

BINAURAL AMPLIFICATION

Our experience over many years with monaural (one aid), Y cord (one aid—two receivers), and binaural (two aids) has demonstrated the latter offers the following advantages.

1. Better directional hearing
2. Stereophonic effect
3. Better distance hearing
4. Improved acoustic orientation in ambient noise
5. Better speech
6. Generally more comfortable handling of conversation, schoolroom activity, etc.

We observe these advantages when comparing our older cases (still monaural) with more recent cases. Parents report a difference in their management of the child when for some reason one aid cannot be worn temporarily. Children express displeasure at being limited to one aid.

There is a minority of cases that cannot tolerate two aids. However, we have seen a number of cases that were fitted monaurally because "the other ear was dead." Happily, with intensive training, the "dead ear" was trained to the point of achieving useful discrimination and thus these children have the advantages of binaural hearing when the audiometric testing indicated that no benefit could be expected from a binaural fitting. To the audiologists who withhold prescription of two aids because of cost we and our parents feel this is the prerogative of the parents. Certainly a surgeon would never suggest half of a surgical procedure because it would cost less. And to the audiologists who would save one ear we would ask, "What for?." This is not meant to be facitious. An untrained ear cannot be held in reserve to function in an emergency. Early training of both ears offers the greatest potential for developing good quality of speech and language.

INTENSIVE AUDITORY TRAINING

In a unisensory program intensive auditory training means developing the use of amplified hearing to its maximum potential. Even *profoundly deaf children* can learn to hear. They can be brought to the point of handling conversational speech—repeating and discussing a story through hearing alone. They are not allowed to rely on speechreading until they are hearing oriented. Eventually they become multisensory. These children just naturally develop the necessary speechreading skill without special instruction.

In early training we know that the child with one sensory receiving modality intact (sight) and one impaired (hearing) will rely on the easier modality and so we force him to listen and to hear by preventing him from watching the speaker's mouth. If our goal is to provide maximal use of residual hearing, he must be *forced* to hear enough to stimulate the motor speech center of the brain and to appreciate what hearing and discrimination can do for him. One does not just put a hearing aid on a child and expect him to hear. Pollack (p. 68) stated that a child's hearing age dates from the time he is fitted with amplification. It sometimes takes months or even a year before there is objective evidence that the child "knows" that he hears. During that time we must "charge" the brain like a battery until sound perception and cognition are converted to a motor speech response.

First of all the child must be alerted to sound. The watch word is "listen." Whether banging a door, blowing a whistle, mooing like a cow, dropping an object on the floor, or saying "Up, up, up," as we lift the child up to the chair, the therapist, mother or anyone helping the child, learns to point to his ear, calling his attention to the sound in an effort to make it meaningful to him. Then ways are contrived to repeat this same situation so that eventually, just like a hearing child, he learns to associate meaning with the sound and to respond appropriately. He is learning to manipulate his world by listening and talking.

FULL FAMILY INVOLVEMENT

In order to succeed in our program, we must have not only full collaboration of the parents, chiefly the mother, but also the conviction that the goal can be achieved. Facing the responsibility of rearing a child who seemingly hears nothing is indeed a formidable task. One of the best means of allaying the fears and apprehension a mother feels when facing the job for the first time is to have her observe other cases successfully on their way. Regardless of the age at which the infant or child receives amplification, the mother or her substitute is made aware that she is to be the teacher during all the child's waking hours. She is instructed about the care of the hearing aid and held responsible for having it in working condition. She will bring the child to us for at least two one-hour individual therapy sessions per week. During these sessions the therapist offers the mother guidelines for her work at home. Mother sits in on demonstration sessions of the therapist working with the child. Teaching materials are suggested or lent to the mother with specific assignments. However, it is emphasized that improvisation appealing to the child's daily interests can be the most meaningful motivation for the child to learn what listening and speaking can do for him. When necessary, a therapist visits the home to demonstrate how to capitalize on daily activities. The mother is asked to keep an informal diary of observations of the child's receptive and expressive responses. This diary often proves to be a concrete means of helping the mother at times of discouragement. She also keeps an activity book containing drawings or pasted-in pictures and snapshots of daily happenings captioned with the appropriate language and revealing the interests of the child. This offers the therapist, family, and friends the opportunity to reinforce through repetition language useful to the particular child. More mature children may also be given a "homework" book with assignments from the therapist for the mother and child, for example, to learn colors, numbers, various categories, rhymes, and idioms. Parents are assigned appropriate literature to aid them in their overall task. However, from demonstration sessions they can best learn directly how to carry out some of the following important directions.

1. Keep eye contact with the child.
2. Get his attention before addressing him.
3. Cover your mouth, or have the child close his eyes or turn his head for specific listening tasks.
4. Use firm intonation, not exaggerated mouth movements.
5. Repeat stimulus with decreased loudness once the child has responded.
6. Repeat stimulus at a greater distance after positive response from the child.
7. Feed back the child's vocal play.
8. Be alert to respond to and to reinforce immediately any attempt at vocal utterance of the child.
9. Correct any unnatural, strained vocalization with the "chewing approach".

CHEWING APPROACH

According to Froeschels' (see Beebe, 1956) theory of the identity of chewing aloud and speaking, the natural way for the vocal apparatus to function is to use it as though we were chewing food while vocalizing. This assures that the musculature involved will be in a state of optimal contraction, i.e., neither hyper- (over) nor hypo- (under) contracted. Hearing children and adults who develop functional voice problems have been treated successfully by applying the chewing approach. They are led gradually from vocalized chewing (nonsense chewing) into chewing meaningful speech, that is talking with the mental attitude of chewing.

We stress the necessity of stimulating the receptive speech centers of the brain of the hearing impaired child with normal speech patterns and yet we know that amplification at best cannot be adjusted to offer compensation for the individual variation of decibel loss in the speech frequencies. The early vocalization and babbling of deaf children often exhibits a natural voice quality but as soon as they try to reproduce the speech patterns they hear through amplification they are apt to speak with strained high pitch and in unnatural melodic patterns. This can be changed into natural voice quality by teaching them vocalized chewing. As we encourage the infant to follow the stages of babbling, lalling and echolalia we introduce the various phonemes in syllabic series with voiced chewing. This is not difficult. Children enjoy it and soon recognize the comfortable feeling of not straining their voices. Articulation per se is not stressed in the early stages of speech production. Hearing children do a lot of talking before their articulation skills are refined. Calling attention to articulation is psychologically and physiologically unsound. Speech melody is the important thing to encourage. Later, when articulation needs to be refined, chewing helps to incorporate a newly learned sound into the stream of speech.

THERAPY ON A ONE TO ONE BASIS

The hearing child speaks because he hears. His acquisition of language skills, unless he lives in a deprived environment, follow a logical sequence. Our training of the hearing impaired child is geared to follow the speech and language development of the hearing child. At whatever age the child is aided and we begin training, we must "zero in," so to speak, on the child's mind and personality—which has been conditioned by his soundless world. Our first effort is to focus his attention so that we can alert him to sound. Mother's role in this first stage and in all subsequent stages is to capitalize on the child's activities and interests so that he acquires cognitive skills as quickly as possible. The child must be guided carefully by therapist and parent in planned stages of language growth which are commensurate with his ability to use and master syntactical forms etc. At certain stages of language acquisition, motor speech skills may deteriorate. This has to be recognized by whoever is in charge of training. A child of superior intelligence deprived of normal hearing is apt to organize his world to his satisfaction without making the effort to use oral communication. This must also be recognized and appropriately handled. Another child may be satisfied to stick to the stage of echolalia or of telegraphic speech. Chronological age, hearing age, psychological types, and so many other factors in addition to the primary condition of impaired hearing have to be taken into consideration when planning a speech and language development regimen. Individual therapy seems the only efficient means of monitoring and implementing these various factors.

EDUCATIONAL PLACEMENT WITH HEARING PEERS

Most of the children trained in our program with the unisensory approach have been fully mainstreamed from the beginning in regular school programs with their hearing peers. The goal of our program is to educate the hearing impaired child to live comfortably in the hearing world. As adults they must be able to cope with people in a complex "integrated" society. In order to do this they must have good oral communication. One of the requisites for acquiring good speech is to be exposed to good speech and language models all day long. This would not be possible were our children segregated with children who have distorted speech and language patterns. We also feel that it is psychologically important to the hearing impaired child to be kept in a normal environment. Emphasis is on all the things he has and does in common with hearing children. With very few limitations, he is encouraged to participate in all the activities of a hearing child. He watches T.V., uses the phone, plays musical instruments—in fact functions like a hearing child and is deaf only without his hearing aids.

At the nursery school level, we ask only that the child be encouraged to participate in all group activity. At 5 years of age, he should have enough language and use of hearing to cope with a kindergarten curriculum. However, since some children are at least a year behind in "hearing age" they might have to repeat kindergarten so that they can mature in use of language.

We have prepared guidelines to aid the teacher in managing the hearing impaired child in the classroom. Early in the year one of the staff visits the classroom to evaluate the child's performance as well as to make constructive suggestions to help the teacher. We also learn from the teachers areas in which we can be helpful during the therapy sessions which continue twice a week after school hours. Teachers are encouraged to keep parents informed about any areas that need special help for which there is not time during school hours. School districts vary as to auxilliary services provided such as speech or hearing therapists, tutors, etc. None of our children have had the advantage of a resource teacher which would alleviate in some instances the responsibility shouldered by the parents and to a degree by ourselves.

Here I would remind you that we and our parents have been "going it alone," that is, none of the schools involved have had any experience mainstreaming a *profoundly hearing impaired child*. Even in cases when more recently hearing therapists have been available, their experience has been limited to moderately impaired hearing. This same observation could be made by many of our colleagues who have joined us in advocating mainstreaming. To name a few: Pollack, Griffiths, Northcott, Grammatico, Bitter, Gantenbein. Hopefully, institutions responsible for training teachers and educational specialists will bring their curriculums up to date, thus taking us out of the pioneer role.

From our vantage point—that is, working in a private practice—we might be considered unrealistic when we say that every hearing impaired child should at least be given the opportunity of exposure to an auditory program. We realize that there are some children who will not be able to develop language through acoustic processing and therefore will have to be educated with an alternative method, but let's be sure that choice has not been made prematurely and/or on false premises. We have succeeded with too many cases whose families had been given dismal prognoses simply because those professionals to whom they turned were uninformed. Do not prejudge the child's capacity to hear or the parents' ability to do their part. Too many hearing impaired of past generations have been denied the opportunity to learn to hear. We should take heed of the remark of Dr. Robert Wieland, Director, Exceptional Child's Center, Fort Lauderdale, Florida, who after surveying various programs concluded, "We have been teaching our children how to be deaf when we should be teaching them how to hear."

BIBLIOGRAPHY

Beebe HH: Practical aspects of chewing therapy. Folia Phoniat 8:2, 1956
Beebe HH: A guide to help the severely hard of hearing child. Basel, S. Karger 1953
Pollack D: Educational audiology for the limited hearing infant. Springfield, Ill., Charles Thomas, 1970
Whetnall E, Fry DB: The deaf child. Springfield, Ill., Charles Thomas, 1964

Grant B. Bitter

20

Mainstream Education for the Hearing Impaired—Promises to Keep . . .

The woods are lovely, dark and deep
But I have promises to keep,
And miles to go before I sleep.
  ("Stopping by Woods on a Snowy Evening"—Robert Frost)

Promises for what purposes? And to whom? Are they not promises to bring about the dignity of mankind? Promises to America's children—to the children of the world; perhaps, ultimately, to the children of the universe!

Indeed, it is hoped that the advancement of human rights within the final quarter of the 20th century, and the impending birth of the 21st century, will not be retarded by the inhumanity of man to man as described by the following historical flashback.

Dateline
Stoneage
  Diagnosis: Patient suffering from continuous, severe headaches and convulsions, evil spirit imprisoned in mind. Prescription: Chip out a circular area in the skull permitting pressure to be relieved and evil spirit to flee (Hewett, 1974).

Dateline
Sparta (450 BC)
  Diagnosis: Male infant born with twisted hand; female infant, twin.

Prescription: Assemble on a cliff on Mt. Taygetus where father will hurl both infants down on the jagged rocks below (Durant, 1966).

Dateline

Rome (100 BC-100 AD) Bulletin: House of Aristocracy, for amusement, come see the "natural fools" and imbeciles entertain the well-to-do (Wallin, 1955). A *prescription* for remediation for the mentally ill (Zillboorg, Henry, 1941):

> Asclepiades: hydrotherapy, massage, sunshine, exercise, and abstinence from meat; do not bleed subject nor place in dark cells and dungeons.
> Celsus: chastise by hunger, chains, and fetters. Keep in total darkness; shave heads; use bleeding and morphine-like medicines.
> Aretaeus: pay attention to how the patient thinks and feels (Hewett, 1974). Obviously Aretaeus was centuries ahead of his time in advocating humane treatment.

Dateline

Middle ages (400 AD-1500 AD) An historical comment:

> The surge of religious conviction brought some protection and consideration for the physically and mentally different, yet their behavior was considered to be of satanic origin. Some of the deviant ones, however were considered to be "Heavenly Infants," or "Infants of the good God." It was a period of gross confusion for the exceptional: to be tolerated as "fools," as innocents; or to be persecuted as witches (Hewett, 1974, Doll, 1962).

Dateline

Eighteenth Century—Hewett (1974) reported that:

> Fifty-nine percent of all children born in London during this time died before reaching the age of five; sixty-four percent were dead before age ten. Many babies were abandoned at birth; those who were rescued and survived were given to nurses at public expense and later placed in workhouses . . . From 1771 to 1777, 32,000 children were admitted to the Paris Foundling Hospital at the rate of eighty-nine per day. It was reported that eighty percent of those children died before completing their first year.

Dateline

Nineteenth Century, United States. *Hear this* from Dorothea Dix:

> More than 9,000 idiots, epileptics, and insane . . . destitute of appropriate care and protection . . . bound with galling chains, bowed beneath fetters and heavy, iron balls attached to drag chains, lacerated with ropes, scourged by rods and terrified beneath storms of cruel blows; now subject to jibes and scorn and torturing tricks; now abandoned to the most outrageous violations. (Zillboorg, Henry, 1941)

Dateline

Twentieth Century—United States, 1961. Hear this from President John F. Kennedy:

> "The manner in which our Nation cares for its citizens and conserves its manpower resources is more than an index to its concern for the less fortunate. It is the key to the future. Both wisdom and humanity dictate a deep interest in the physically handicapped, the mentally ill, and the mentally retarded. Yet, although we have made considerable progress in the treatment of physical handicaps, although we have attacked on a broad front the problems of mental illness, although we have made great strides in the battle against disease, we as a nation have for too long postponed an intensive search for solutions . . . ." (President's Committee on Mental Retardation, 1962).

Dateline

United States, 1974. Hear this from Robert T. Stafford, U.S. Senator (R-Vt)

> ". . . recent court decisions have reminded the nonbelievers among us—that all Americans have the right to equal educational opportunities. Indeed, the recent court decisions have directed our attention to the fact that the handicapped, along with all other Americans:
> - Have the right to public education, regardless of the degree of disability.
> - Have the right to just compensation for labor.
> - Have the right to appropriate treatment at public institutions.
> - Have the right to fair protection from harm."

Dateline

Tennessee, 1974. Hear this from Dr. Benjamin E. Carmichael, Commissioner of Education:

> "Under the leadership and sponsorship of the Tennessee Department of Education, the initial phase of an ambitious plan for providing comprehensive educational services to the hearing impaired are being implemented in Tennessee . . . . Following national trends in special education, Tennessee is expanding its programs for the handicapped beyond the traditional concept of residential instruction. Recent progressive legislation has dramatically acknowledged the state's responsibility for providing comprehensive educational services to all handicapped children. This is being done primarily through the collaborative efforts of local school systems and the state. This legislation underscores the high priority of normalization and mainstreaming with maximum integration of handicapped children into the regular classroom. It empowers local school systems to deliver the comprehensive continuum of regular and special educational services required to increase potential for successful integration.
>
> . . . the primary goal is to meet the individual needs of all hearing impaired children and adults. The program acknowledges education at the earliest possible level as the cornerstone for helping each handicapped child attain maximum developmental potential (Carmichael, 1974).

Obviously, the transitional journey of mankind from the cruel battles of the "survival of the fittest" through the chasm of superstition, and ignorance to the present day of enlightenment has not been one of systematic order. It has been made possible through an outpouring of knowledge and intelligence through the untiring efforts of people of science, education, religion and government whose convictions and contributions have had, and are now having, far-reaching effects in bringing about the dignity of man.

The Tennessee Plan as previously described is one of many programs designed to provide social and educational opportunities for children that will revolutionize educational programs and practices. Indeed, they are "acid tests" in proving the nobility of man in the quest for unselfish advocacy of children's rights in our kind of democracy.

To assist in expediting the mandates which have been issued by legislative and judicial bodies, school boards and educators throughout the country in meeting the challenge of the mainstreaming concept, the staff of project NEED (Normal Educational Environment for the Hearing Impaired) at the University of Utah, Department of Special Education, carried out a three-year special program whose primary objective was to develop a package of mediated materials that would be useful in orienting regular classroom teachers, public school administrators, support personnel, parents and many others to the manifold needs of hearing impaired children.

The motivating philosophy underlying the Project NEED concept was the simple premise that hearing impaired children have the right to dignity and individuality; and, indeed to an opportunity to become full participating citizens within their culture to the degree permitted by their abilities and capacities and the conditions within their environment. This approach is called Maximum Cultural Involvement, and emphasizes utilization of four significant dimensions of the child's environment, i.e., the *family,* the *community,* the *church,* and the *school* in qualifying him for meaningful cultural achievement (Bitter, 1973).

There was intense national participation from educators, specialists, parents and others in preparing the orientation materials for the purposes of facilitating the integration of hearing impaired children into the educational and social mainstream.

Identified as Systems O.N.E. *(Orientation to the Normal Environment), the nine sound filmstrip modules designed and produced by the staff of Project NEED (Normal Educational Environment for the Hearing Impaired) have universal educational versatility. The materials offer orientation information for regular classroom teachers, resource specialists, parents, administrators, special educators, and others who might be or who are presently involved in the educational programming of hearing impaired children.

The modules provide a source of new knowledge to some and a meaningful review for others. Used skillfully, they are capable of serving as facilitators of dynamic group interaction. Thus, their appropriate utilization becomes an opportunity to share ideas about attitudes, strategies, and educational processes needed in generating an orderly systems approach to the meaningful placement of hearing impaired children into regular classrooms.

The SYSTEMS O.N.E. package contains:

one (1)	introductory booklet
nine (9)	narration guides
nine (9)	cassette tape narrations to accompany filmstrips
nine (9)	filmstrips on integration, which are approximately 10 minutes in length.

Following is a brief description of each module.

Language—To orient the regular classroom teacher to the concept of language development as it pertains to hearing and hearing impaired children; classroom techniques for improving language development.

Classroom Management—To orient the regular classroom teacher to the causes of frustration in the hearing impaired child and strategies to decrease or eliminate undesirable behaviors caused by frustration and anxiety.

Reading—To orient the regular classroom teacher to the aspects of reading in terms of the hearing impaired child. General classroom techniques for improving reading competency in the hearing impaired child.

Peer orientation—To orient the regular classroom teacher to possible strategies for involving hearing classmates with the hearing impaired children in the class.

Classroom communication—To orient the regular classroom teacher to ways of facilitating speechreading and practicing basic auditory training in the regular classroom.

Family orientation—To orient family members to their roles in developing mainstream readiness in hearing impaired children. Included are suggestions on how the family might be involved in mainstream activities in the school, and the community.

Speech—To orient regular classroom teachers to the speech difficulties of hearing impaired children; ways to maintain and improve speech in the regular classroom.

Administrative guidelines—To orient administrators to the organizational parameters of a mainstream program; discusses liaison, parent involvement, and recommendation for teacher selection.

Hearing aids—To orient the regular classroom teacher to the types of hearing aids; basic trouble-shooting techniques discussed along with minor hearing aid repair suggestions.

The following concepts are basic to the effective use of SYSTEMS O.N.E.:

1. Systems O.N.E. is most effective when used with the guidance and assistance of a person who is knowledgeable in mainstreaming procedures and is an experienced educator of the hearing impaired.
2. Mainstreaming is a process, as well as a goal.
3. The process of mainstreaming should be thoroughly explained through inservice orientation and supplemented with supportive services and continuous monitoring through evaluation and supervision.
4. The process of mainstreaming is enhanced through positive attitudes and constructive work by all who are involved including administrators, teachers, support personnel, and parents.

5. The success of mainstream programs depends, in part, on interdisciplinary team effort, cooperation and communication.
6. Successful mainstreaming also depends, in part, upon the proper fitting and consistent use of appropriate hearing aids.
7. Children should be evaluated carefully prior to being mainstreamed to insure proper placement and delivery of support services.
8. Hearing impaired children should have the opportunity to participate in a regular school program to some degree regardless of the degree of hearing loss.
9. In the process of mainstreaming, hearing impaired children who are involved should actively participate in classroom experiences. Attendance in a regular classroom without appropriate participation is not necessarily an indicator of educational and social progress.

The SYSTEMS O.N.E. material is provided to help fulfill promises in regard to the individual achievement of hearing impaired children—of all children in fact. This program is intended to stimulate and utilize the environment in

> "Broadening the intellectual, emotional, social, educational, vocational and spiritual horizons of hearing impaired children and their hearing peers with the hope that they may become mature, self-reliant, independent, productive citizens, giving to the world in service that which only they can give as unique and worthy human beings." (Bitter, 1973)

Such an awesome and thrilling task must be the shared responsibility of educators, scientists, specialists, political leaders, churchmen, families within every community in the nation—in pursuit of cultural excellence in the keeping of our promises and our commitments.

> The woods are lovely, dark and deep,
> But I have promises to keep,
> And miles to go before I sleep.
> (Robert Frost)

Promises—For what purposes? To bring about the dignity of man! Promises—To whom? To our children who are our eternal investments. What price are we willing to pay?

---

*May be ordered from: Educational Media Center
207 Milton Bennion Hall
University of Utah
Salt Lake City, Utah 84112

BIBLIOGRAPHY

Bitter GB: Facilitating the integration of hearing impaired children into regular public school classes. The Volta Rev 75: 1973 The Alexander Graham Bell Association for the Deaf, Washington, D.C.

Bitter GB, Johnston KA: SYSTEMS O.N.E.: Salt Lake City, Utah, Educational Media Center 207 Milton Bennion Hall, University of Utah, 1974

Carmichael BE: The tennessee plan: A new program for delivery of services to school districts. The Volta Review, A.G. Bell, Washington, D.C., February, 1974

Doll E: A historical survey of research and management of mental retardation in the united states. Readings on the Exceptional Child: Research and Theory, Trapp and Himmelstein New York: Appleton Century Crafts, 1962

Durant W: The Life of Greece. New York: Simon & Schuster, 1966

Frost: Stopping by Woods on a Snowy Evening

Hewett FM, Forness R: Education of Exceptional Learners. Boston, Allyn and Bacon, Inc., 1974

Kennedy JF: President's Committee on Mental Retardation. 1962, p. 196

Stafford RT: The handicapped: Challenge and decision. Excep Child 486, 1974

Wallin JE: Education of Mentally Handicapped Children. New York,. Harper & Row, 1955

Zillboorg G, Henry GW: A History of Medical Psychology. New York, W.W. Norton, 1941

Gary W. Nix

Summary

In reviewing the information presented in this volume, a broader scope than the title *Mainstream Education for Hearing Impaired Children and Youth* is readily seen. The volume might have been titled *Educational Programming for Hearing Impaired Children and Youth* since mainstreaming is viewed within the perspective of educational alternatives and the gestalt of programming.

It is the purpose of this summary to synthesize the information presented by the contributors in the volume. Considerable agreement among the experts and concordance with research findings permit some operational statements to be made. Areas of disagreement among the contributors and conflicting research data must await further research for resolution.

The current state of the art is not advanced and, as solutions become evident to questions which at this point remain unanswered, the whole of educational programming will be moved forward. The education of hearing impaired children has undergone an accelerated evolution. It has been influenced by the quantum gains made in the field of audiology or perhaps a better term would be "hearing science". The trend of deinstitutionalization now affecting all of special education is accelerating the movement to regional or local day programming for severe to profoundly hearing impaired students. An important influence has been the human rights movement.

Green divided the restrictions faced by the hearing impaired individual into two basic categories. The first category consisted of restrictions imposed by the disability such as the inability to appreciate good music. The second category of restrictions were those imposed by our society on the individual. He may not be permitted to attend a regular school, serve on a jury, enter military service, or perhaps is underemployed. The hearing impaired person may impose restrictions upon himself resulting from a poor self concept acquired through the interactions of the individual with parents, peers, and others in their environment. Education "in the least restrictive environment" seeks to minimize the restrictions imposed upon the individual either directly or indirectly by society.

McGee viewed an expanded milieu as an opportunity for the hearing impaired individual to develop broader perceptions than that available in a restricted environment in which there are few people available for consistent interaction. The expectancy level for communicative and academic performance is increased.

Bitter felt living at home supplies the hearing impaired child with the invaluable experiences of family interaction. Hearing impaired children learn about family life by sharing in the fun, the pain, the responsibilities, and the confrontation of family give and take. He referenced the fact maternal deprivation has been shown to retard a child's growth and development. The detachment of the child from the mother can produce lasting emotional problems.

On a personal note, the editor has previously been employed as a child care worker (house parent) in the preschool-primary dormitory of a residential school for the deaf. The experience of physically restraining a crying, kicking, desperate four year old hearing impaired child to keep him from running from the dormitory in order to join his parents in their drive home is matched only by the experience of seeing the emotional trauma of the parents as they leave their little one.

After one Thanksgiving holiday period, one of the children did not return to the school. The school social worker was dispatched to bring the truant primary level child back to the institution. As her car arrived at the dilapidated, rural family home, the hearing impaired boy saw her and began running across a freshly plowed field. The social worker apprehended the truant and returned him to the institution. Two facts stand out. First, the family did not want to be separated from the boy nor he from his family. Secondly, even though we provided him with much better living quarters and three balanced meals per day, we did not substitute for his family and the love provided on a daily basis by his mother, father, and siblings.

A recent survey of deaf adults by the Wisconsin Department of Public Instruction (1974) documented the emotional trauma experienced by preschool hearing impaired children when separated from their intact families. The respondents to the questionnaire had attended the Wisconsin School for the Deaf (p. 70).

The emotional trauma evident in both the hearing impaired child and his family when separation occurs produces a very clear implication. Services must be provided as close to the family as possible.

Matter noted living at home provides the opportunity for hearing impaired youth to obtain part-time employment as baby sitters, paper boys, parking lot attendants, and other responsible positions. Through mainstreaming, the hearing impaired youth develops in a more normal social and learning environment.

Cosper stated the expanded environment of mainstreaming places the hearing impaired youth in contact with a broad spectrum of hearing peers. He is likely to encounter bullies, cliques, snobs, know-it-alls, loners, as well as the friendly and considerate student.

A number of benefits which can accrue to the mainstreamed hearing impaired student are summarized below.

1. Provision of normal age appropriate speech, language, and social models
2. Reduction in the amount of gesture language initiated by the child
3. Motivation and reinforcement for the development of good speech and speech perception
4. Reduction of the excessive dependence which may have developed between the mother and child
5. Addition of a verbal mediating link between the action of play and cognitive development
6. Faster academic pacing is available and achievement level expectations are raised
7. Greater variety of high school courses to meet differing needs and interests than found in most high schools for the hearing impaired
8. Availability of a broad range of co-curricular activities with hearing youth. Co-curricular interaction can increase self-esteem and a feeling of belonging to a greater society than that available in the restricted environment

Not all hearing impaired children are candidates for a mainstream placement. There exists some disagreement among the experts as to the relative importance of the parameters of age and hearing impairment as reflected by the pure tone audiogram.

Ross stated the best single predictor of a hearing impaired child's communicative performance is the degree of hearing loss. In the chapter on assessment, he substantiated his claim with the supportive data in Tables 7-1-7-3. Since adequate communication is a requisite of success in the mainstream environment, a more profound hearing impairment will diminish the chance for success.

Northcott in reviewing current research (Kennedy, 1974; McCauley, 1974; Rister, 1974) did not feel the degree of hearing loss to be equated with the ability to function in a mainstream placement.

Cosper noted the majority of mainstreamed students coming from programs for "the deaf" have severe to profound hearing losses which is contrary to popular belief.

Bitter presented research by Jones and Byers (1971) which concluded the hearing deficit does not appear to be the most important parameter for predicting success.

McGee observed the degree of hearing impairment as reflected by the pure frequency audiogram is not predictive of the development of functional residual hearing in children below the age of four.

Although the experts disagree on the relative importance of the use of the audiogram and actual hearing level as a predictor of mainstream success, considerable agreement is found on the importance of functional hearing.

Sanders presented the dilemma faced by the hearing impaired infant. The infant is faced with the task of acquiring language as a generative function which requires rule learning and rule using. Rule learning can only be deduced naturally through the auditory pathway. The development of a child's auditory perception is essential if the child is to develop communicatively in as near normal manner as possible.

The point was made by Sanders that auditory perception is an active rather than a passive process. Auditory perception and functioning are therefore not simply determined by the degree of hearing sensitivity possessed by the individual. He called for a total commitment to the maximal exploitation of residual hearing.

Gantenbein made a plea for schools to accept the responsibility for providing good audiologic management through the hiring of an educational audiologist. Audiologic management, he felt, should not be left to the parents, teachers, and/or teacher aides.

Hanners reported that audiologists have not generally accepted the challenge and opportunities presented by early intervention systems. Current clinical practices frequently result in long delays between identification of the disability and the fitting of a hearing aid.

In order to achieve successful mainstreaming, Simmons-Martin presented the need for a chronological age disparity between the hearing impaired child and his classmates of one year or less.

Northcott also noted the need for minimal age disparity in order to achieve a successful placement.

On the other hand, Cosper, Auble, and Gantenbein felt chronological age variation is not the problem which it would appear to be.

A summary of the important parameters for a successful mainstream placement upon which the contributors appear to agree includes the following.

1. Early detection of the hearing impairment and enrollment in a family-oriented special education program
2. Amplification provided as soon as the hearing impairment is diagnosed
3. Full-time hearing aid usage during waking hours

4. Minimal disparity between the hearing classmates and the child's
   A. Listening age
   B. Developmental age (social, emotional, physical)
   C. Linguistic age
   D. Academic skills
   E. Reading level
5. Average or better in intelligence
6. A secure and outgoing personality which exhibits a resilient, gregarious nature
7. Receptive and expressive auditory-oral communication skills at a level sufficient to anticipate reasonable success in the regular classroom
8. The capacity to learn through large group instruction when new material is presented
9. Supportive parents and family members
10. A variety of specialists available to serve the child and his family in counseling, monitoring the placement, and providing any necessary remediation

Green stated it is easier to structure a positive mainstream situation for a child of three than for a youth of thirteen. Early mainstreaming was seen as not only easier to achieve but as having a number of positive effects on the child's psychological development as well.

Bitter through his Maximum Cultural Involvement model uses environmental parameters to develop the child's positive self-concept, social adequacy, and competent educational skills. He presented the environmental interaction of mainstreaming as the process through which a child achieves social, linguistic, academic, etc. adequacy. Yet, a child must have a modicum of competence in the same areas in order to function successfully in a mainstream environment.

The advantages of early intervention for developing the entry level skills necessary for success in a mainstream placement were stated by several of the authors and were related to the neurophysiological development of the child by Sanders. The objective of converting a remnant of residual hearing into functional hearing is best achieved through early and consistent amplification coupled with intensive training which gives repeated exposure to the auditory pattern of all new language concepts. The use of audition for the development of speech perception and production was seen as a critical element to the successful assimilation of the hearing impaired child.

Not all hearing impaired children who are candidates for a mainstream placement are best served by an early, continuous placement in a regular classroom from the nursery level on. The child must possess the necessary entry level skills and a special class placement can provide the intensive training necessary for the remediation of skill deficiency. Northcott delineated three natural periods for consideration of a mainstream placement: 1—kindergarten/first grade; 2—third/fourth grade; 3—junior high school.

In spite of early identification, early amplification, consistent binaural hearing aid usage, and a maximum early intervention effort by the child, his parents, and a multidisciplinary team of professionals, some children are not realistic candidates for a mainstream placement. Parents can, and frequently do, experience feelings of guilt if their child is not mainstreamed.

Professionals faced with parental involvement and pressure in educational placement decision-making may accede to the parents' wish (or frequently demand) for a mainstream placement which is premature or inappropriate. By doing so, the professionals become a party to the debacle which follows. Premature or inappropriate mainstream placement can have the opposite effect of the desired objectives. Ross and Golf noted the harvest of educational problems which can accompany such a placement. The child may fail to develop communicative, academic, and social competence. He experiences failure, frustration, and isolation. Golf felt such a placement may, in fact, "de-normalize" a child. Both the child and his family experience shattered expectations.

The mandate of placement in the least restrictive environment possible does not mean that all hearing impaired children should receive their education in a regular class placement. Mainstreaming is viewed as one educational alternative which should be available to hearing impaired children. It may or may not be the desired alternative for a particular child.

Northcott proposed that children in the age range of birth to age six with one or more of the following characteristics *not* be considered candidates for placement in a setting with non-handicapped peers.

1. Late identification requiring immediate and intensive special education services
2. Severe multihandicapping conditions
3. Extreme social or emotional immaturity
4. Irregular hearing aid usage

Hearing impaired children and youth for whom a change in educational placement from a mainstream situation to enrollment in a special class can be identified by one or more of the "failure indices" outlined by Golf in her chapter. Such indices as the development of a poor self concept, evidence of social promotion, emotional problems, difficulties with reading, language, and math skill development, and, of course, low grades, should "red flag" a hearing impaired student's educational placement. As is the case with hearing children, intelligent hearing impaired students may be bored in a slow paced regular classroom and can be "turned off" toward school and learning.

Cosper noted some of the problems which affect the academic or social adjustment of the hearing impaired child or youth are frequently parent-related: alcoholism, a step parent, lack of a father figure, overprotection. The school counselor or social worker may be able to assist in the solution of the difficulty.

McGee addressed himself to some of the difficulties in program implementation. A necessary function of the mainstream specialist is to monitor the integrated student's performance in the regular classroom. It is a difficult task, at best, if the monitor is also responsible for a full-time self-contained classroom. Therefore, a resource teacher or mainstream specialist should not be encumbered with a full-time class. If the student is to be partially mainstreamed, the schedule may have to be readjusted in order to permit the teacher of the hearing impaired to work with the child when he is available.

It is an unfortunate fact not all regular class teachers want hearing impaired students. The mainstream specialist must locate those classroom teachers who have a receptive attitude. The specialist assists the regular classroom teacher in creating a receptive climate prior to the placement of the hearing impaired child in the regular classroom.

The resource specialist must face the problem of determining which parts of the general curriculum the student is capable of handling and conferencing with the parents, administrators, and other members of the multidisciplinary team. The solution of problems as they arise will also be the resource specialist's primary responsibility.

Cosper remarked on the "hearing loss blues" which mainstreamed hearing impaired children may suffer on occasion. The "blues" may be precipitated when the student may not have done well in band or by losing in the try-outs for cheerleader, wanting a particular date, or obtaining a desired job.

Unfortunately, one of the most difficult problems encountered in the implementation of a mainstream program is the determination of which children are to be considered candidates for a regular class placement. Instrumentation and selection procedures need further development. It is likely strength in one of the important parameters may compensate for a weakness in another parameter and thus permit a successful mainstream placement to be made. The Rudy-Nace Transitional Instrument in *The Hearing Impaired Child In A Regular Classroom,* edited by Northcott (1973) permits parameter compensation (pp. 128-133). The instrument has been validated but the actual correlation of the instrument with the achievement of mainstreamed students awaits further investigation.

Instrumentation which rates a hearing impaired student on all of the critical parameters for a particular regular class placement would enable researchers to use the compensation factor in the development of a profile for the child. A number of successful mainstream profiles might be possible while other profiles might indicate an unsuccessful placement. It may be likely some characteristics cannot be compensated. The instrumentation developed thus far does not include a rating of the mainstream environment into which a student is to be placed. Attention must be given to such parameters as: teacher vs student-centered communication, large vs small group instruction, individualized vs traditional curriculum, communication environment including the classroom noise level.

Assessment practices prior to educational placement vary widely in quality and degree. Hanners found at least two audiologists who had made educational placement decisions based upon a limited pure tone audiogram from a single test visit. The children were pronounced "too deaf to learn language orally" and referred to manual language classes. Additional cases cited by Hanners suggest important decisions regarding amplification and school placement are often made on very limited audiological information.

Sanders suggested the criterion for measuring auditory function must be communicative behavior and not pure tone audiometry. He also suggested a child's communicative capacity to communicate orally cannot be adequately assessed until he learns the basic processing rules.

Ross noted the instrumentation used at the Willie Ross School. Speech is evaluated through the Goldman-Fristoe and Fisher-Logeman tests. The staff at Willie Ross have also enlisted the assistance of normal listeners in hearing and rating speech intelligibility from word lists recorded on tape by the students.

Cosper added the use of evaluations based upon academic grades, written and verbal reports from the student's current teacher. A multi-year graph of the student's performance on school wide achievement testing provides valuable input. If possible, the student could enroll in a summer school which uses the same curricular materials encountered in the potential mainstream placement.

Assessment should be a continuous process with educational placement considered to be tentative and subject to change. Students may be moved from partial mainstreaming to full mainstreaming or vice versa. If necessary, partially mainstreamed students might return to a full-time self-contained classroom placement.

Itinerant teachers from the Willie Ross School assess a mainstreamed student's functioning by spending a full day accompanying the child to all of his classes. He observes the child's responses to classroom instruction and communicative interaction with the other children. The itinerant teacher judges how intelligible others find the child's speech, consults with all relevant school personnel, and either requests or administers standardized tests of academic and language performance.

Unanimity is seen among the contributors regarding the important role of the hearing impaired student's parents in the educational process. Simmons-Martin stated the best preparation for mainstreaming other than direct education of the child is early parent education.

Green supported the practice of early intervention and the ready availability of counseling for the parents in handling their feelings. She felt

Summary

parents can contribute to better child growth on social, emotional, and psychological bases.

Ross stated the conviction the traditionally poor performance of hearing impaired children is largely due to the lack of or ineffectiveness of early intervention programs.

As noted in Northcott's chapter, parent education is one of the key ingredients in a successful early intervention program. Early intervention specialists train the parents to work with their child in order to build expressive and receptive communicative skill and linguistic concepts.

Simmons-Martin commented on the diversity of parents of hearing impaired children. Some parents learn and use educational principles quite well while a more structured "cookbook" approach is necessary for others.

Northcott proposed a "Bill of Rights for Every Parent of a Hearing Impaired Child." In her view, the parents' role has changed from a passive consumer of services emanating from the school to an active participant in educational decision making and monitoring the child's acquisition of essential skills. Parents have assumed the role of child advocates in acquiring increased resources for the implementation of programs stressing the individualization of services. The Parents' Bill of Rights includes the right to an intact family.

Bitter presented a list of recommendations to parents of adolescent hearing impaired youth which was developed by Rosenthal (1966). Parents were charged to not shield the youth from new experiences but prepare him for new social situations whenever possible in order to make him feel more at ease. While acquainting some people with the youth's communicative problems, the parent can emphasize their offspring is a person like anyone else.

The resource teacher of the hearing impaired has a challenging role to fill in the successful mainstreaming of the student. Resource teachers must have good interpersonal skills in order to develop a close working relationship with the staff of the regular school. Matter presented several suggestions for the resource teacher in becoming "a part of rather than apart from" the rest of the school faculty. She suggested the resource teacher do the following:

1. Mix with other faculty members and hearing students during free hours
2. Work on faculty committees with regular classroom teachers
3. Speak positively about the achievements of the hearing impaired students in order to emphasize their capabilities to the regular staff when in the lounge or lunchroom
4. Reflect positive statements made by a mainstreamed student back to the regular classroom teacher
5. Serve as a counselor to the hearing impaired student as well as an academic tutor
6. Serve as a homeroom teacher for a class of hearing students

Golf stated the resource teacher should work within the regular classroom whenever possible. If there are hearing children who need the same type of academic tutoring, they should be included in small group work with the hearing impaired. Such an approach will reduce the labelling of hearing impaired children as either "special" or a "failure". The willingness to work with both hearing and hearing impaired children in a team approach establishes better staff relationships. Golf cautioned against the resource teacher setting himself above the regular classroom teacher as the "expert."

The resource teacher can ease later mainstreaming for the hearing impaired student who has inadequate reading and language skills through preteaching as suggested by Matter.

Bitter pointed out many educators recommend phasing a hearing impaired student into a mainstream placement. As the student develops his academic and social competence, the student is assigned to the regular classroom for a greater part of the day.

From the editor's experience, mathematics is frequently a good subject for the first academic experience in the regular classroom. It is a highly visual subject with less verbal loading than subjects such as reading and social studies. If educational television is used in the regular classroom, it will be necessary for either the resource teacher or regular class teacher to preteach the lesson. One incident serves to illustrate this point. A hearing impaired boy was seated at the front of the regular classroom watching an educational telecast on "set concepts." The video teacher in reviewing sets asked the set of all girls in the room to stand up. Since the camera was not on the video teacher's face, Cory could not speechread the instructions. Unfortunately, Cory was the only boy in the front row. When he detected the other front row students rising with his peripheral vision, Cory stood also much to his immediate embarrassment.

Cosper discussed the difficulties faced by the junior high student in a mainstream placement. The hearing impaired youth must adjust from having one or two teachers to having a different teacher for every subject. Each teacher has a personal style of presenting material. Some teachers use a lecture mode and follow the textbook closely while other teachers make frequent use of records, audio tapes, and video tapes. In checking pupil knowledge, some teachers test for recall knowledge and some test for the application of knowledge to hypothetical situations.

The resource teacher is particularly challenged at the high school level. With students following individualized programs, the number of regular class teachers involved can be rather large. It is sometimes difficult for the high school resource specialist to preteach subjects about which he knows little. Advanced chemistry, physics, foreign languages, etc. may best be met through extra tutoring sessions given by the regular teacher of the subject.

One of the greatest needs in the education of the hearing impaired is the employment of a systems approach to service delivery. As Gantenbein pointed out, teachers of the hearing impaired cannot provide for all the educational needs of hearing impaired students. Other specialists in education (learning disabilities, behavioral disorders, etc.), psychology, audiology, social work, and medicine, to name but a few, need to be involved with and in the school for the solution of a student's problems. Some normally hearing children have difficulty with reading and verbal communication. Not all of the learning problems of a child necessarily spring from his hearing disability.

Hanners found the present procedures of audiologic management to be unsystematic and fragmented in the early intervention programs surveyed. All of the programs revealed delays between identification and the initiation of service of twenty months or more. She proposed a model service delivery system which includes the audiologist as a member of the system throughout all levels. The audiologist is viewed as the resident expert in hearing, its measurement, and utilization.

The field of the education of the hearing impaired has been widely known for its controversies. The oral/manual controversy and the day/residential controversy have probably received the most attention. Other controversies have existed in the teaching of language (natural/structured) and the teaching of speech (analytic/synthetic). Advocates of a particular approach have promoted it as "the best way" to educate hearing impaired students.

The contributors to this volume represent a broad spectrum of professionals in the area of the hearing impaired. They advocate a systematic approach to the education of the hearing impaired with the provision of a service continuum which includes a variety of educational alternatives one of which is mainstreaming.

Sanders made a plea for educational alternatives based upon the needs of the particular child under consideration. Some children will not develop auditory function to a degree which is sufficient for communication in a near normal manner. For those children a complete system of manual communication such as Seeing Essential English to be used in conjunction with auditory and oral communication training is advocated. This does not, according to Sanders, obviate the fact that for children with sufficient auditory perception, language is best learned by the auditory-oral approach.

Golf presented a model for an age/level continuum of services from birth to age twenty-one. The continuum includes services ranging from full mainstreaming to self-contained, residential and from auditory-oral to total communication.

Ross outlined a service continuum which similarly provides a range of educational alternatives. The "best method" or alternative is the one which meets the student's needs at a particular time. In implementing the service continuum, it is necessary to have comprehensive and continuing assessment of both the student and the school setting. The student's placement is considered tentative and can be changed when it is in his best interest. The model educational cascade has been implemented at the Willie Ross School.

Leslie included the Deno Service Cascade which has found general acceptance in the field of special education. It provides for education "in the least restrictive manner possible."

It may be the growing acceptance of the provision of a continuum of services will be the death knell of the major controversies which have plagued the education of the hearing impaired for so long. Professional energies and research can be channeled into child advocacy and refining the assessment techniques for placement of the hearing impaired student into the proper educational alternative for his set of needs at that point in time.

A variety of new classroom organizational patterns have begun to emerge. Bitter defined the three most frequently mentioned. The standard mainstream model involves the placement of a hearing impaired child in the regular classroom for all or part of the school day. The cross mainstream model calls for the mutual exchange of pupils between the regular and special class. The reverse mainstream model brings hearing children into the classroom for part of their instructional day.

McGee noted some problems with the cross mainstream model. Everyone concerned must be convinced such mainstreaming is in the best interests of the students. The arrangement can increase the amount of time required for management and planning by all staff members. Several teacher support systems are required and the program costs as much as a traditional program so cost reduction arguments cannot be used in selling the program idea to the school administration.

Connor presented a variant of the reverse mainstream model which involves the enrollment of hearing children in the special school on a full-time basis. The Lexington School for the Deaf has overtly rejected the concept deaf children are to be educated apart from hearing children. However, in so doing, it has not rejected the basic reasons for requiring specialized teachers and services.

During the 1968-1969 school year, the Lexington School admitted normally hearing students into its three- and four-year-old nursery classes. A progressive phasing in of hearing children has occurred. Concurrently, a full-day instructional program is provided to mixed classes through the primary grades and a half-day program in the three- to five-year-old classes.

The Lexington School operates a Teen Center four nights a week with a one to one or two to one ratio of hearing and hearing impaired youth between 16 and 25 years of age. It provides an opportunity for social integration with hearing youth which stands in contrast to the frequent "deaf club" environment found in many metropolitan areas of the United States.

The Community School provides for the continuing education needs of hearing and hearing impaired adults in mixed classes. It has been well received and will be expanded.

The Lexington model for mainstreaming the special school is innovative and appears to be working well. It is a model which other day/residential schools may adopt to provide their students with some of the benefits of mainstreaming. A number of questions have been answered by the Lexington program and a number of conclusions have been reached by Connor.

1. The special schools can be a part of the mainstream yet remain special.
2. Parents of hearing children will send their children to a special school if it provides a quality education which best meets their children's needs.
3. The competancies and qualities which make an excellent teacher of the hearing impaired can also serve to provide excellent teaching of hearing children.
4. Critical observers, standardized tests, and clinical analyses support the integrated education of hearing and hearing impaired children.

Gantenbein presented a service delivery model for meeting the needs of hearing impaired children in a public school setting. He described a visual-oral alternative to the auditory-oral program component. A diagnostic-developmental department serves the Berrien County hearing impaired children who are seriously brain damaged, emotionally impaired, mentally impaired, or otherwise multihandicapped. Five classroom mainstreaming plans which are used in the Berrien County Day Program were presented in the chapter by Gantenbein.

Simmons-Martin described the model demonstration home program at the Central Institute for the Deaf. The techniques of parenting used in the parent-infant program permit flexibility in meeting the needs of the child and the capabilities of the parent. Parent counseling assists the parents in coping with their emotions. Whenever possible, grandparents, aunts and uncles, siblings, and others in the family constellation are included in the parent training sessions.

Beebe discussed the role of the speech pathologist in preparing hearing impaired children for and supporting them in the mainstream. The Beebe Clinic is a private practice which successfully utilizes a unisensory auditory approach. The unisensory approach involves intensive auditory training of even minimal residual hearing with the elimination of visual clues whenever possible. The students are placed educationally with hearing peers and receive supportive therapy on a one to one basis. The chapter includes a discussion of the chewing approach to develop and maintain a natural voice quality.

"Administrative readiness" was viewed by Bitter as a critical factor in the successful implementation of a mainstream program. The administrative staff must have a very real commitment to developing a mainstream component as one of the educational alternatives available to the hearing impaired children in their program.

Connor presented the components of an administrator's decision and suggested a realistic approach to influencing the decision on adding a mainstream option. Careful attention to the administrator's probable concerns will enable the informed parent or professional to be more effective. Frequent questions are

1. Is there a well thought out, specific plan concerning the proposed program arrangement?
2. Have local, state, and/or federal resources been identified which will support the program?
3. Is the time frame realistic?
4. Are the parents of hearing impaired children supportive and interested in enrolling their children in a mainstream program?
5. How will the inservice preparation of regular class teachers be accomplished?
6. Where has mainstreaming been implemented and what were the results?
7. Will the new program component jeopardize other experimental programs?

Cosper considered some of the problems faced by public school administrators in reducing class loads in order to mainstream hearing impaired students, additional equipment purchases, provision of an adequate resource room, and promoting harmony between the regular and special staff. The location of the resource room in a quiet part of the building away from the band room, gymnasium, and cafeteria is important for environmental sound level control.

Hanners indicated the need for a shift in the funding of audiologists from a fee structure to full funding support. This was viewed as necessary due to the restricted number of children which an educational audiologist will see annually.

Northcott suggested several possible funding sources for the support of early intervention mainstream programs. State aid reimbursement of local school district expenditures is possible in many states for nursery and kindergarten level programs. Federal funds under the Elementary and Secondary Education Act (Titles I, III, VI, Part B or C) are available. Foundations can and do give fiscal support to early intervention programs. Local tax dollars may be the best source of long-term program support.

Connor listed administrative guidelines for the implementation of a mainstream alternative. As also noted by Auble, the basic organizational patterns may involve limited options in the initial phase. Perhaps, only a resource room and a self-contained classroom would be provided. The new program should be staffed only with fully certified and experienced personnel. An administrator should consider whether or not the mainstream

Summary

resource program will meet the needs of the students it is to serve. The pooling of resources into regional programs may permit more educational alternatives to be provided. In order to give a program a fair trial, several years are needed.

In conclusion, a number of operational statements, recommendations, and salient points need to be capsulized.

1. A systems approach to educational programming must be provided.
2. Services should begin as soon as the hearing impairment is discovered.
3. Binaural amplification, whenever possible, and the intensive training of the infant's residual hearing is essential for maximum communicative development.
4. A multidisciplinary team approach for diagnostic and intervention services is the most effective.
5. Mainstreaming as soon as a student is ready for such a placement is desirable if a suitable regular class and specialist support is available.
6. Inappropriate or premature mainstreaming can produce social isolation, academic failure, and in general a "de-normalizing effect."
7. Mainstreaming is both a process and an educational goal. It is *not* an educational panacea and educational alternatives must be provided in a service continuum.
8. Parents have a vital role to fill and must be actively involved in the hearing impaired student's education at all levels. The intact family must be maintained unless institutionalized, 24-hour residential care is necessary due to the family's inability to properly care for the child.
9. The improvement of diagnostics is greatly needed for assessing the critical parameters necessary for a mainstream placement.
10 All educational placements should be considered tentative with monitoring of each placement by the multidisciplinary team.
11. The modification of present professional preparation programs in the education of the hearing impaired to include the specific preparation of early intervention and resource specialists is needed.
12. A subspecialty of audiology needs to be created in order to prepare audiologists to function within educational programs on a full-time basis with a particular emphasis on the audiologist's role as a member of the multidisciplinary early intervention team.
13. Regular class enrollment needs to be reduced in schools which provide a mainstream alternative in order to more effectively accommodate hearing impaired children.
14. Inservice education programs must be implemented for teachers of the hearing impaired who have not been trained as resource specialists but will be expected to assume such a role.
15. Continuing research on the effects of mainstreaming on the child's total development is needed.

16. Early intervention programs should be tax-supported.

BIBLIOGRAPHY

Northcott WH (ed): The hearing impaired child in a regular classroom. The Alexander Graham Bell Association for the Deaf, Inc., Washington, D.C., 1973

Cook JJ: A Ten Year Follow-Up of Graduates From Educational Programs for the Hearing Impaired in the State of Wisconsin. Program Accountability in Special Education, Monograph No. 3, Hearing Impaired Survey, Wisconsin Department of Public Instruction, Madison, Wisconsin, 1974

INDEX

Academic achievement
　in demonstration home program, 220
　differences between expected and actual, 105
　hearing impairment and, 15
　mainstreaming and, 81-85
　summary of speech, hearing, language assessments and, 103
Academic facilities, Shorewood, 160-164
Academic tutors, 14, 171
Accountability, school, 113
Achievement, *see* Academic achievement
Acoupedic programs, preschool, 15
Active process
　auditory perception as, 258
　perceptual process as, 40
Adjustment patterns, of persons with impaired hearing, 29-32; *see also* Educational adjustment; Social adjustment
Administration, 6, 181-190
　cautionary notes on, 181-183
　guidelines for, 186-188, 268
　of normalization programs in public schools, 201-203
　See also Administrators
Administrative readiness, 12-13, 267
Administrators, 188-189
　appropriate delivery of services as concern of, 12
　problems faced by, with high school students, 153
　at Shorewood, 165-166
Adolescents, parents of hearing impaired, 18; *see also* Hearing impaired high school students
Adults, number of handicapped (1974), 88
Age
　enrollment, in nursery schools, 231-232
　of onset of hearing impairment, average decibel loss and, 117
　See also Chronological age
Alcoholism, costs of, 87-88
Amplification
　daily testing of amplification equipment, 70-71
　importance of early, 15, 176
　insuring optimal functioning of, 48
　in Systems O.N.E., 251
　See also Binaural amplification
Anxiety, hearing impairment and, 77, 78
Assessment, 161-162
　of failing mainstreamed children, 172
　placement and, 3, 4
　prior to mainstreaming, 101-108
　See also Diagnostic services; Testing
Assimilation
　as goal, 107
　integration vs., 101
　See also Mainstreaming
Audiograms
　functions of, 41
　reliance on, 178, 258
Audiologic services, 4, 53-73, 258
　delays in, 69-70
　fragmented, 69
　importance of, 230

271

lack of systematized, 68-69, 265
model of, 70-73
need for continuous, 71-72
for preprimary hearing impaired children, 71, 124
present state of, 53-68
Audiologists
concerns of, 40
as educators, need for, 269
See also Audiologic services
Audiometers, pure-tone, 103-104
Audiometric deafness, 46, 48
Auditory approach, 14-15
to language development, 229
Auditory behavior (listening), as learned behavior, 44, 45
Auditory materials, *see* Amplification
Auditory maturity, 95
Auditory/oral approach
multiple handicapped auditory/oral classes, 234-235
orientation toward, 128
used with hearing impaired high school students, 157-160
used with preschoolers, 198-199, 232
Auditory perception
as active process, 258
expectancy in, 41-42
Auditory training in unisensory approach, 241-242
Aural rehabilitation, communicative improvement with, 156

Behavioral management programs, as components of normalization, 201
Berrien Springs program, 191-195
Binaural amplification
communicative development and, 269
in unisensory approach, 241
Birth-to-three years of age, *see* Preprimary hearing impaired children

Cascade model of services, 24-25, 266
developing the model, 228-229
educational services, 231-235
overhauling of, 227-228
social services, 231
supportive services, 230-231
Chewing approach, unisensory and, 241-242
Children, rights of, 87, 88, 183-184; *see also specific types of children; for example:* Failing mainstreamed children; Hard-of-hearing children; Preprimary hearing impaired children
Chronological age
of hearing impaired high school students, 149-151, 259
one-to-one therapy and, 244 Church, the, Maximum Cultural Involvement in, 92-93, 251
Classrooms
communication in and management of, in Systems O.N.E., 252
multiple-handicapped auditory/oral, 234-235
transitional, 172-174, 233
See also Placements; Regular classroom placements; Regular classroom teachers; Resource room support
Co-curricular activities, participation in, at Shorewood, 164-165
Cognition, neurophysiology and, 94-95
Colleges, mainstreaming in, 14
Communication
binaural amplification and development of communicative ability, 269
classroom, 252
degree of hearing loss and communicative performance, 257
establishing, within age appropriate hearing peers, 136
in demonstration home program, 219-220
improvement in, of hearing impaired high school students, 156
normalization of communicative skills, 150-151
receptive and expressive, 150
teaching/learning models of, 46-48

total, defined, 116; *see also* Total communication approach
See also Sign language; Speech; Speech development; *and entries beginning with term: language*
Communication media, modification and reinforcement of, 151
Community in Maximum Cultural Involvement, 93-99, 251
Competency-based education, 88
Continuum of services, 6, 172-175, 265-266
Correctional institutions, population of, 11
Counselors
 of hearing impaired high school students, problems of, 153-154
 Shorewood, 166
Cross-mainstreaming, 13, 266
Curricula
 Lexington School, 211-213
 model of, for preprimary hearing impaired children, 125
 Shorewood, 162-163, 165-166
 Type IV plan, 141

Day programs
 deinstitutionalization and, 255, 265
 enrollment in (1965), 2
 local-regional oral, 174
 See also specific day programs; for example: Cascade model of services
Deaf, defined, 114
Deafness
 audiometric, 46, 48
 functional, 46
Decibel loss, age of onset of hearing impairment and average, 117
Deinstitutionalization, 182, 255, 265
Demonstration home program, 7, 217-226, 267
 communication skills in, 219-220
 language development in, 219
 social and emotional maturity in, 220-226
 verbal intelligence and academic skills in, 220

Dependency, minimization of, as goal of Maximum Cultural Involvement, 98
Detection, *see* Early detection
Diagnostic services, multidisciplinary approach to, 269; *see also* Audiologic services; Early detection
Divorces, impact of, 87
Dropout rate, 12

Early childhood education specialists, 127-28; *see also* Resource teachers; Teachers
Early detection, 16-19, 172
 audiologic services and, 70-71; *see also* Audiologic services
 effects of, 176
 importance of, 75
 social adjustment and, 78
 unisensory approach and, 240-241
Early entry skills, 259-260
Education, relationship between special and regular, 88; *see also specific aspects of education; for example:* Curricula; Schools
Education specialists, early childhood, 127-128; *see also* Teachers
Educational adjustment of hearing impaired high school students, 152
Educational expediency, educational integrity vs., 11-21
Educational services, cascade model of, 231-235; *see also* Schools
Educational system, shortcomings of, 11-12
Emotional maturity in demonstration home program, 220-226
Employment opportunities for hearing impaired high school students, 165
Enrollment
 age of nursery school, 231-232
 day program (1965), 2
 nursery school, 114
Entry skills, early and late, 94-96, 259-260
Environment
 Berrien Springs, 194-195

least restrictive, 4, 182, 186
Normal Educational Environment for the Hearing Impaired Project (NEED Project), 250-251
Orientation to the Normal Environment (Systems O.N.E.), 7, 251-253
physical setings for preprimary impaired children, 120-121
self-concept and home, 95; *see also* Family *See also* Maximum Cultural Involvement
Equal rights for children, 87, 88
Exceptional children, segregation of, 12, 13
Exceptional deaf children, characteristics of, 80
Expressive communication, 150

Facilities, Shorewood, 160-164; *see also* Services
Failing mainstreamed hearing impaired children, 169-178, 260
Family
effects of mainstreaming on, 81
Maximum Cultural Involvement in, 92, 251
orientation of, in Systems O.N.E., 252
social adjustment and, 256-257
unisensory approach and involvement of, 242-243
See also Parents
Financial rationale of mainstreaming, 26-27
Fingerspelling, 118-119
for children up to three years old, 117-118
in total communication approach, 232-233
Functional deafness, 46
Functional hearing, converting residual into, 259
Functional high school students, 147-149
Funding
of audiologic services, 72-73
of mainstream programs, 268
of schools for preprimary hearing impaired children, 120-121
tax-supported, 270

Generative function, language acquisition as, 42-43
Guidance counselors, *see* Counselors
Guidelines, administrative, 186-188, 268

Handicapped, the inhumanity toward, in history, 247-250
number of (1974), 88
rights of, 7
Hard of hearing, defined, 114
Hard-of-hearing children, study of, 102
Hearing
acuity of, as established by pure-tone audiometers, 103-104
assessment of, 103
converting residual into functional, 259; *see also* Residual hearing
placement and level of, 104
teaching deaf children how to hear, 239-246
Hearing aids, *see* Amplification
Hearing impaired children, role of residual hearing in training, 45-48
Hearing impairment
age of onset of, average decibel loss and, 117
defined, 114
Hearing loss
environmental clues to identifying, 17
negative values associated with, 76-77
Hearing management programs, as components of normalization in public schools, 199-200
Hearing peers
assistance from, 17
benefits derived from intermingling hearing impaired children with, 16, 17
establishing communication with age appropriate, 136
of hearing impaired high school students, 155-156

Index

of hearing impaired three year olds, 123-124 placement with,
unisensory approach and, 245-246
type of orientation needed by, 16
High school students, *see* Impaired high school students
Home environment, self-concept and, 95; *see also* Family

Illiteracy, 88
Impaired high school students, 5, 147-156
chronological age comparisons of, 149-151, 259
educational adjustment of, 152
modification and reinforcement of communication media and, 151
placement of, 151-152
problems faced by administrators and, 153
problems faced by hearing students when associating with, 155-156
problems faced by teachers/counselors and, 153-158
at Shorewood, 157-168
Incarceration, costs of, 12
Income of handicapped adults, 88
Individualized education at Shorewood, 158, 161
Information in perceptual process, 42
Institutions
deinstitutionalization, 182, 255, 265
for hearing impaired (1965), 2
population of correctional, 11
programs in, 28-29
Instruction, *see* Teaching
Integration, assimilation vs., 101
Integrity, educational expediency vs. educational, 11-21
Intelligence, verbal, 220; *see also* Communication
Interactions, *see* Hearing peers; Social relations
Itinerant teachers, role of, 14

Junior high school students, *see* Impaired high school students

Kindergartens, 232-233

Labeling, adverse effects of, 11, 12
Language, *see* Sign language; Speech; Speech development
Language ability, personality development and, 81
Language acquisition, 14
as generative function, 42-43
by osmosis, 176-177
Language concepts, exposure to auditory patterns of new, 49
Language development
assessment of, 103
auditory approach to, 229
crucial years in terms of, 231
in demonstration home program, 219
residual hearing and, 234
with resource teachers, 16
in Systems O.N.E., 251
written language, 156
Language instruction, auditory stimulation in, 50-51
Late entry skills, 259-260
Learned behavior
auditory behavior as, 44, 45
social maturity as, 80
Least restrictive environment concept, 182, 186
Legislation, mainstreaming, 1-3, 33-35, 185
Lesson materials, relevancy of, to children's experience, 49
Lexington School model, 6-7, 209-215, 266-267
background of, 210-212
objectives of, and results obtained with, 212-214
Listening (auditory behavior), as learned behavior, 44, 45
Litigation, mainstreaming, 33-35, 185
Local-regional oral day classes, 174

Mainstreamed impaired children
characteristics of preprimary, 121-124
failing of, 169-178, 260

Mainstreaming
    administrative readiness and, 12-13
    approaches to, 13-17
    bandwagon support for, 25-26
    at college level, 14
    defined, 1, 24, 101, 169
    dollar-support for, 26-27
    factors determining success of, 18-19
    legislation and litigation dealing with, 1-3, 33-35, 185
    psycho-social support for, 27-32
Mainstreaming readiness, 229, 232, 233, 269
Marginal deaf children, characteristics of, 80
Maternal deprivation
    early school entries and, 96
    effects of, 256
Maturity
    auditory and visual, 95
    emotional, 220-226
    social, 79-85, 220-226
Maximum Cultural Involvement, 87-100, 251, 259
    in Church, 92-93, 251
    in the community, 93-99, 251
    premise of, 91
    school, family and, 92, 251
    social crisis and, 87-91
Monitoring processes for preprimary hearing impaired children, 124
Mothers, *see* Maternal deprivation
Multidisciplinary approach to diagnostic services, 269; *see also* Audiologic services
Multiple handicapped auditory/oral classes, 234-235
Multisensory programs, as components of normalization, 200

Negative values, hearing loss associated with, 76-77
Neo-oralism, 118
Neurophysiology, cognition and, 94-95
Normalization, 198-206
    of communication skills, 150-151
    mainstreaming and, 177
    in public schools, components of, 198-206
Nursery schools
    enrollment in, 114
    enrollment age in, 231-232
    mainstreaming in, 78-79
    parental participation in, 126-227

One-to-one therapy, unisensory approach and, 244-245
Oral approach, *see* Auditory/oral approach
Oral programs, 235
    nature of good, 150-151
Oralism, neo-oralism, 118

Parent programs
    as components of normalization in public schools, 199
    in demonstration home model, 217-218, 221-225
Parental participation, 113, 235
    in nursery schools, 126-127
    in speech pathology programs, 230-231
Parental role
    in education of hearing impaired children, 17-18
    importance of, 262-263, 269
    mainstreaming and, 177-178
    in social adjustment, 77-78
Parents
    demonstration home program and, 212-213
    of hearing impaired adolescents, 18
    normalization and, 198
    rights of, 4-5, 113
    See also Family
Parents' organizations, 113
Participation, *see* Parental participation
Peer orientation in Systems O.N.E., 252
Peers, *see* Hearing peers
Perception
    residual hearing and, 40-45
    self-perception, 81
Personality, physique and, 75-76
Personality development, language

Index 277

ability and, 81
Physical settings
  of Berrien Springs program, 194-195
  for preprimary hearing impaired children, 120-121
Physique, personality and, 75-76
Placements
  in cascade model, 236
  hearing level and, 104
  with hearing peers, unisensory approach and, 245-246
  of hearing impaired high school students, 151-152
  key to, 102-103
  of preprimary hearing impaired children, 114-115
  prescriptive, 15-16
  relying on teachers and audiograms for, 178, 258
  Rudy-Nace Transitional Instrument to determine, 4, 261
  shortcomings of, 12
  successful, 258-259
  tentative nature of, 269
  See also Regular classroom placements
Play patterns of preprimary hearing impaired children, 125
Preprimary hearing impaired children (from birth to six years of age), 111-133
  acoupedic programs for, 15
  assumptions dealing with, prior to placement, 114-115
  audiologic services for, 71, 124
  auditory-oral approach used with, 198-199, 232
  characteristics of mainstreamed, 121-124
  critical variables to be considered for, 124-126
  early childhood education specialists and, 127-128
  fingerspelling and, 118-119
  methods of instruction for, 115-116, 126
  nature of sign language and, 116-118
  parental participation in management of nursery schools and, 126-127; *see also* Kindergartens; Nursery schools
  parents of, 113
  physical settings for, 120-121
  reasons for mainstreaming, 119-120
Preschool socialization process, 78-79
Prescriptive placement, basis of, 15-16
Primary hearing impaired children (six-to-twelve year olds), 135-145
  Fairfax County Program for, 138-139
  problems with, 137-138
  problems and promises of Type IV plan for, 143-144
  Type IV plan for, 139-141
  workings of Type IV plan for, 141-143
Psychiatric deaf children, characteristics of, 81
Psycho-social aspects of mainstreaming, 4, 75-85
Psycho-social rationale of mainstreaming education, 27-32
Pure-tone audiometers, 103-104

Readiness
  administrative, 12-13, 267
  communicative improvement and, 156
  factors in, 94
  mainstreaming, 229, 232, 233, 269
  reading, 94
  in Systems O.N.E., 252
Receptive communicative skills, 150
Regular classroom placements, 2
  in Berrien Springs program, 193-194
  determination of, 261
  language acquisition and, 14
  in 1970s, 1
  with resource room support, 170
Regular classroom teachers
  in Berrien Springs program, 194
  mainstreaming of high school students and problems faced by, 154
  Shorewood, 161, 162
  type of orientation needed for, 16
Regular education, relationship between

special and, 88
Research, need for continuing, 269
Residential programs, 28-29; *see also* Institutions
Residual hearing, 39-52
   converting functional into, 259
   language development and, 234
   learning to hear with, 239-240
   making maximal use of, 3, 230
   perceptual process and, 40-45
   training and, 45-50, 269
Resource room support, 13, 170
Resource teachers, 170-171
   components of programs of, 13
   language development with, 16
   role of, 263-265
   at Shorewood, 166
Reverse mainstreaming, 13, 266
Rights
   of children, 87, 88, 183-184
   of parents, 4-5, 113

Schooling of handicapped adults, 88
Schools
   audiologic programs in, 71
   early and late entries in, 94-96, 259-260
   Maximum Cultural Involvement in, 92, 251
   multisensory programs in, as components of normalization, 201
   records of, parents' right to examine, 113
   vandalized, 88
   See also Classrooms; Day programs; Institutions; Kindergartens; Nursery schools; *and specific programs and models*
Segmental components of speech, emphasis on, 49
Segregation of exceptional children, 12, 13
Self-concept, 256
   home environment and, 95
Self-esteem, 76
Self-perception, 81
Senior high school students, *see* Impaired high school students
Sentences, emphasis on use of, 49
Services
   cascade model of, *see* Cascade model of services
   continuum of, 6, 172-175, 265-266
   diagnostic, multidisciplinary approach to, 269; *see also* Audiologic services; Early detection
   start of, 269
Sign language
   nature of, 116-118
   Seeing Essential English as (SEE), 232, 233, 265
Six-to-twelve year olds, *see* Primary hearing impaired children
Social adjustment,
   family role in, 256-257
   parental role in, 18, 77-78
Social maturity, 79-85, 220-226
Social relations
   effects of impairment on, 77
   of preprimary mainstreamed children, 123-124
Social services, cascade model of, 231
Socialization process, 78-80
Special education, 88
Speech, segmental and suprasegmental components of, 49
Speech development
   assessment of, 103
   communicative improvement and, 156
   in Systems O.N.E., 252
Speech pathology programs, 230-231
Speech perception, speech production and, 50
Spelling, *see* Fingerspelling
Staff, *see* Administrators; Audiologists; Teachers
Standard mainstreaming, 13
Stimulation
   need for, 42
   as part of language instruction, 50-51
Students, *see* Impaired high school students; Preprimary hearing impaired children; Primary hearing

Index

impaired children
Suicides, in 1973, 87
Supervision
  of normalization programs, 201-203
  in Type IV plan, 142
Supportive services, cascade model of, 230-231
Suprasegmental components of speech, emphasis on, 49
Systems approach to educational programming, 269

Tax-supported funding, 270
Teachers
  in Berrien Springs program, 192-193
  in cascade model, 236-237
  development of, for Type IV plan, 142-143
  expectations of, 171
  of hearing impaired high school students, problems of, 153-155
  itinerant, 14
  in Lexington School model, 213
  reliance on, 178
  role of, in educating hearing impaired children, 17
  Shorewood, 160-163, 165-167
  tendencies of, to slow teaching pace, 158
  training of, 269
  training of, for preprimary hearing impaired children, 127-128
  See also Regular classroom teachers; Resource teachers
Teaching aids, 16-17
Teaching
  of deaf children to hear, 239-246
  of language, auditory stimulation in, 50-51
  with materials relevant to children's experience, 49
  methods of, for preprimary hearing impaired children, 115-16, 126
  team, 165-168, 204-206
Teaching/learning models of communication with hearing impaired children, 46-48
Team teaching, 165-168, 204-206
Technology, mainstreaming, 1

Tennessee Plan program, 250-253
Testing
  with A.B.C. Inventory Test, 147
  of amplification equipment, 70-71
  with Boehm Test of Basic Concepts, 102, 122
  with Fisher-Logeman Test, 106, 262
  with Goldman-Fristoe test, 106, 262
  with Hand Test, 80
  with Metropolitan Readiness Test, 148
  with Rudy-Nace Transitional Instruments, 4, 261
  with Stanford Achievement Test, 105, 148
  with Vineland Social Maturity Scale, 80
  See also Assessment
Therapy, one-to-one, 244-245
Total communication approach
  in day programs, 174
  defined, 116
  in kindergartens, 232-233
Total education program, 157
  as result of team effort, 165-168
Training
  auditory, 241-242
  changes in audiologic, 72
  residual hearing, 45-50, 269
Transition classes, 172-174, 233
Tutors, academic, 14, 171
Type IV plan, 139-141
  problems and promises of, 143-144
  workings of, 141-143
Typical deaf children, characteristics of, 80

Unisensory approach to teaching deaf children how to hear, 239-246

Vandalism, school, 88
Verbal intelligence, 220
Visual maturity, 95

Written language, communicative improvement with, 156

Zero-to-six years of age, *see* Preprimary hearing impaired children